IMAGES
of America
EARLY COUNTY

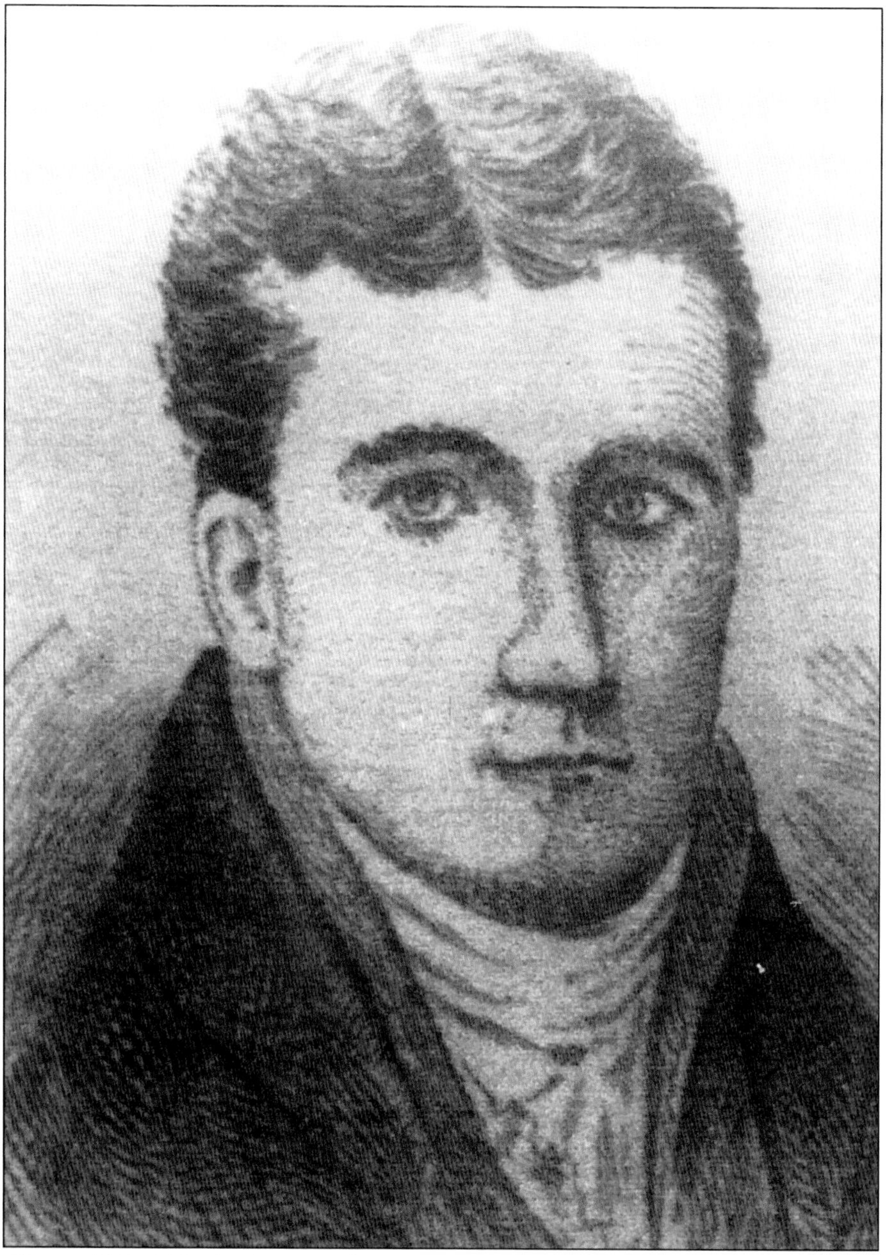

Peter Early, 1773–1817. An American lawyer, jurist, and politician, Peter Early had a distinguished career. He served in the 8th Georgia Congress, was a judge of a Superior Court, and was elected the 28th governor of Georgia in 1813. As governor, he was instrumental in committing money on several occasions from the state treasury to help raise and supply additional troops from Georgia to the American military forces during the latter half of the War of 1812. In 1818, Early County, Georgia, was named in his honor. (Courtesy of the Archives of the Early County Museum.)

On the Cover: Neoclassical Revival. The courthouse on the town square in Blakely, Georgia, was already more than 35 years old when this photograph was snapped in 1941. (Courtesy of Georgia Archives Vanishing Georgia Collection, EAR 35-82.)

IMAGES
of America

EARLY COUNTY

Tina Owen on behalf of the
Early County Museum

ARCADIA
PUBLISHING

ISBN 978-0-7385-8810-0

Published by Arcadia Publishing
Charleston, South Carolina

Printed in the United States of America

Library of Congress Control Number: 2011927661

For all general information, please contact Arcadia Publishing:
Telephone 843-853-2070
Fax 843-853-0044
E-mail sales@arcadiapublishing.com
For customer service and orders:
Toll-Free 1-888-313-2665

Visit us on the Internet at www.arcadiapublishing.com

This book is dedicated to the Early County Museum Board, which includes director Lynn Drew, John Edmondson, Kaye Hall, Charles Garrett, Phillip Moore, Tina Owen, Priscilla Perkins, and Ruth Washington, for having invested so much time and effort into creating a place to protect Early County's treasures.

Contents

ACKNOWLEDGMENTS

A project such as this is always a collaborative effort. The cooperation of the Early County community has been truly heartwarming; it has also made this a better and more representative volume. My particular thanks go to Johnny Scarborough and his generous participation in all phases of this publication. Without him, this volume would never have been possible. Grant Mauldon was my computer "go-to" guy and lent countless hours of advice and troubleshooting. Ann Jarrett's proofreading was invaluable in producing an accurate and cohesive book.

Unless otherwise noted, all images are courtesy of the Archives of the Early County Museum. Historians Delores Eubanks and Virginia Harvey, who have also shared with us their memories and historic information as they participated in museum activities, furnished many of the museum images. Numerous individuals, who delved into their own collections searching for family photographs, supplied other photographs. Still others were given by Lucy Hilton-Maddox Memorial Library and by the Georgia Archives Vanishing Georgia Collection. The Early County Historical Society has been invaluable in sharing historical information. Much of the information in this book was derived from publications of the Early County Historical Society.

INTRODUCTION

Located in southwest Georgia, Early County is rich in history and is labeled as the "Garden Spot of God's Country." Early County was not included in the original charter that created the colony of Georgia but was formed from land obtained from the Creek Indians in 1817. The flags of Spain, France, England, the Confederate States of America, and the United States of America have all flown over the county. In 1818, Early County territory included the Georgia counties of Calhoun, Clay, Decatur, Dougherty, Grady, Miller, Mitchell, and Seminole.

Early County was named for Peter Early, a Virginia native who was governor of Georgia from 1813 to 1815. Blakely, the county seat, was named for Capt. Johnston Blakeley from North Carolina, who was lost at sea with his ship, the *Wasp*, during the War of 1812. Blakely was incorporated as a town in 1871 and as a city in 1900. (Notice that "Blakely" the town and Captain "Blakeley" are spelled differently.)

Central to Blakely is the beautiful, historic Court Square, which houses the current courthouse, fondly known as the "Grand Ole Lady." It was constructed in 1905 and was the fourth one built in Blakely. With entrances on all four sides, the Neoclassical Revival structure sits squarely in the center of Blakely's town square and business district. On its grounds stands a wooden Confederate flagpole, erected in 1861 and the only one still standing in the United States. There is also a monument to the peanut carved of stone atop a pedestal. An inscription notes the economic value of the legume to the area. During the fall, the night air smells of freshly dug peanuts ready to be harvested and shelled. Each year on the last Saturday in March, Court Square is host to the Peanut Proud Festival, which has gained national recognition.

Early County has several historic landmarks. The Kolomoki Mounds State Park is located in the north central part of the county. It contains seven mounds built during the 12th and 13th centuries by the Swift Creek and Weeden Island Indians. The temple mound dates to the year 800 CE and is the largest in the United States. Each year on the second Saturday in October, the park hosts the Kolomoki Indian Festival, with demonstrations of primitive and pioneer skills.

Built in 1891, the Coheelee Creek Covered Bridge is still standing in the western section of Early County. It measures 96 feet long and is the southernmost covered bridge in the United States. In 1976, the bridge was placed in the National Register of Historic Places. It is a popular tourist attraction.

All of the small towns and communities that join Blakely in making up Early County emphasize country life at its best. Here, community pride is big, giving is abundant, and life is so good; it is the "Garden Spot of God's Country!"

One

Early Times

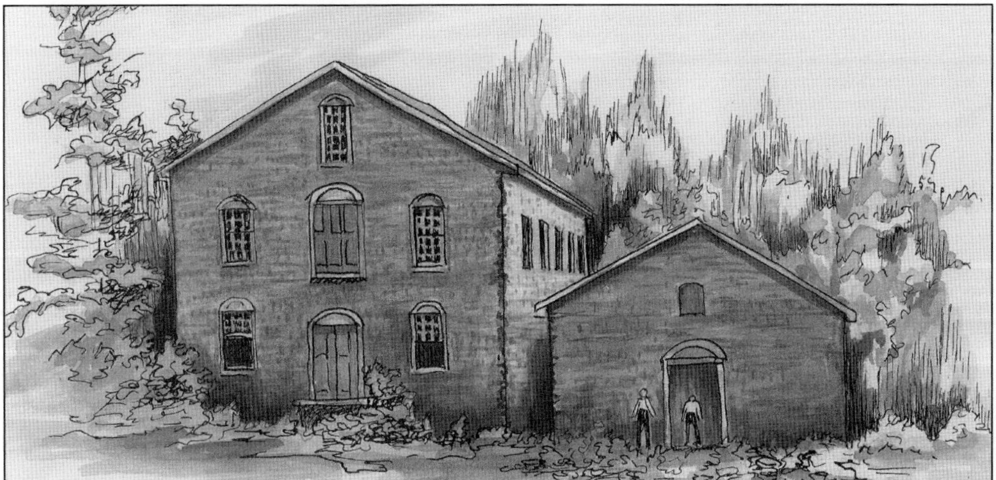

The Old Factory. In 1855, Anthony Hutchins and a group of local citizens built the mill in this drawing. Named Early County Manufacturing Company, the mill was built of handmade bricks that were fired in Early County. Powered by waterfalls on Harrod's Creek, it was in operation for two decades until 1876 and spun local cotton into thread, which was shipped to Columbus, Georgia, to the W.C. Bradley Company. Standing unoccupied, the old mill burned in 1927. The ink drawing of Early County Manufacturing Company was done by the author, and details of the building were inspired by a photograph from a 1927 *Early County News* issue.

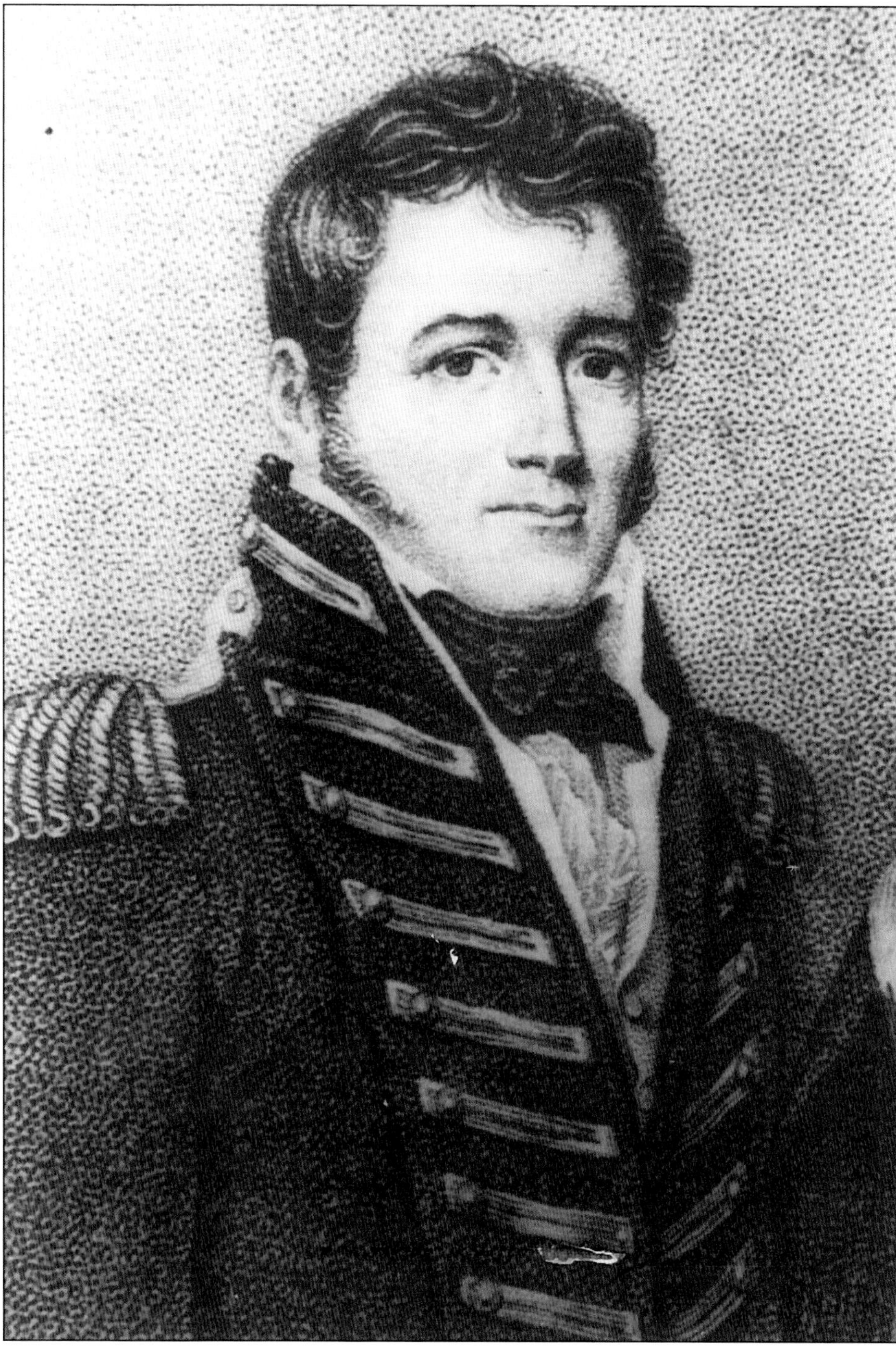

CAPT. JOHNSTON BLAKELEY. Born in Ireland, Capt. Johnston Blakeley (1781–1814) immigrated to America with his family. He joined the Navy and had a distinguished career as an officer. He was placed in command of the cruiser *Wasp* and set sail in 1814 to cruise the area near the English Channel to track British commerce. He and his crew disappeared at sea. The city of Blakely, incorporated in 1870, was named for Captain Blakeley.

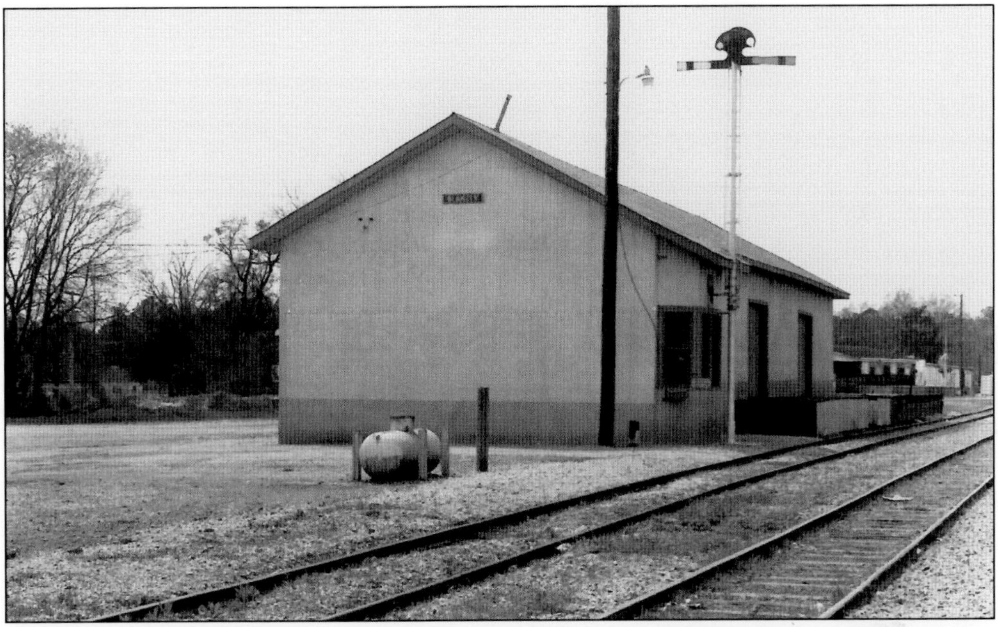

Railroad Depot. In September 1881, after raising $10,000, work began on the train depot building. The building was completed a few months later. *Early County News* reported, "Track laying on the railroad still progresses slowly toward our town. They have passed the halfway ground and will be here after a while." In the same issue, the newspaper reported, "the telegraph has come into the community."

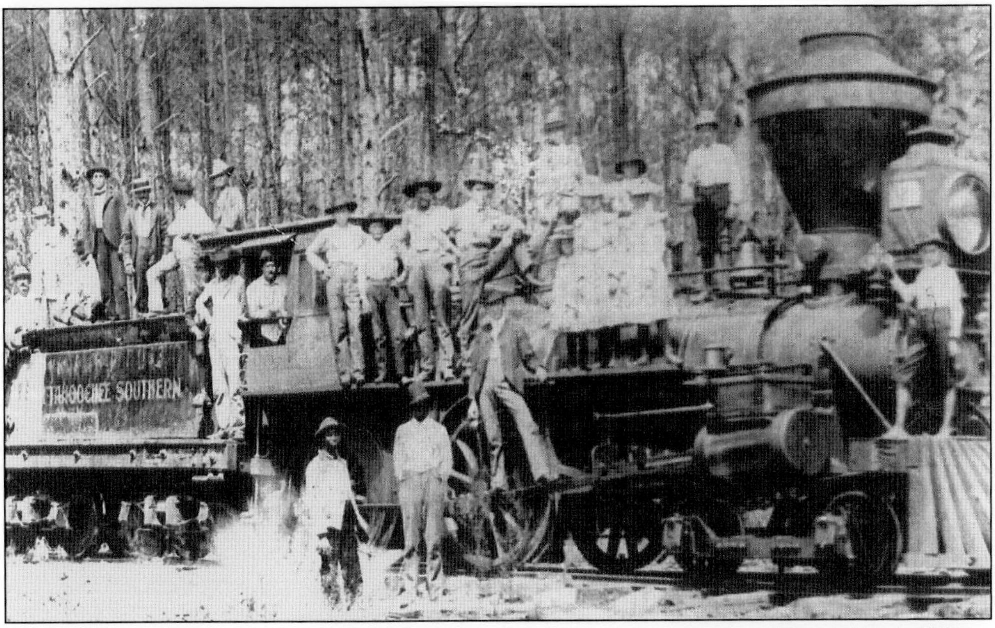

The Train Arrives. The first Chattahoochee Southern train arrived on November 1, 1881, at the new depot on North Cuthbert Street. Trains from Alabama and Albany met in Blakely at 9:45 a.m. and 6:15 p.m. every day. Everyone in town met the trains. It was the "social" thing to do. A "mini-bus" conveyed passengers from the depot to the Livingston House, the Merchant's Hotel, and to Hotel Thompson on the square a few blocks away.

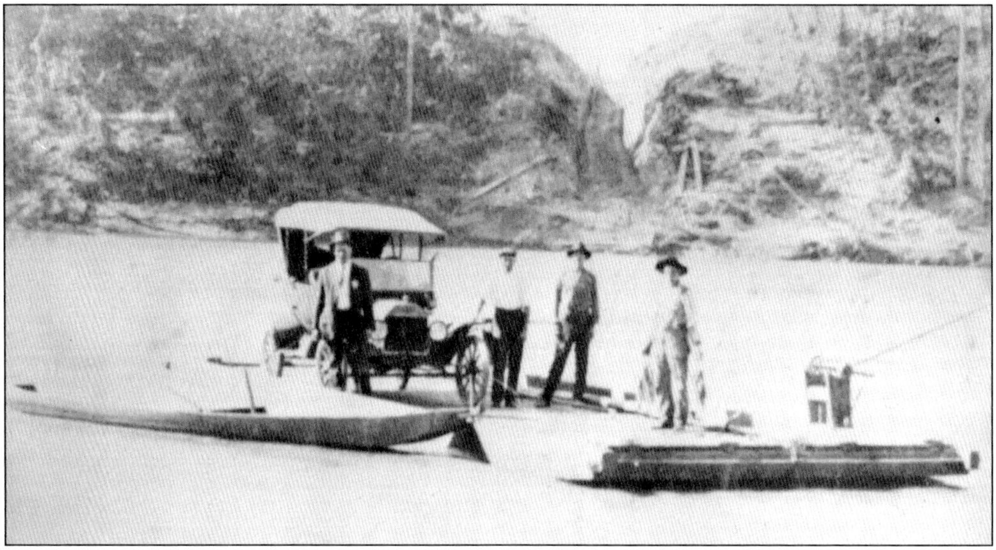

Chandler's Ferry. A narrow dirt road suitable for horse and buggy, mule and wagon, or Model T Ford ran down to the ferry crossing the Chattahoochee River. At the very southern tip of Georgia and Alabama, it was the nearest road from Jakin to Dothan. The high clay banks on either side of the river made the trip a very dangerous one in rainy weather. (Courtesy of Georgia Archives Vanishing Georgia Collection, EAR 100-82.)

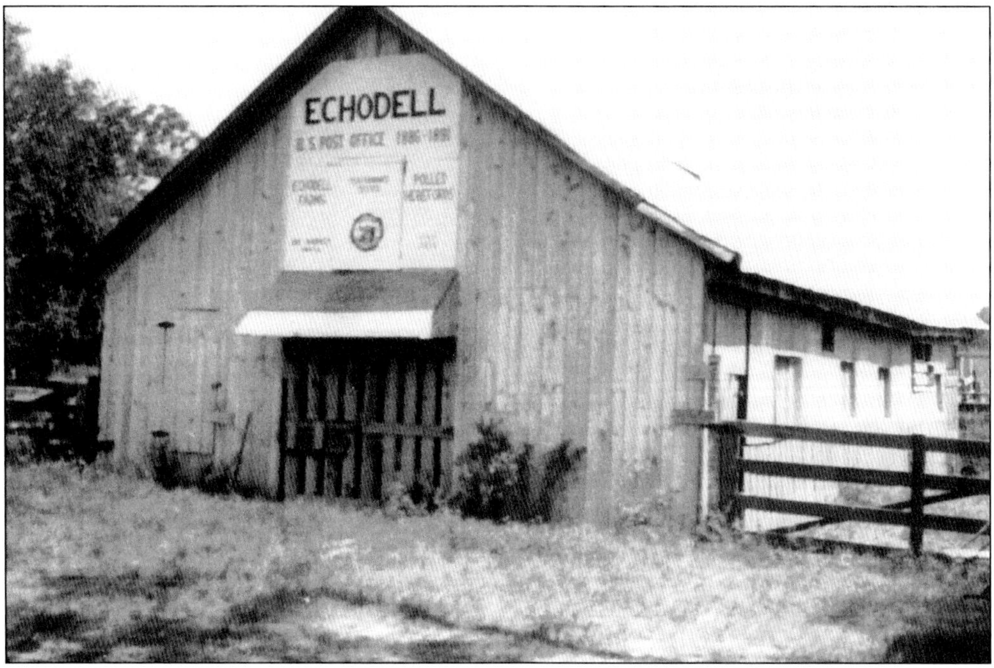

Echodell Post Office, 1886–1891. After nine years of having a post office named Saffold in the southernmost part of Early County, the name was changed to Echodell in 1886. When William Hodges became the postmaster in 1887, the post office was located at his store Echodell, located on River Road about a mile south of the road that became Highway 84 West. The post office name was changed to Josephine in 1891, and eventually, the building was vacated to be used for horses and cows. (Courtesy of Virginia Harvey.)

Kolomoki Mounds. At the time of its highest development from 350 to 600 CE, Kolomoki was perhaps one of the most populous Indian settlements north of Mexico. The Kolomoki site, now a part of Kolomoki Mounds State Park, includes seven mounds, with the largest standing nearly 60 feet high. Smithsonian excavations (1894–1897) concluded that the mounds dated to the Mississippian Period (800–1600 CE). However, archaeologists now recognize that the main occupation of Kolomoki dates to the Woodland Period (1000 BCE–900 CE). In her diary, Rebecca Panton, a Chattahoochee trader's daughter in the early 1800s, mentions being told by her Indian guide that Creek Indians traveled every year to Kolomoki for the Green Corn Festival. The two photographs show the temple mound in 1941 (right) and in the 1960s (below).

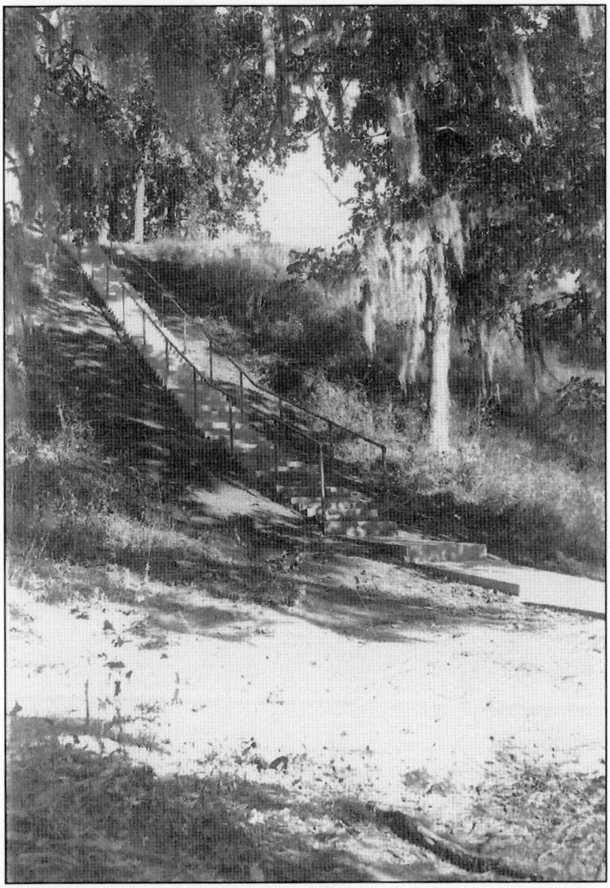

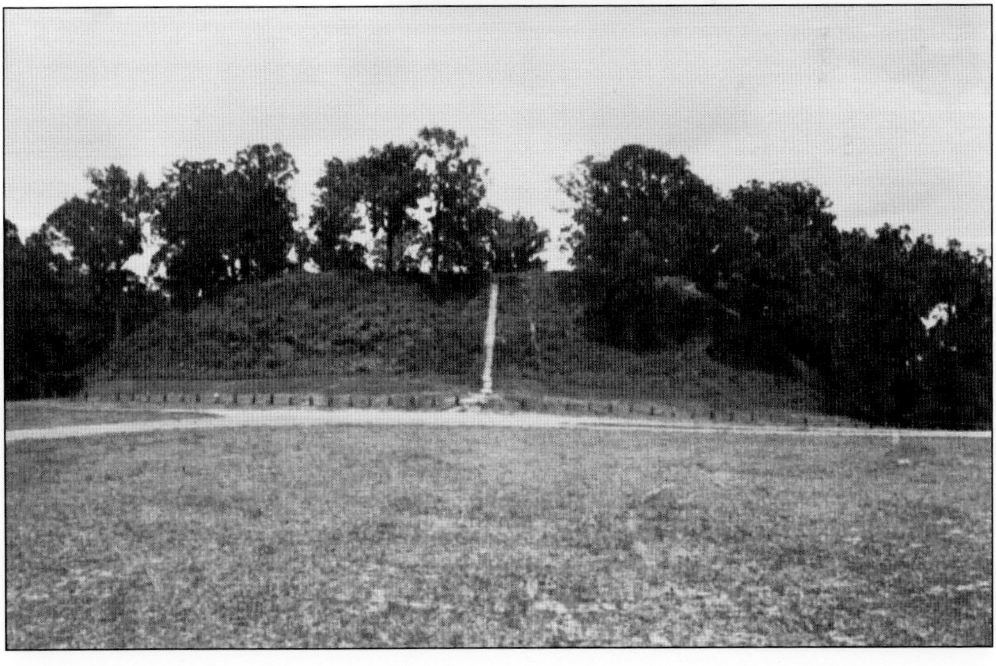

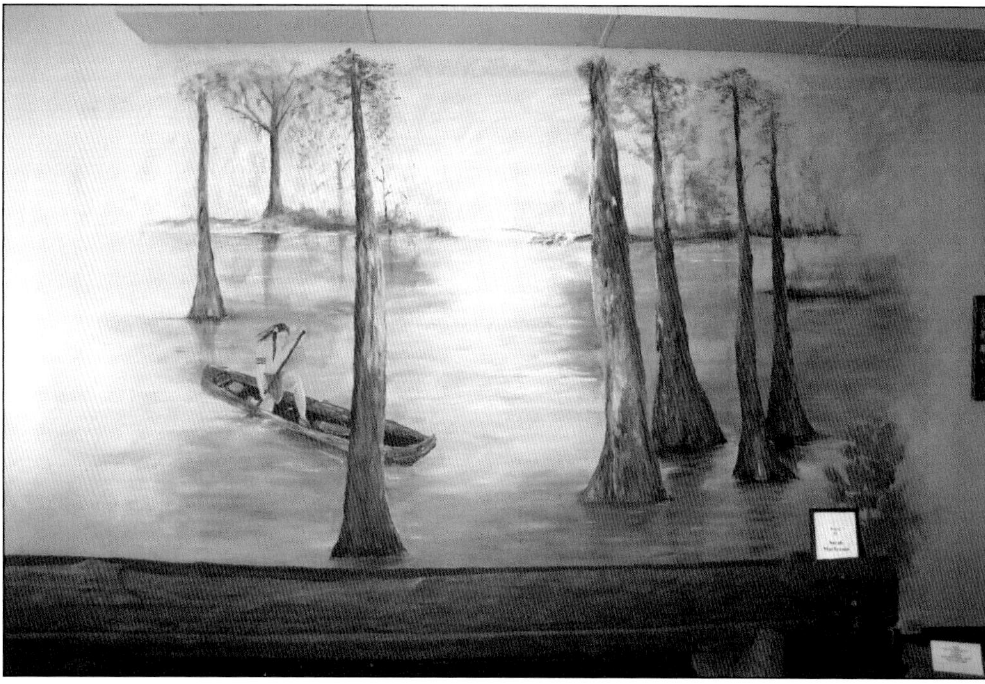

Dugout Canoe. Dating to possibly the 1700s, this hand-hewn canoe was pulled from Spring Creek in Early County when the water was low during the August drought in 1986. Workers clearing the creek bed on Nick Collins's property near Damascus uncovered the artifact in the mud. It is speculated that Indians or early pioneers used the canoe to transport supplies and furs up and down the creek from the Flint River. The canoe is on display at the Early County Museum on North Main Street. The drawing for the mural in the background was created by local artist Samuel Tully Lightsey and painted by Blakely artist Sarah Murkerson. A mural on the exterior wall of the Early County Museum creates a historically accurate scene that depicts the activities of Indians at the site of the seven mounds of Kolomoki. It captures the attitude of a Creek Indian father showing his son the wonders of nature. The mural below was created by muralist Wes Hardin of Dothan, Alabama.

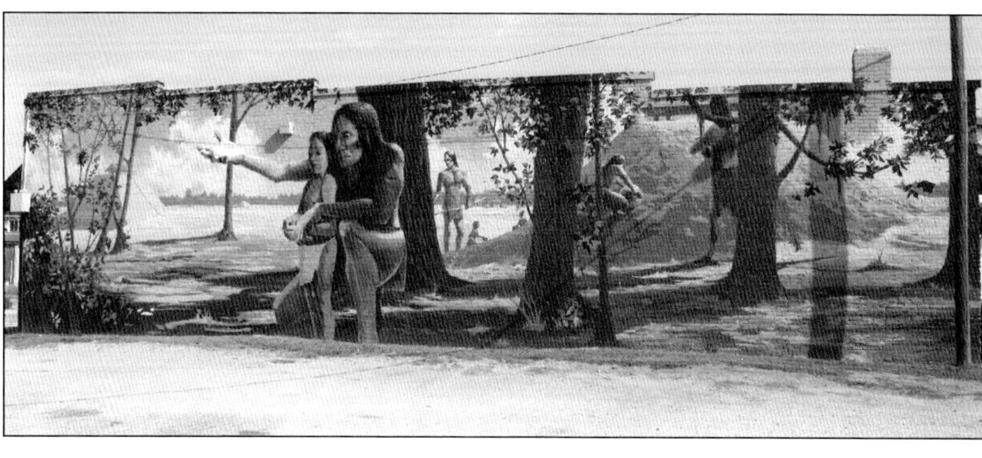

Jesse Brown, 1759–1835. Jesse Brown came to the Early County area before the Indians ceded the territory to the government. His burial site, now Cedar Springs Cemetery, was originally in the front yard of his home. In 1776, at 17 years of age, he became a soldier. He served in the Continental Army for seven years. He was included in the land lottery grants drawn in the Cherokee Land Lottery on July 1, 1833. His descendants still live in Early County.

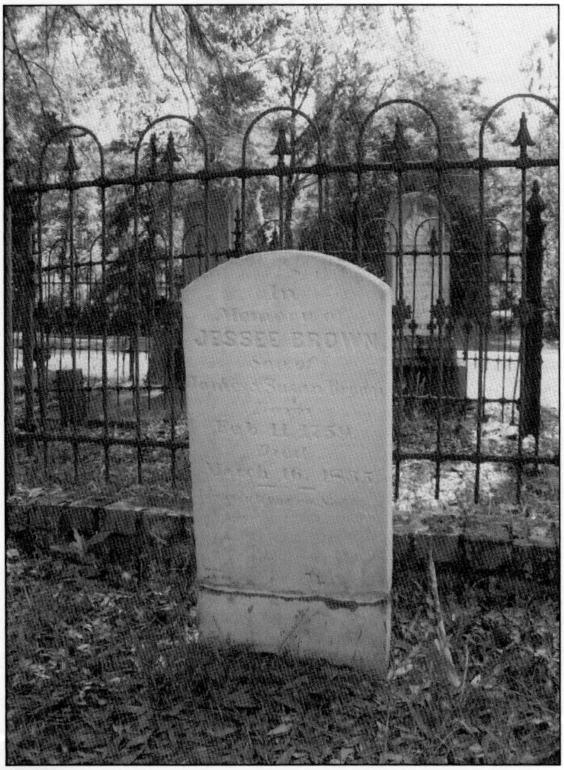

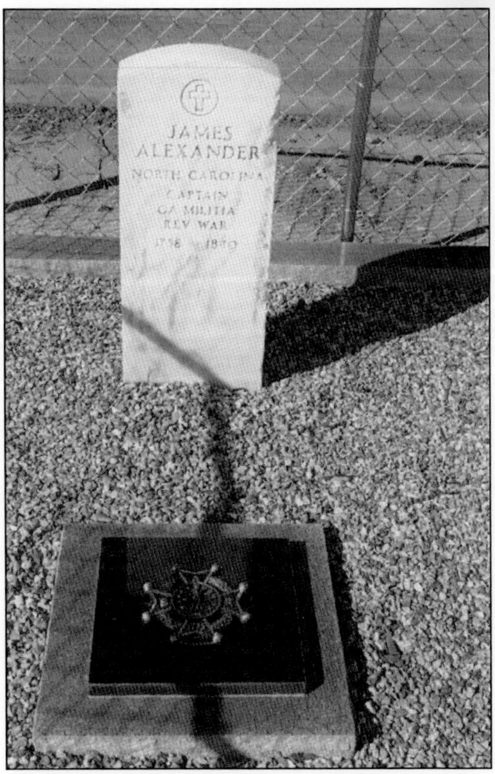

James Alexander, 1758–1840. An isolated grave stands alone on Hattaway farmland near the Chattahoochee River. James Alexander, a Revolutionary War soldier, was a captain in the Georgia militia. Records indicate that he fought at the Battle of Kettle Creek, at which Georgia was freed of Tory domination on February 14, 1779. A high-ranking officer of the Tories, referred to as "Grayson," was shot dead by Alexander after Grayson's capture.

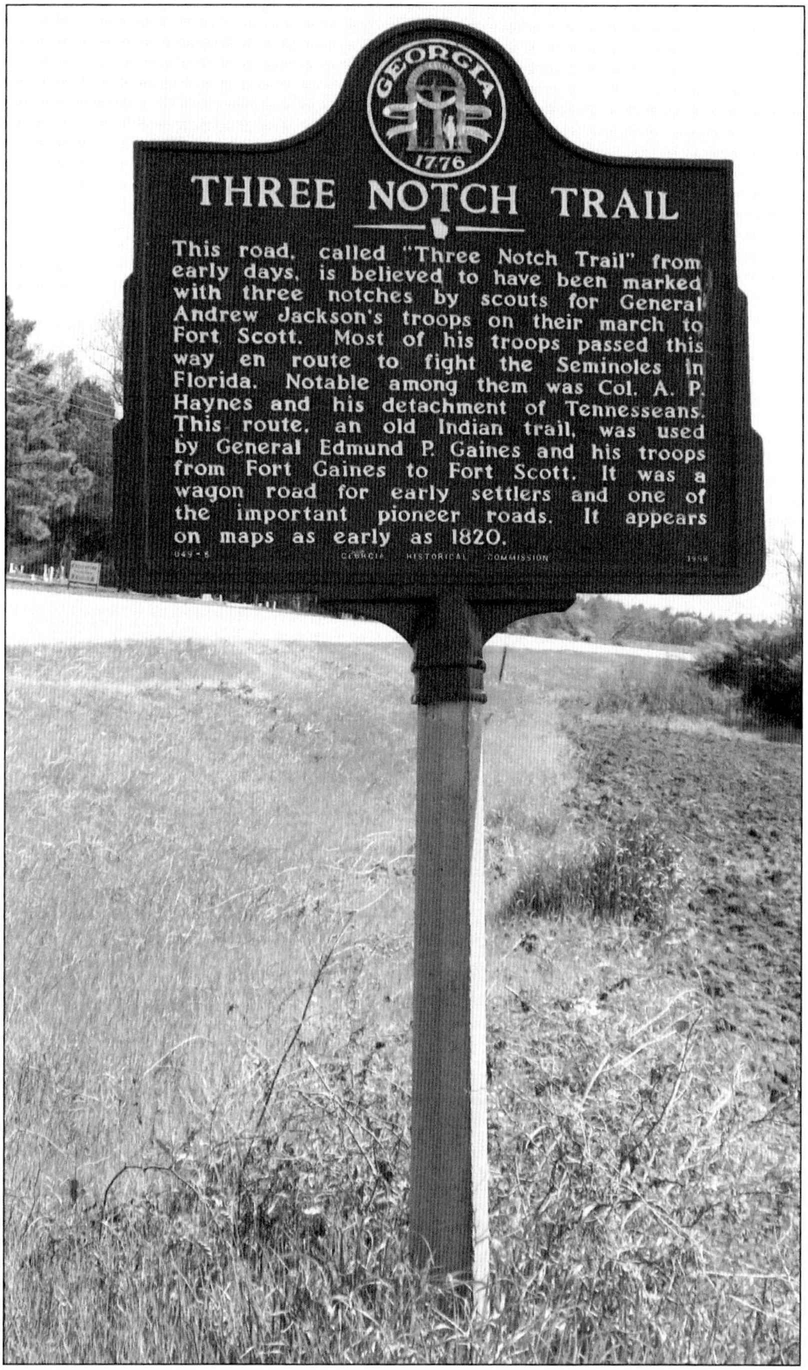

THREE NOTCH TRAIL. Tradition has it that Gen. Andrew Jackson and his men, during his conflicts with the Indians in 1813 and 1818, passed back and forth between Fort Scott and Fort Gaines. This trail, with three notches marked on trees, was originally an old Creek Indian trail. It was marked and widened by General Jackson's scouts to provide passage for ammunition and supplies for the troops on the way to fight Seminoles in Florida. Later, it was a pioneer road and a wagon road for early settlers. Enterprise Freewill Baptist Church Cemetery is in the background.

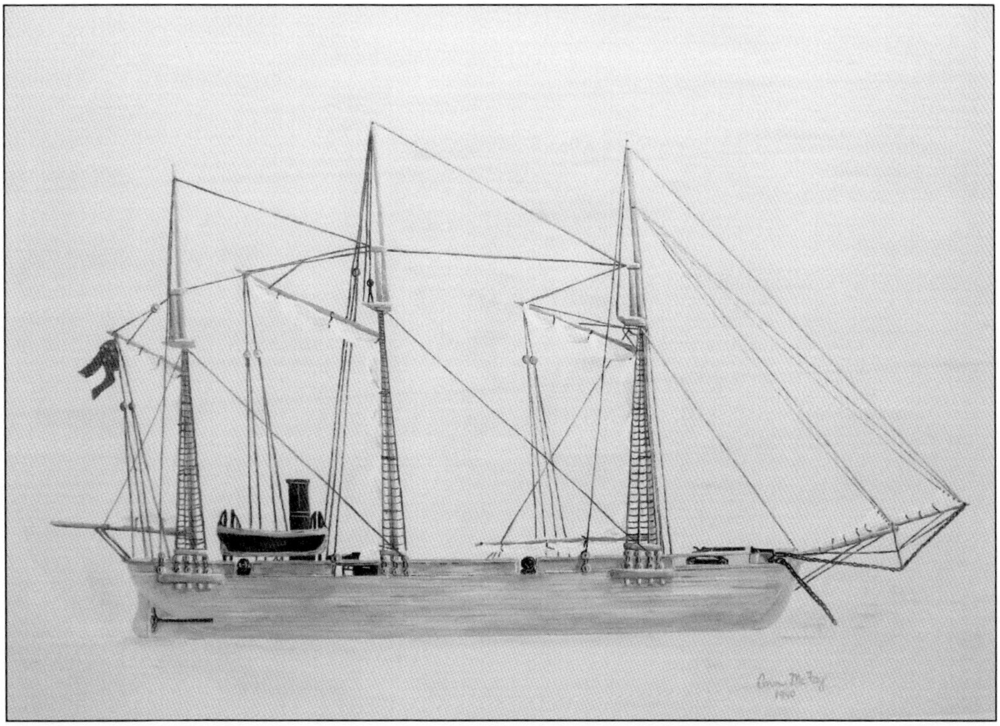

GUNBOAT. The Confederate gunboat *Chattahoochee* was built in the Saffold, Georgia, Confederate Naval Yard in Early County in 1861. The boat saw little service and was burned and sunk in the Chattahoochee River by Confederate forces in 1865 so that it would not end up in enemy hands. A 30-foot section of the stern and its steam engines were recovered in 1964 and are in the National Register of Historic Places in the Columbus, Georgia, Civil War Naval Center. The painting of the gunboat is on display at the Early County Museum and is used with the permission of the artist, Anne McFay Boyd.

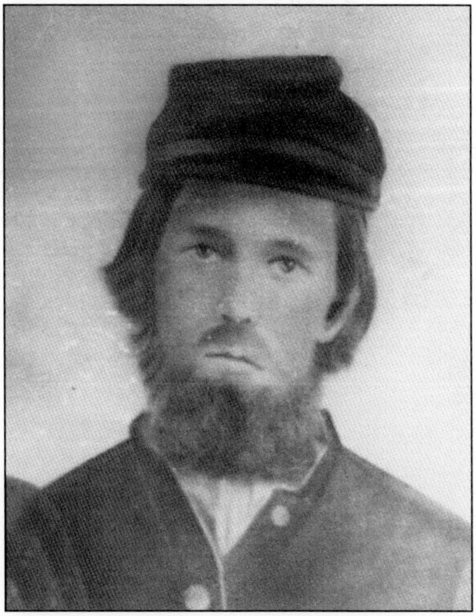

CIVIL WAR SOLDIER. Edward Joshua Houston, pictured here, was an early settler in Early County. He was born in 1818 and lived on the county line of Early and Miller Counties. He was a Civil War soldier in Company K, 51st Georgia Infantry of the Confederate States of America. Returning from the war, he gave the land for the Houston Cemetery, which was on a high knoll just across the road from his home. He died at the age of 70 and was buried in the cemetery. (Courtesy of Mr. and Mrs. Johnny Dixon.)

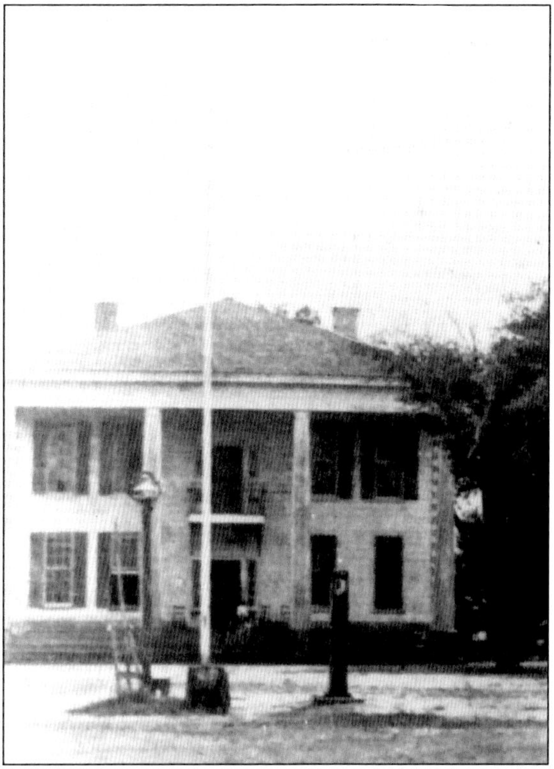

Courthouses of Early County. The first courthouse in Early County was a log structure and was used for the first time in 1827. It was sold for $13 and moved to make way for a two-story wooden structure in 1834. The third courthouse, shown here, was erected in 1857–1858 by Thomas Williams for $4,650 and sold for $155 to make way for a fourth courthouse, built in 1904.

Neoclassical Revival. The dramatic visual impact of the architecture of the building surrounded by lesser buildings, grass, and trees created a beautiful outdoor room to be enjoyed for generations of Early Countians. This photograph also appears on the cover. (Courtesy of Georgia Archives Vanishing Georgia Collection, EAR 35-82.)

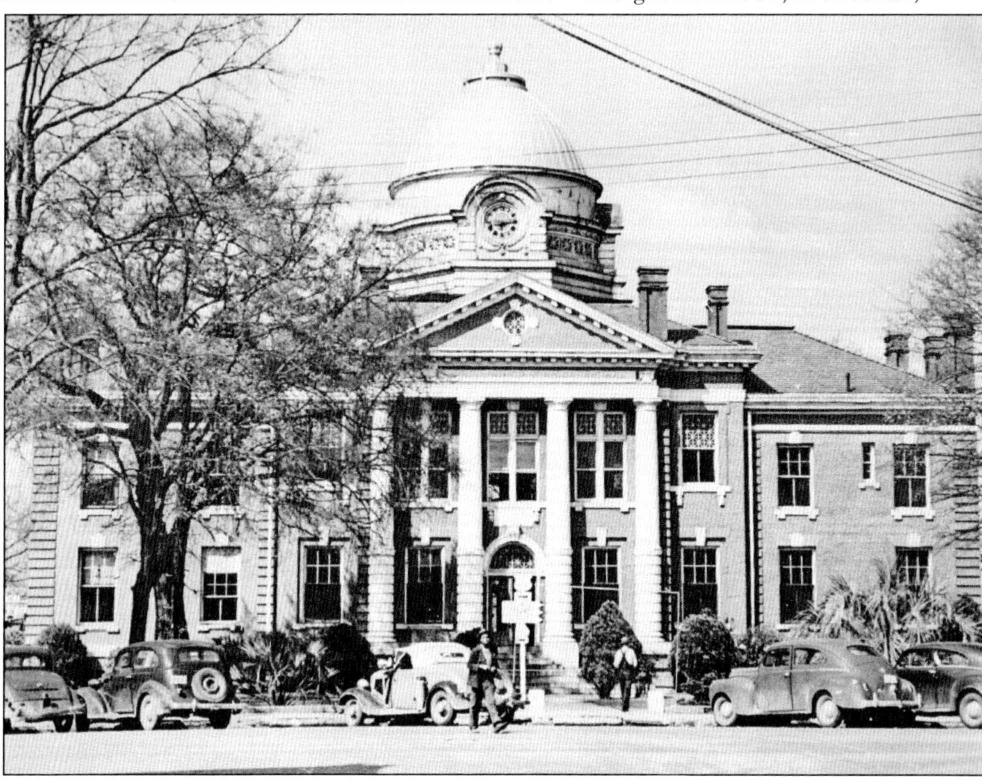

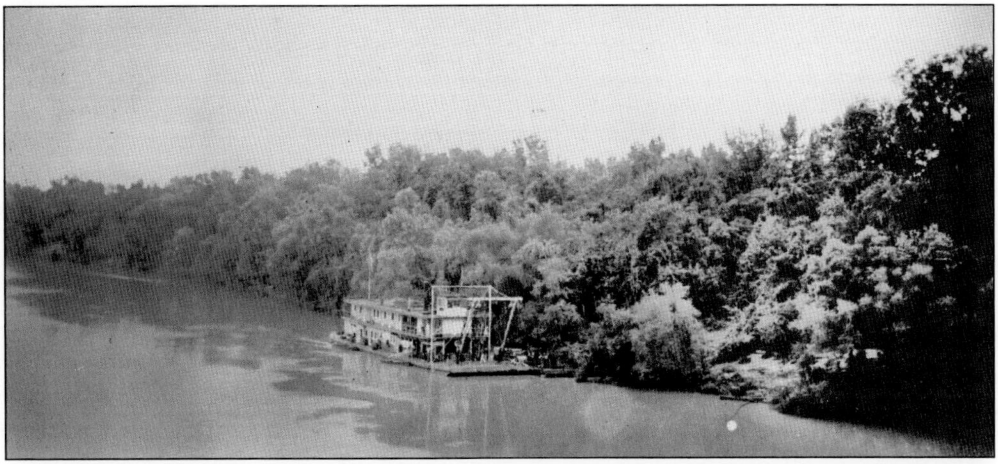

The "Hooch." The Chattahoochee River creates the western border of Early County. During the early years of the 1900s, it was a busy trade route as riverboats and cotton barges fought their way through the murky, swirling waters north to Columbus to unload their goods. Here, a boat used for a different purpose on the river at Saffold makes it way between the overhanging branches to clear out logs and debris. River use declined when the railroad appeared in the 1880s. (Courtesy of Georgia Archives Vanishing Georgia Collection, EAR 70-82.)

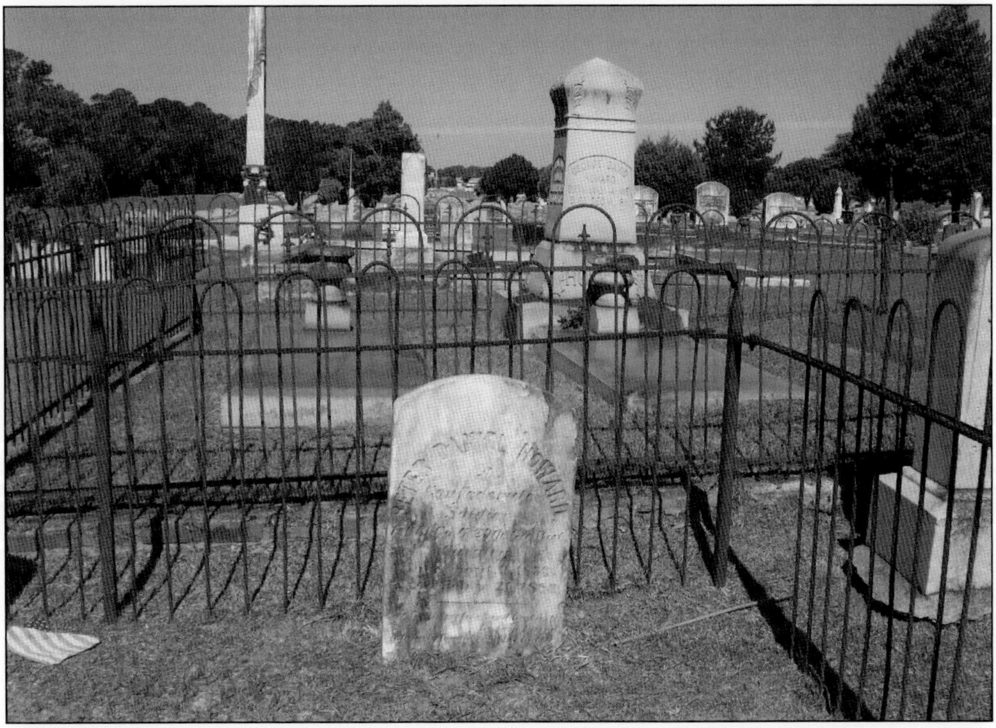

City Cemetery. Just inside the gate of the city cemetery (pictured), the original building of First Baptist Church, named Macedonia, was erected facing east after convening a committee in 1852. The committee, made up of J.W. Perry, Peter Howard, James Buchannon, Benjamin Collier, W.H. Wade, and Joseph G. Collier, had a church constructed that was one of the largest and most imposing structures of its day. When the cemetery grew up around it, the city of Blakely bought the site, and the church built a new structure on the corner of Church and River Streets.

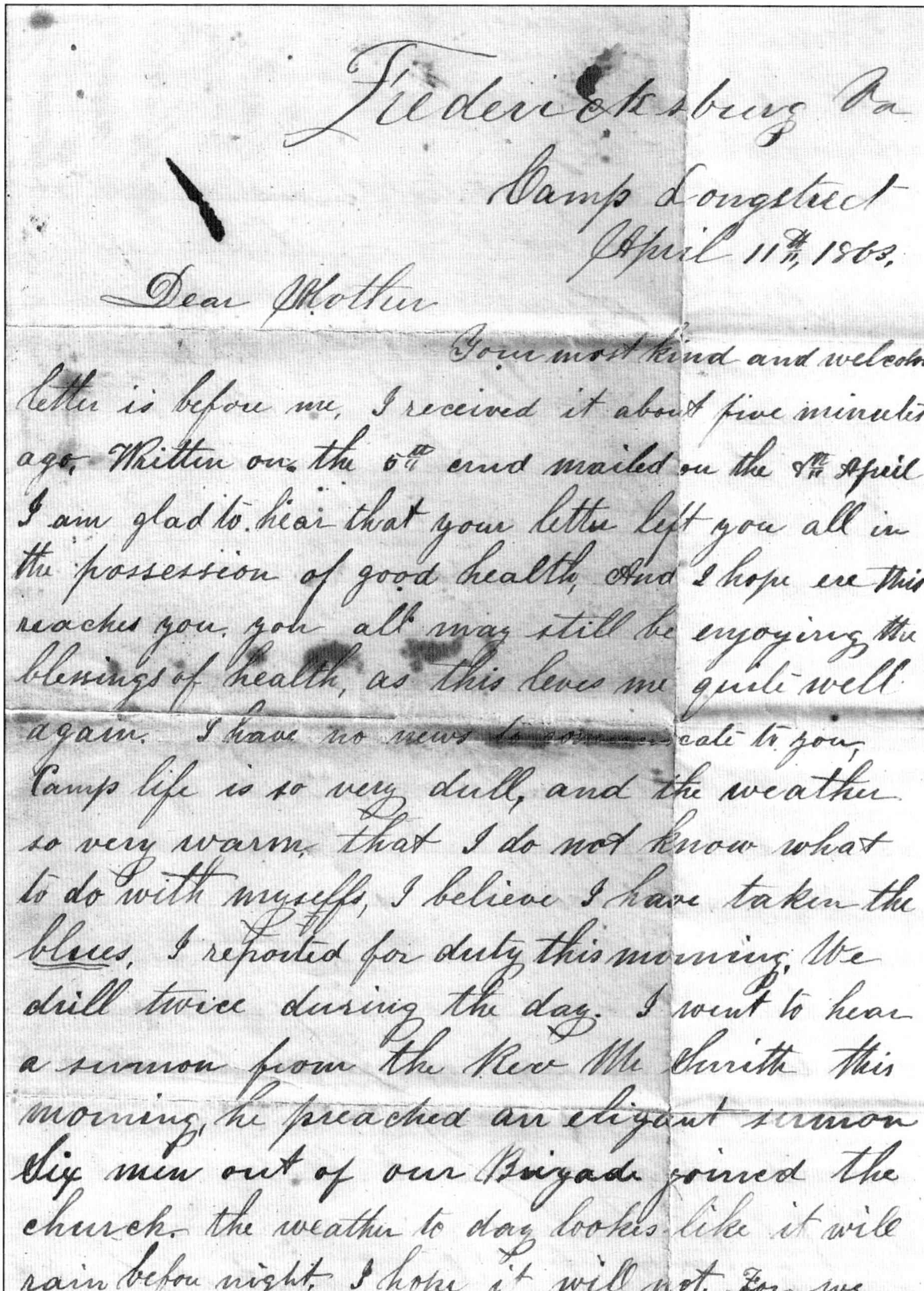
Fredericksburg Va

Camp Longstreet

April 11th, 1863.

Dear Mother

Your most kind and welcome letter is before me, I received it about five minutes ago. Written on the 6th and mailed on the 8th April I am glad to hear that your letter left you all in the possession of good health, And I hope ere this reaches you, you all may still be enjoying the blessings of health, as this leaves me quite well again. I have no news to communicate to you, Camp life is so very dull, and the weather so very warm, that I do not know what to do with myself, I believe I have taken the blues, I reported for duty this morning. We drill twice during the day. I went to hear a sermon from the Rev Mr Smith this morning, he preached an elegant sermon Six men out of our Brigade joined the church. the weather to day lookes like it will rain before night. I hope it will not, For we

A Letter Home. From Camp Longstreet in Fredericksburg, Virginia, on April 11, 1863, Confederate soldier Paul Joyner writes home to his mother, Elizabeth Joyner, "The weather is very warm. I reported for duty this morning. We drill twice during the day. I went to hear a sermon from the Reverend Smith this morning. He preached an elegant sermon. Six men out of our Brigade joined the church. The weather today looks like it will rain before nightfall. I hope it will not. I believe I have taken the blues." Paul was discovered to be an ancestor of A.D. Harris of Blakely. He served during the duration of the war for the Richland Volunteers, Columbia, South Carolina, in Capt. William Carson's company.

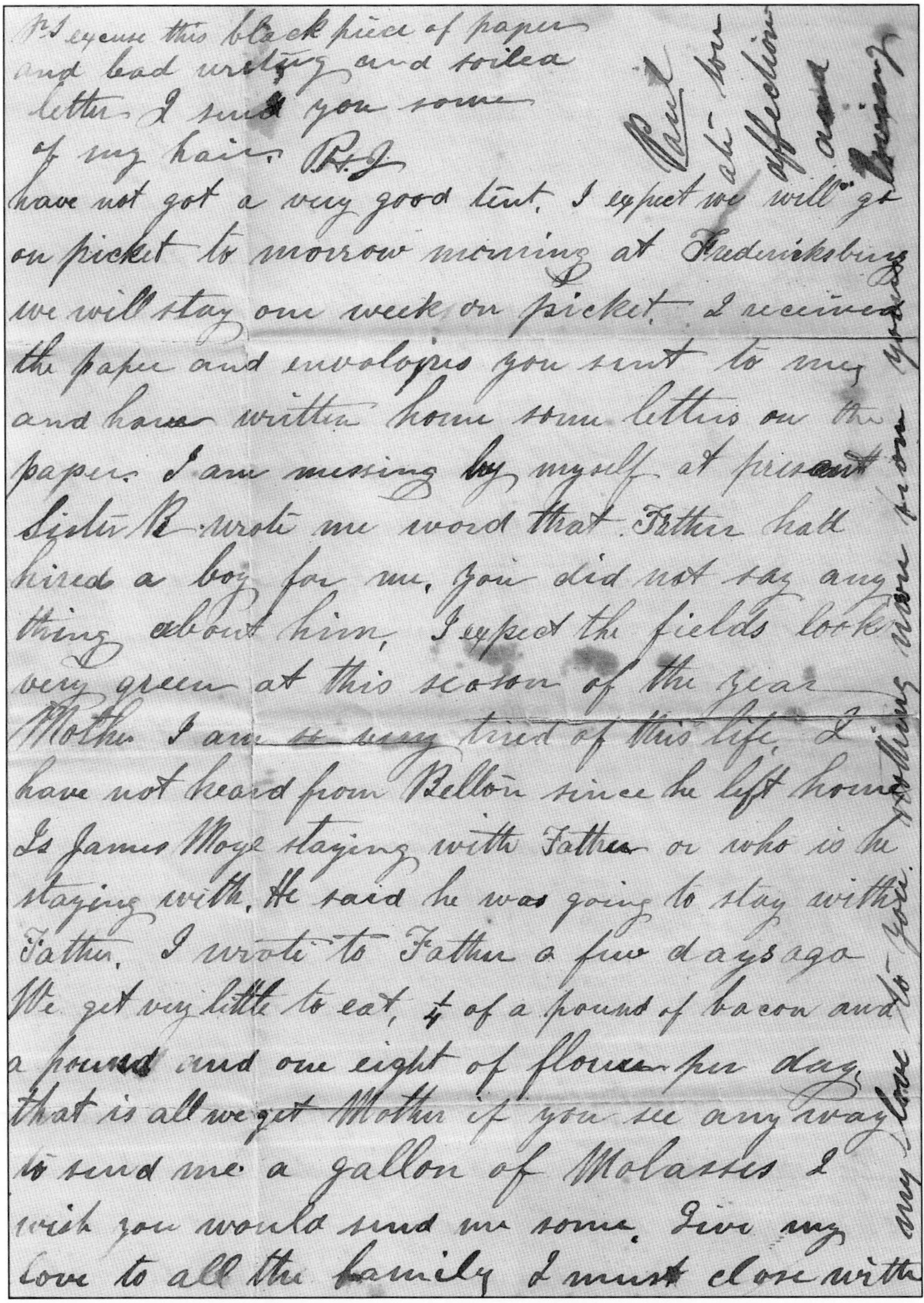
P.S. excuse this black piece of paper and bad writing and soiled letter. I send you some of my hair. P.J.

have not got a very good tent. I expect we will go on picket to morrow morning at Fredericksburg we will stay one week on picket. I received the paper and envolopes you sent to me and have written home some letters on the paper. I am messing by myself at present Sister R wrote me word that Father had hired a boy for me. you did not say any thing about him. I expect the fields look very green at this season of the year Mother I am so very tired of this life. I have not heard from Belton since he left home Is James Moye staying with Father or who is he staying with. He said he was going to stay with Father. I wrote to Father a few days ago We get very little to eat, ¼ of a pound of bacon and a pound and one eight of flour per day that is all we get Mother if you see any way to send me a gallon of Molasses I wish you would send me some. Give my love to all the family I must close with

ARE THE FIELDS GREEN AT HOME? On the back of the page of easily readable script, Paul asks about the family and the weather and follows up by asking about his brother Belton. He writes, "We get very little to eat, ¼ of a pound of bacon and a pound and an eight of flour per day . . . that is all we get. Mother if you see any way to send me a gallon of molasses I wish you would send me some." Paul was wounded twice on the battlefield and later captured at the Battle of Gettysburg. A dedication to another of his family is on the stained glass window by the organ in First Baptist Church of Blakely.

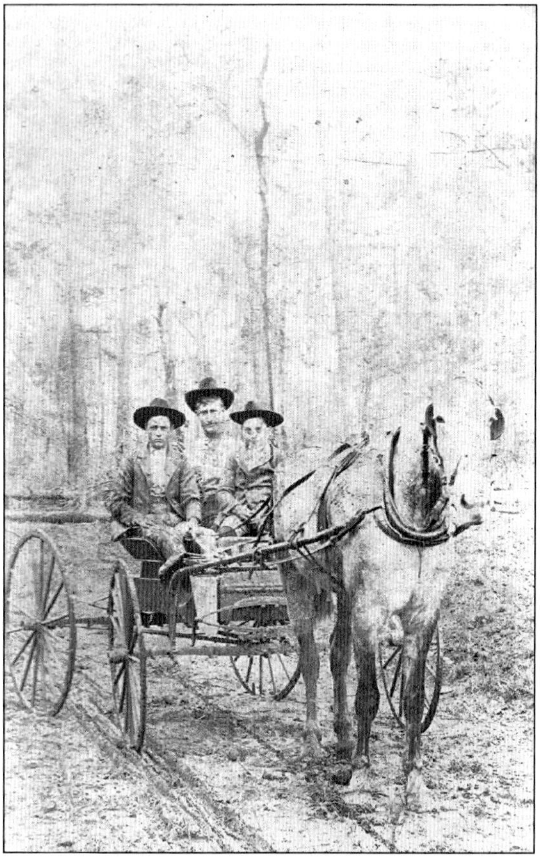

The Buggy. Until the automobile took over as the popular means of transportation, buggies and wagons transported Early County citizens about town and around the countryside. Buggies are American-designed, and this one transports Aileen Robinson, her uncle Jim Frank Robinson, and an unidentified person on a wet road in the Urquhart community. (Courtesy of Mr. and Mrs. John L. Harris.)

Land Surveyors. Georgia's most well-known example of land surveying began with the Georgia Land Lottery of 1805. Land surveyors were called in to measure and regulate the 250-acre parcels of land that were to be sold off by lottery. It was a treacherous job, because most of the land sold off had been "ceded" by the Cherokee and Creek tribes. The tribes fought the seizure of their lands and, in fact, won a decision from the Supreme Court, which both the local state government and Pres. Andrew Jackson ignored. (Courtesy of Georgia Archives Vanishing Georgia Collection, EAR 73-82.)

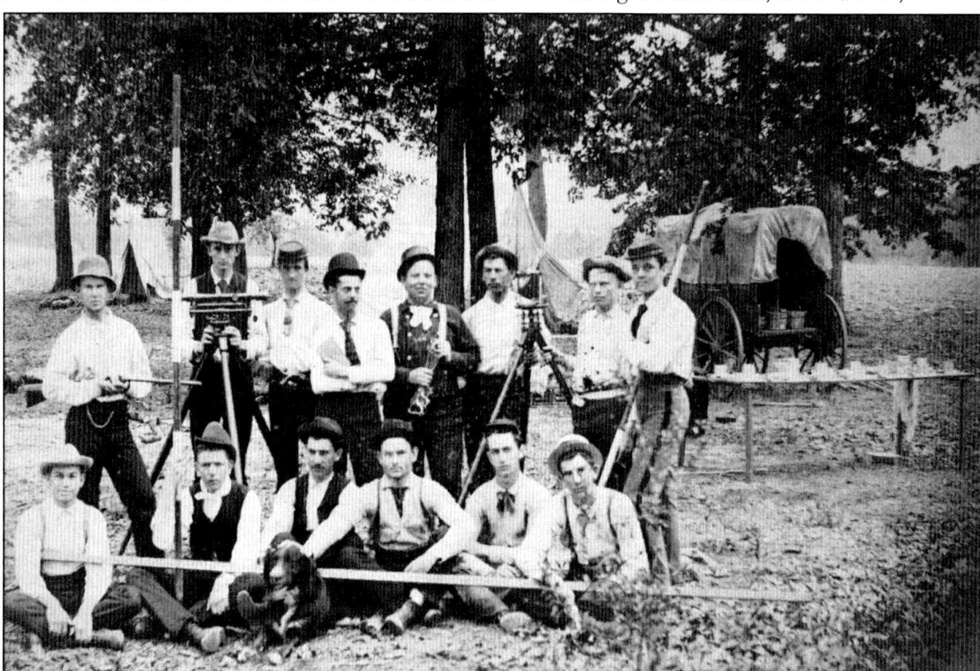

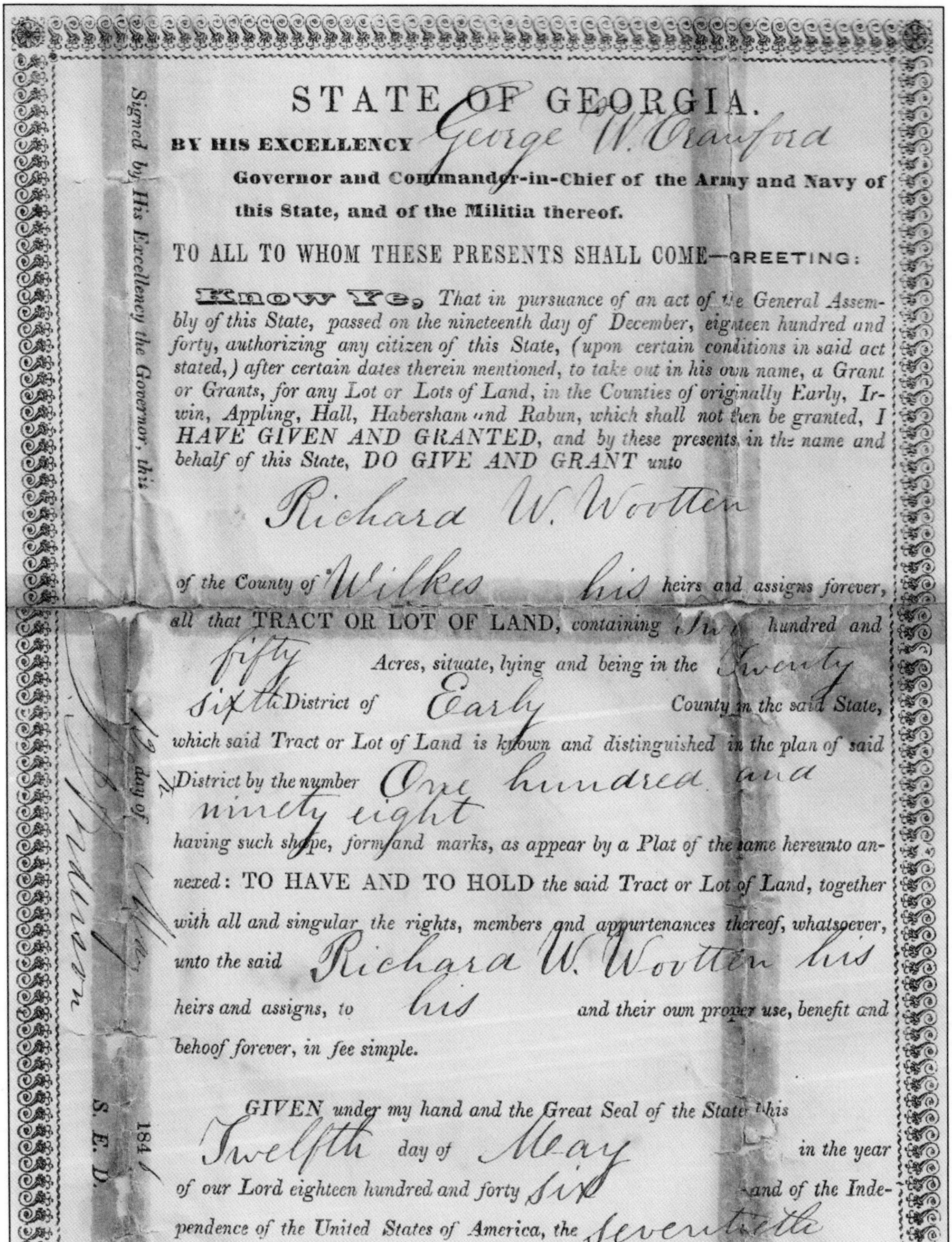

STATE OF GEORGIA.

BY HIS EXCELLENCY George W. Crawford

Governor and Commander-in-Chief of the Army and Navy of this State, and of the Militia thereof.

TO ALL TO WHOM THESE PRESENTS SHALL COME—GREETING:

Know Ye, That in pursuance of an act of the General Assembly of this State, passed on the nineteenth day of December, eighteen hundred and forty, authorizing any citizen of this State, (upon certain conditions in said act stated,) after certain dates therein mentioned, to take out in his own name, a Grant or Grants, for any Lot or Lots of Land, in the Counties of originally Early, Irwin, Appling, Hall, Habersham and Rabun, which shall not then be granted, I HAVE GIVEN AND GRANTED, *and by these presents, in the name and behalf of this State,* DO GIVE AND GRANT *unto*

Richard W. Wootten

of the County of Wilkes his *heirs and assigns forever, all that* TRACT OR LOT OF LAND, *containing* Two *hundred and* fifty *Acres, situate, lying and being in the* Twenty sixth *District of* Early *County in the said State, which said Tract or Lot of Land is known and distinguished in the plan of said District by the number* One hundred and ninety eight *having such shape, form and marks, as appear by a Plat of the same hereunto annexed:* TO HAVE AND TO HOLD *the said Tract or Lot of Land, together with all and singular the rights, members and appurtenances thereof, whatsoever, unto the said* Richard W. Wootten his *heirs and assigns, to* his *and their own proper use, benefit and behoof forever, in fee simple.*

GIVEN under my hand and the Great Seal of the State this Twelfth *day of* May *in the year of our Lord eighteen hundred and forty* Six *and of the Independence of the United States of America, the* Seventieth

Signed by His Excellency the Governor, this 12 *day of* [illegible] *184*6

S. E. D.

Wooten Land Lottery. The site of 250 acres of land, number 198, is described in this land grant document from the State of Georgia. It reads, "TO HAVE AND TO HOLD the said Tract of Lot of Land, together with all and singular the rights, members and appurtenances thereof, whatsoever, unto the said Richard W. Wooten . . . GIVEN under my hand and the Great Seal of the State this Twelfth day of May in the year of our Lord eighteen hundred and forty Six and the Independence of the United States of America, the Seventeenth." The last Harvey to own this land grant was Dot Harvey in the early 1940s. (Courtesy of Virginia Harvey.)

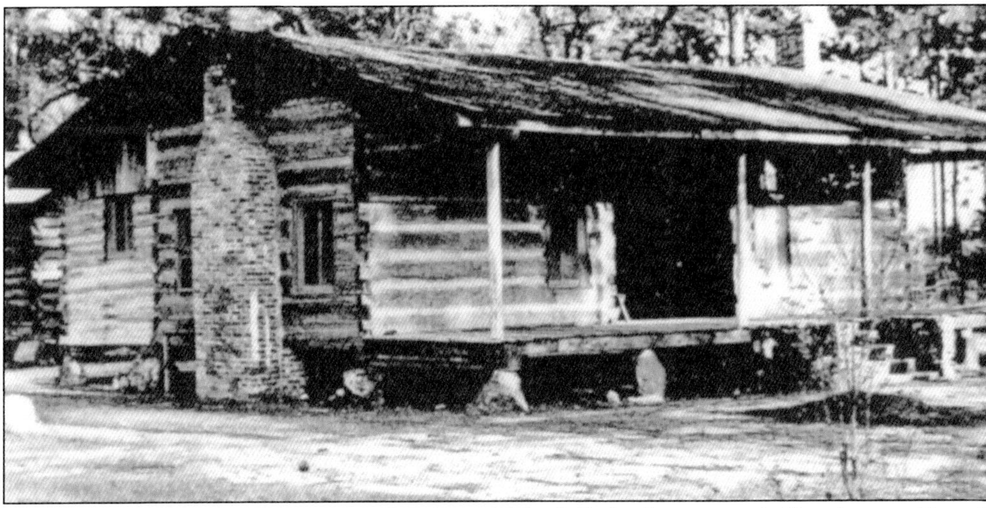

DOUBLEPIN LOG CABIN. Across River Road from Echodell, the former antebellum home of Joseph Q. Harvey, is the authentic log cabin restored by Virginia Harvey. It was originally brought to Early County from a site in Jackson County, Florida, and is historically identical to log homes built in Early County. Originally constructed in the early 1800s, it was probably a stagecoach stop at a crossroads. Smokehouses like the one below were used by country families to store pork, beef, and fish. Hickory fires were built inside the house on the dirt floor. Green wood created a lot of smoke and gave the meat a special taste. The meat was hung from the rafters by jute cords and cut down when needed.

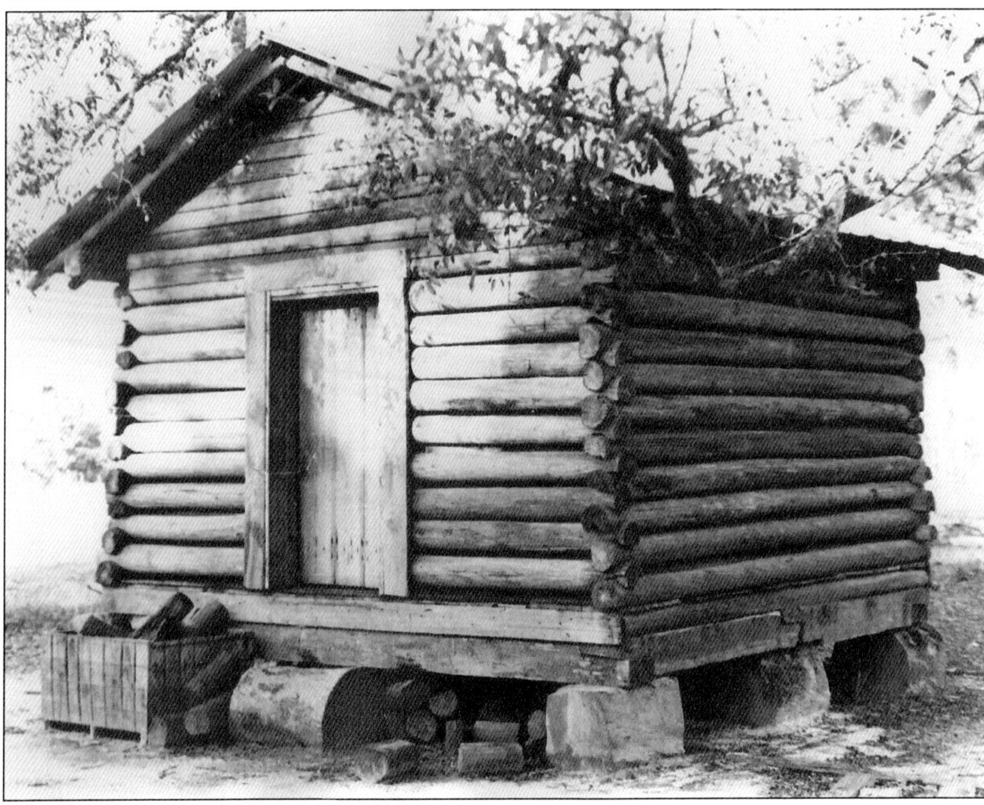

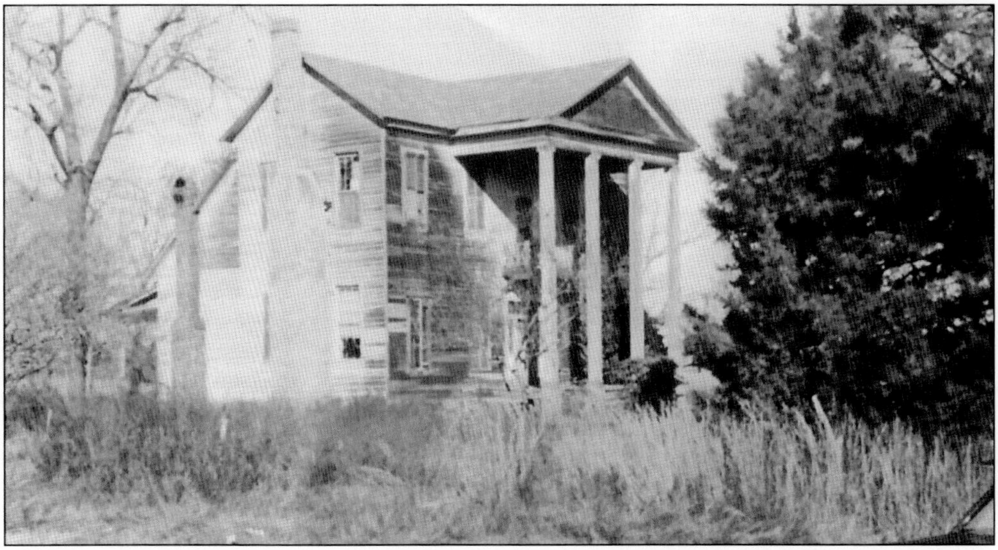

ECHODELL. Built in 1840, Echodell (above), just north of Jakin, drifted into ruin after being built and lived in by three generations of descendants of Dempsey Harrell. It is located on Old River Road and is a showplace reminiscent of the "Old South." Subsequent owners were Dr. A.D. Shewmake and Jule Peterman. Below, Mr. and Mrs. Joe Harvey have restored it to its original splendor. (Both, courtesy of Virginia Harvey.)

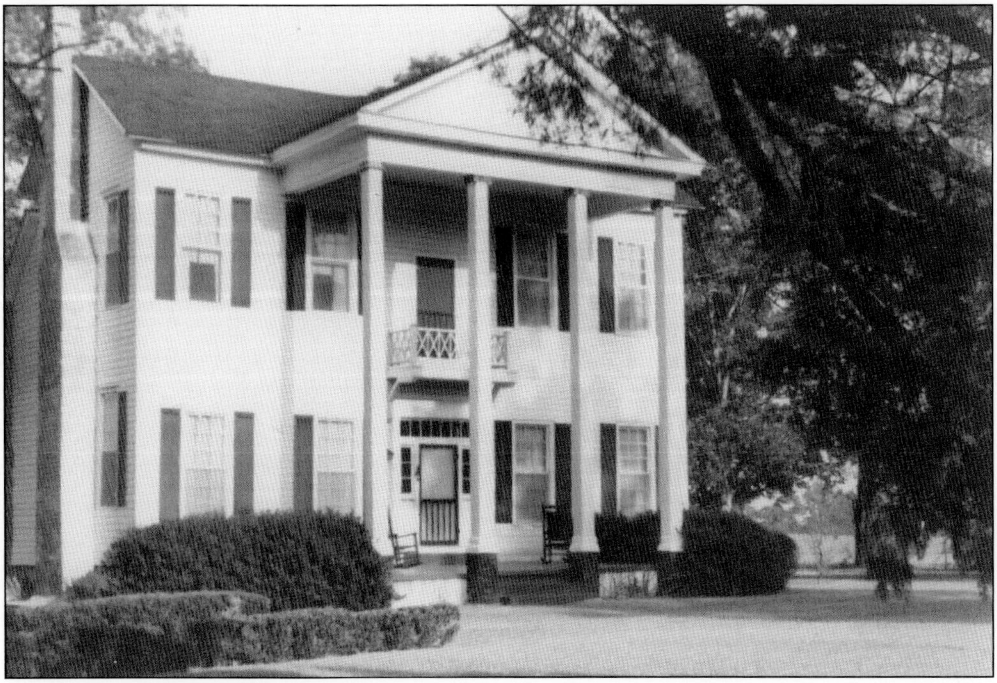

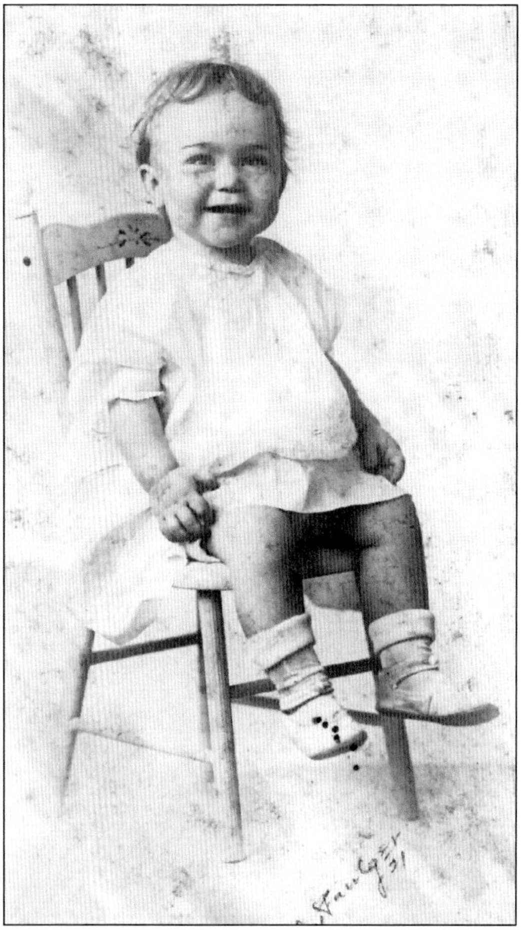

BABY VIRGINIA. On July 29, 1920, John Quitman Harvey and Mattie Lu Brannan Harvey were blessed with a little girl. Growing up in South Carolina, Virginia Harvey, her parents, and her younger brothers and sisters moved back to Jakin in 1939. Over the years, Virginia worked in bookkeeping and accounting. This occupation prepared her for the involvement she had with documenting the history of Jakin, Georgia, a small town in south Early County. She was deeply involved with the Early County Historical Society in publishing its three historical volumes about Early County and with the locally printed book *Remember Jakin*.

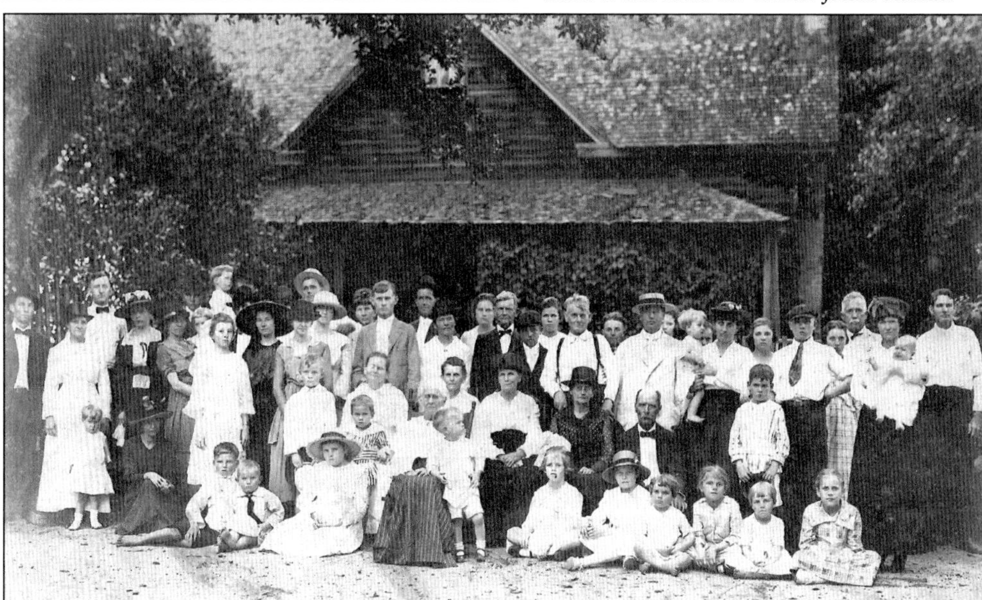

MINTER REUNION. Near Jakin, at the old home place, Cynthia McLain Minter (husband John M. Minter) gathered the extended family for a reunion. John's brother Constantine Alonza Minter, according to the *Early County News* of August 28, 1884, was the first white child to be born in Early County. In the lower part of Early County, he bought three lots of 250 acres each: lot 238 in 1872 for 20 bushels of corn; lot 239 for $5.25 in 1878; and lot 203 for $5 in 1878. So for $10.25 and 20 bushels of corn, he bought 750 acres of land. Part of the land is the land on which Jakin stands.

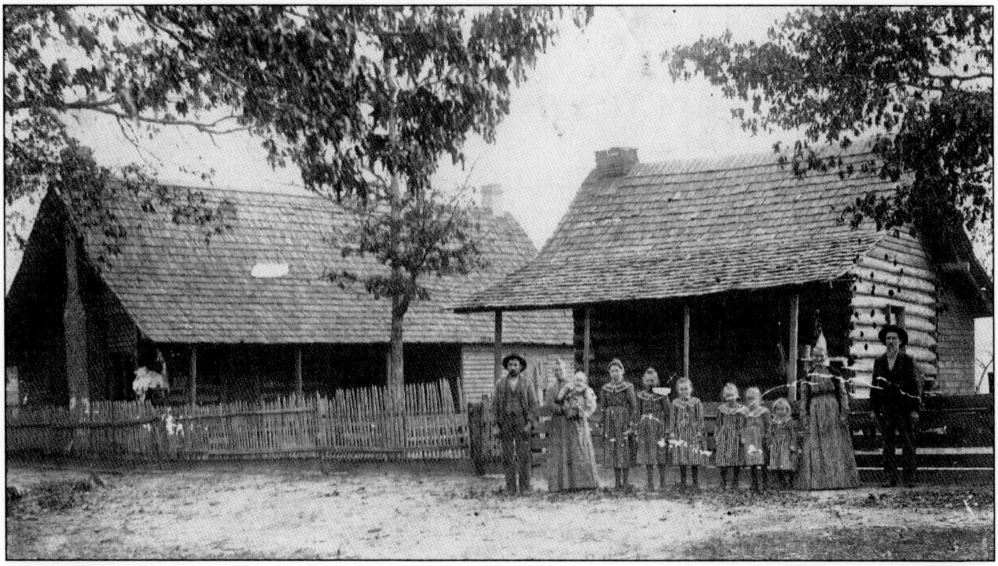

The Jenkins Family. On Jenkins Road, the log home of Louis Wingate Jenkins and Jemima Bates Jenkins was made of hand-hewed logs and shingles covering the roof. The large home was separated from the kitchen, since fire was a common occurrence when stoves overheated. Also, the heated wood stove in the kitchen would cause the whole house to overheat. The family members lined up in front of the home are, from left to right, Louis Wingate Jenkins; Jemima "Jennie" Bates; baby Louis Artemous; Mattie, Jennie Lou, Nettie, Ola Lavenia, Still, and Lonnie Jenkins; Martha Jane Stubbs; and John Taylor Jenkins.

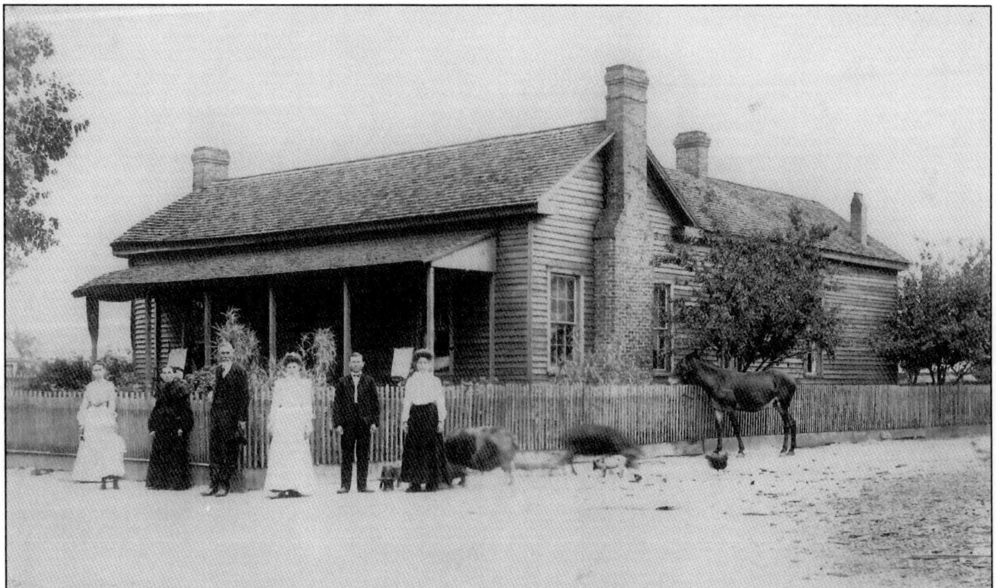

The King Family. Oswald King (center with beard), reared in Early County, was one of nine children. His father, Dr. John James King, trained in medicine and, along with eight of his brothers, defended the cause of the Southern states when summoned in 1860. Miraculously, all eight brothers returned safely. Dr. King practiced medicine and raised a family and was founder of several churches in Early and Clay Counties. (Courtesy of Mr. and Mrs. Bobby King.)

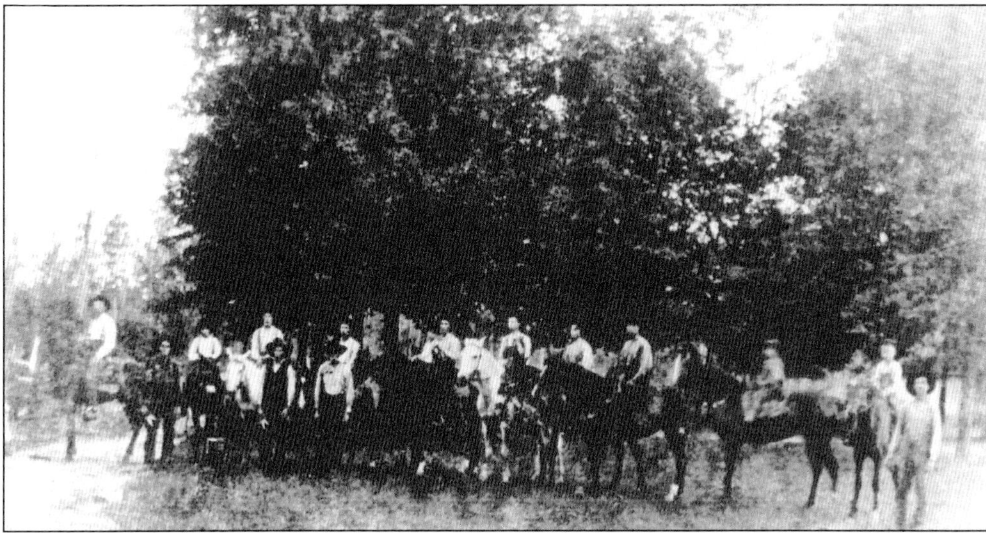

Gathering Wool. In 1906, men and boys on horseback participate in the roundup of the sheep at J. Brown Mosely's home in Jakin. Those pictured are, from left to right, Earl Mosely, Mozelle Mosely, J. Brown Mosely, Ev Pyles, Howard Easom, Bill Johnson, John Pyles, Bart Hayes, Tom Harvey Sr., Ed Fiveash, Pat Fiveash, and Arver Mosely. Sheep were raised in Early County in the early 1900s. Sheepshearing was done by hand using scissor-like shears. Starting with the belly, the shearers would try to keep the belly wool separated from the main fleece, because the belly wool is uneven and filled with dirt and trash. The following are little-known facts: one fleece from a sheep is enough wool for a man's suit; it takes a shearer two to five minutes to shear the wool in one large piece; sheepshearing goes back 1,000 years.

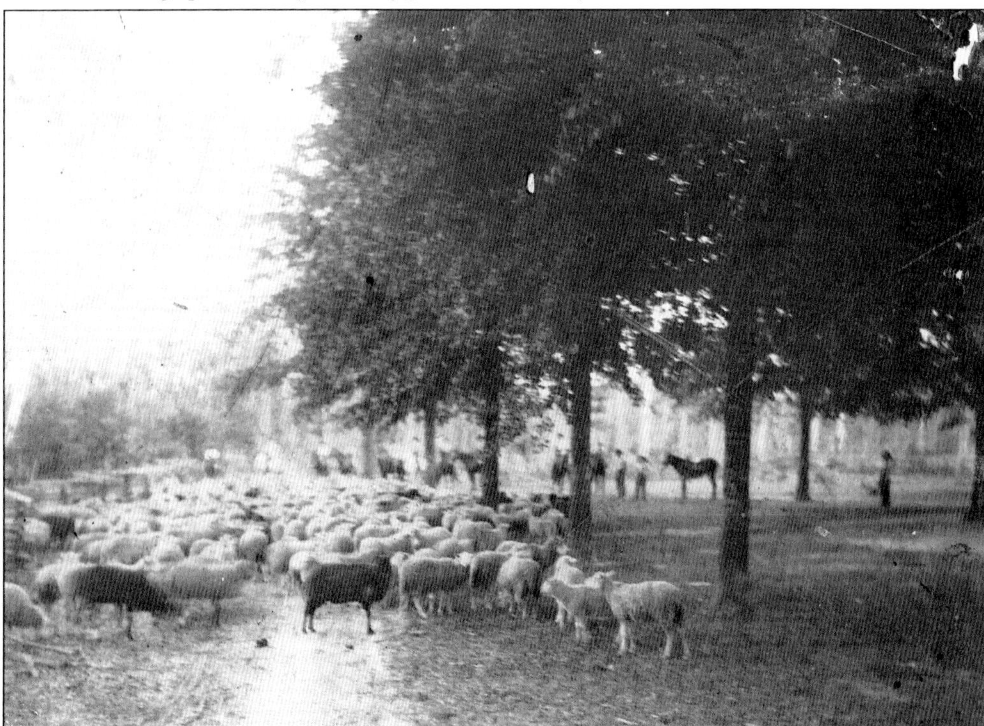

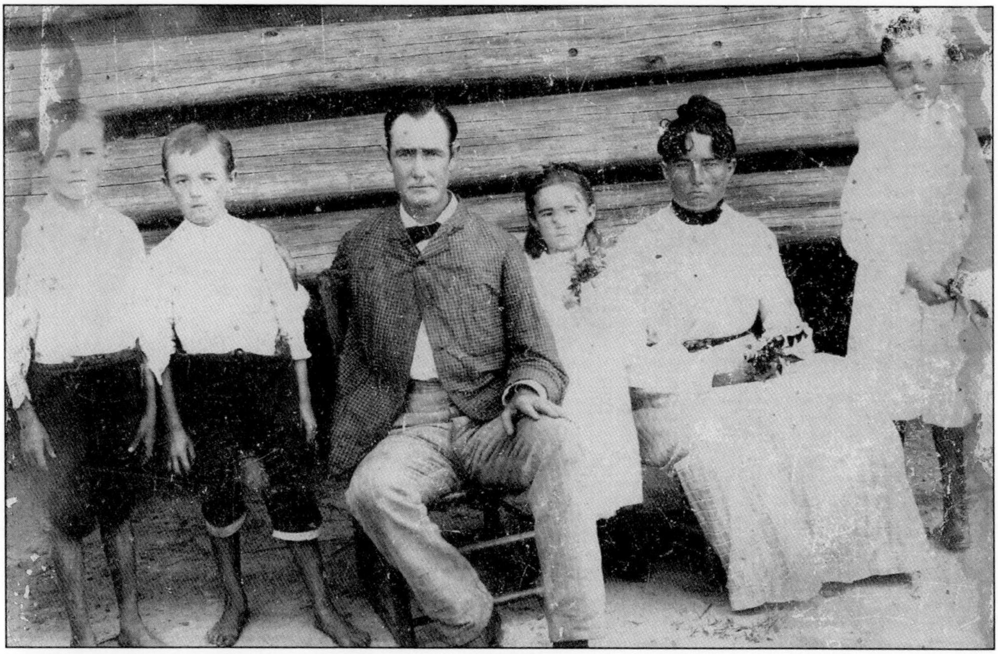

Log Cabin Living. Early log cabins had dirt floors and huge fireplaces, and inhabitants used water that was carried from the nearest creek. In the Cuba community, J.P. Pounds and his wife, Camilla Elizabeth Pounds, gather their children for a rare photograph. The six-year-old standing between her parents is Ethel Pounds. Their two boys in the picture are Jack "Buddy" Pounds (left) and J.P. (Jr.?) Pounds. The girl to the right is not identified. Please note the short chairs; this was probably because settlers used shorter tables during that time. The second photograph is the Loyless-Pearl home, located on River Street in Blakely. The log cabin was built in 1843 by Hightower Loyless and his wife, Mary Perry Loyless (sister of Joel Perry). (Above, courtesy of Mr. and Mrs. Phillip Moore.)

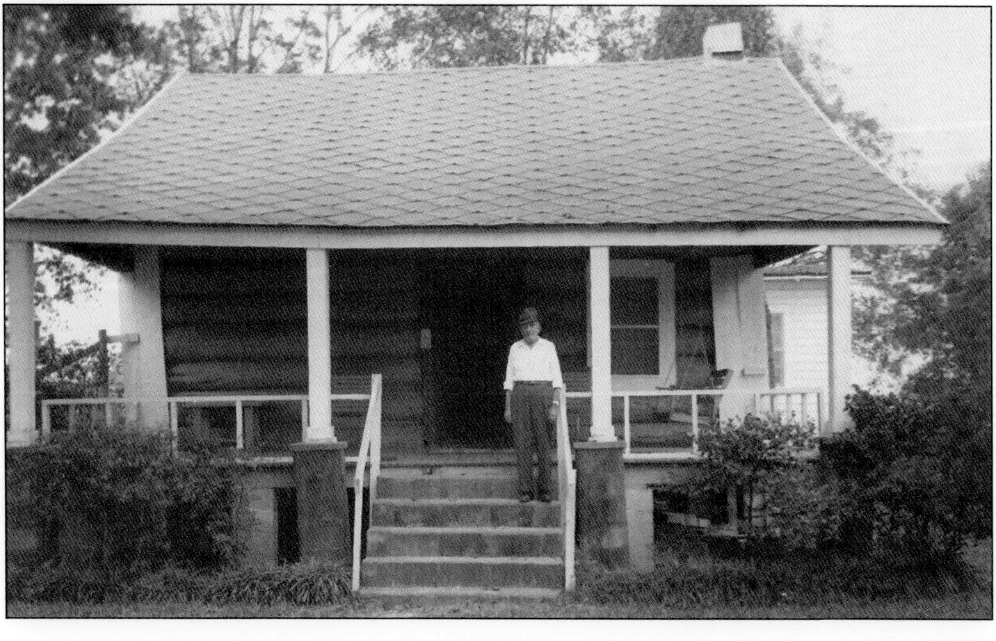

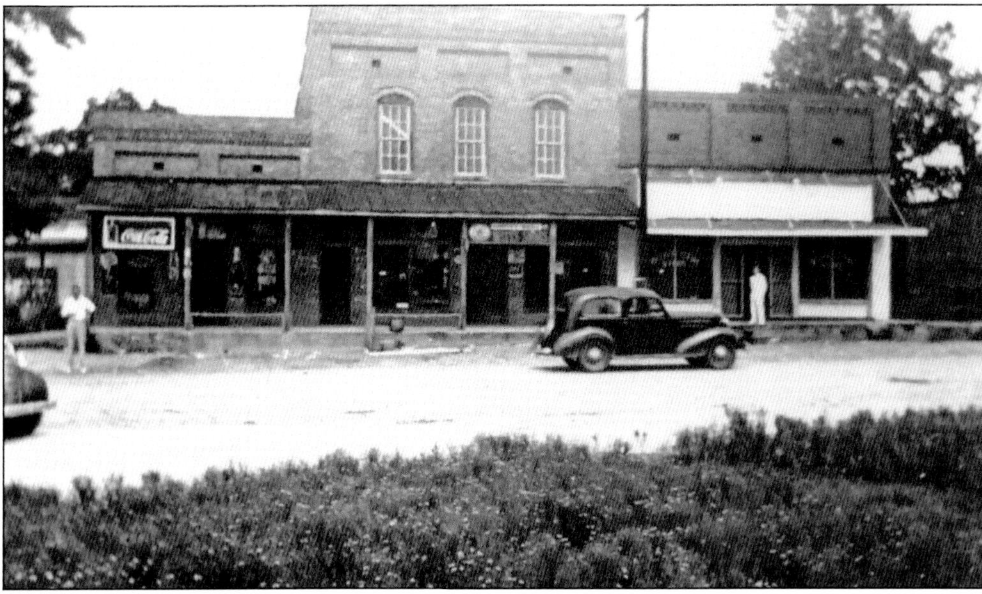

West Side of Pearl. In Jakin during 1910, T.G. Harvey Jr. built a two-story building of brick. The downstairs floor contained general merchandise, hardware, and farming tools, which were all for sale. Upstairs was a meeting hall for community activities, including debates, theater performances, and, at one time, even a skating rink. Tied to the Harvey Building were the Allen Bivens store (on the left) and a grocery store operated by W.V. Miller Sr. and J.W. Miller (on the right). The picture from the late 1930s also shows Glynn Siniard and his 1938 Chevrolet. On the steps, below, from left to right, Will Reeves, L.O. Runnels, Joe Nunnery, and Buddy King sit under a sign that verifies that the O.H. Mosely estate was established in 1894, about 15 years before this brick store was built.

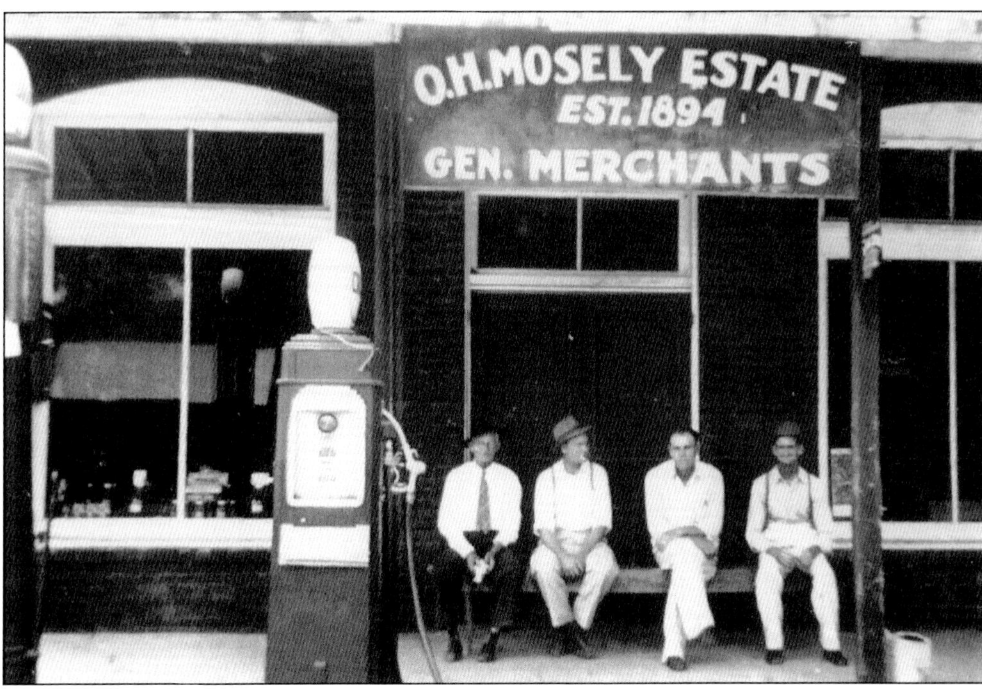

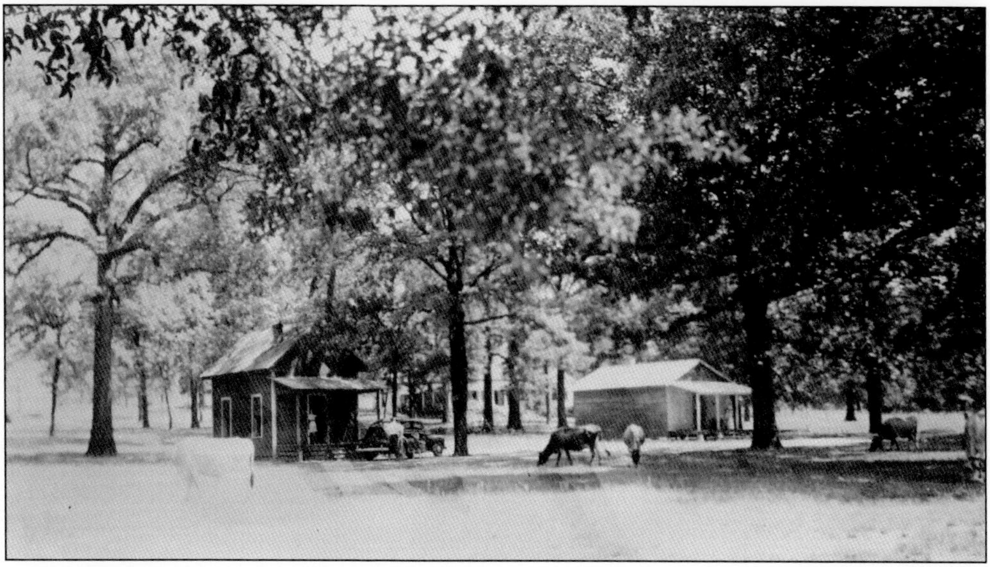

Cedar Springs Post Office. Cedar Springs got its name from a group of natural springs east of the village. One of the oldest communities of the county, the cemetery dates back to 1825. The first settlement in the community was at Green Old Mill Creek, which came to be known as Sheffield Mill Creek. The photograph above shows the original little post office with cattle roaming free around it. The white house on the right is a tenant house. The restored post office (below) is located just north of Cedar Springs. (Above, courtesy of Georgia Archives Vanishing Georgia Collection, EAR 58-82.)

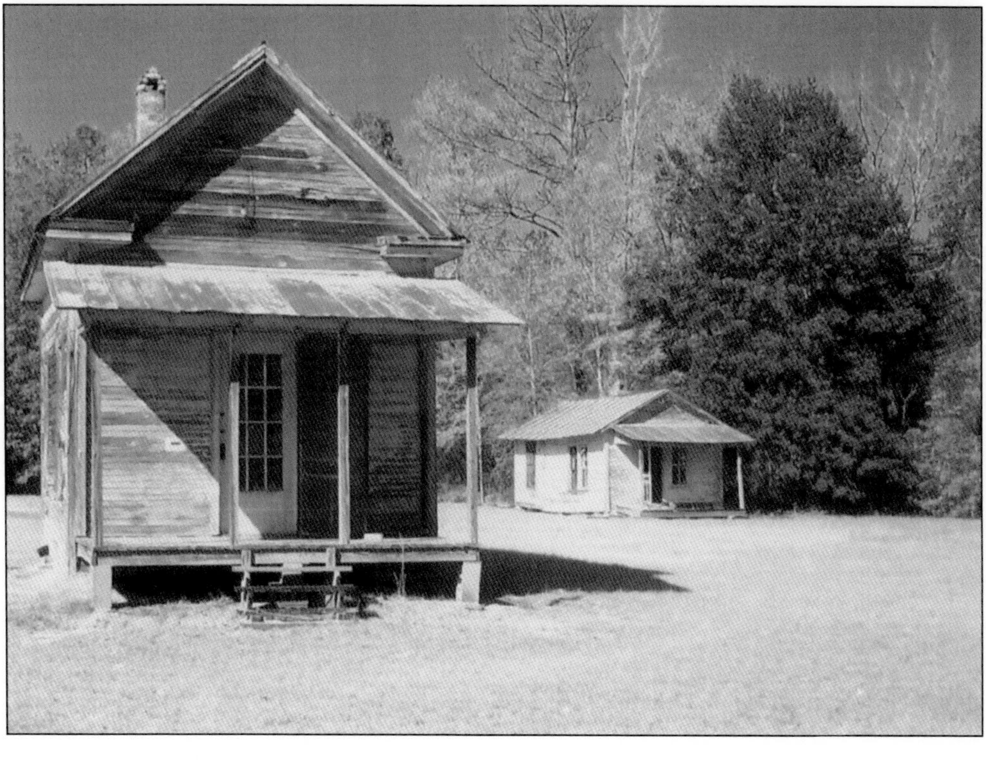

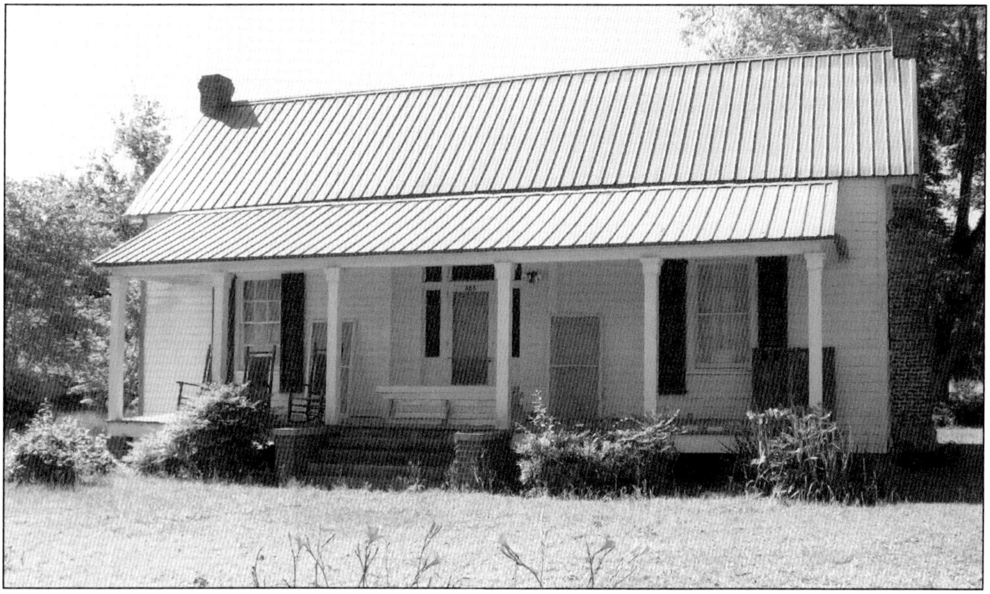

The Oldest Home. Known locally as the Hammond Home, this simple, classic home on Chattahoochee Avenue is the oldest home in Blakely. Erected in 1843, it has been restored by a direct descendant of the Hammond family, George Cliffton Hammond Jr. His father, George Sr., was born in the house. At one time, it was the home of Joel Perry (1818–1872), an Early County historian who died in the house. Perry's wife, Allie Standifer Perry, daughter Angerona, and son-in-law James Alexander continued to live there after his death.

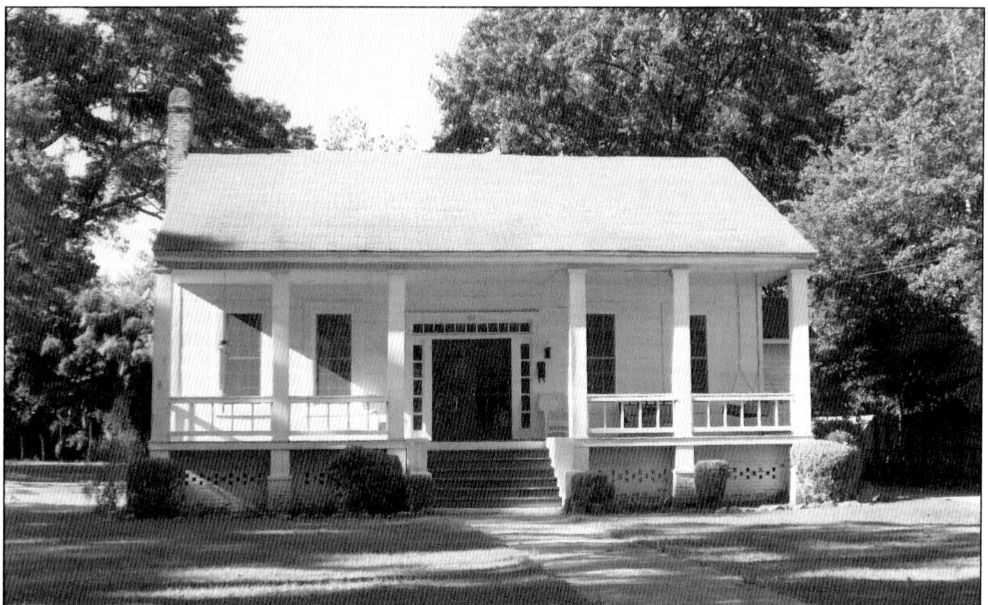

The Vinson House. The Stewart-Vinson house, at 421 River Street, was built by the father of James Marion Stewart, who lived there as a boy. James's daughter was Mrs. Cecil Brown. A niece, Mrs. Joe Vinson, owned the house and resided there for over 50 years. The house has a porch integrated under the main roof of the house. Square columns frame the front entrance, which has double, multi-light, full-glazed doors with a transom and sidelights.

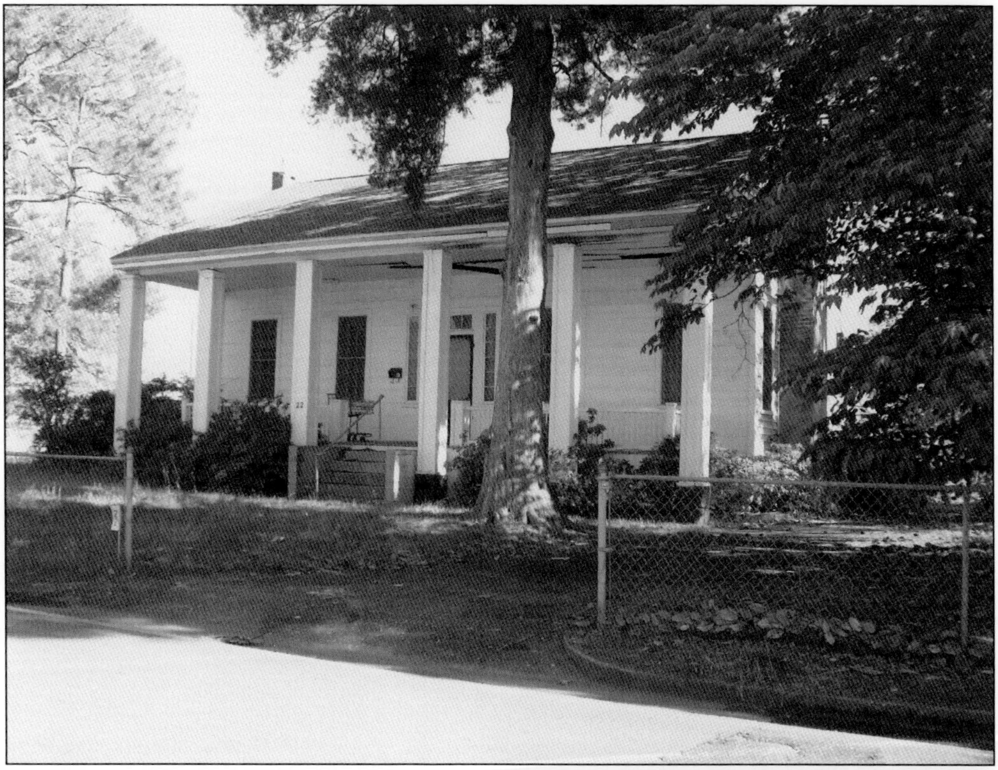

THE BOLLING ROBINSON HOUSE. Bolling H. Robinson (right) served as a first lieutenant in Company G, 13th Regiment Georgia Infantry, during the Civil War. He served in the Georgia Assembly in 1845 as a senator and in 1859–1860 as a representative. He was First Worshipful Master of Magnolia Lodge No. 86. His former home, which also belonged to Sam Stein, J.E. Womack, John Weaver, and Mr. and Mrs. R.E. Glass at different times, will be restored by Blakely Home Town as a service to the community. (Right, courtesy of Georgia Archives Vanishing Georgia Collection, EAR 70-82.)

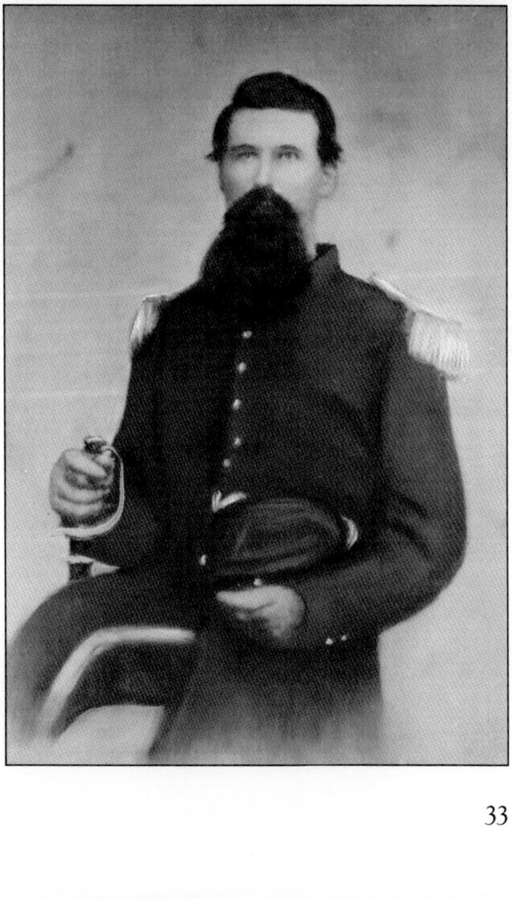

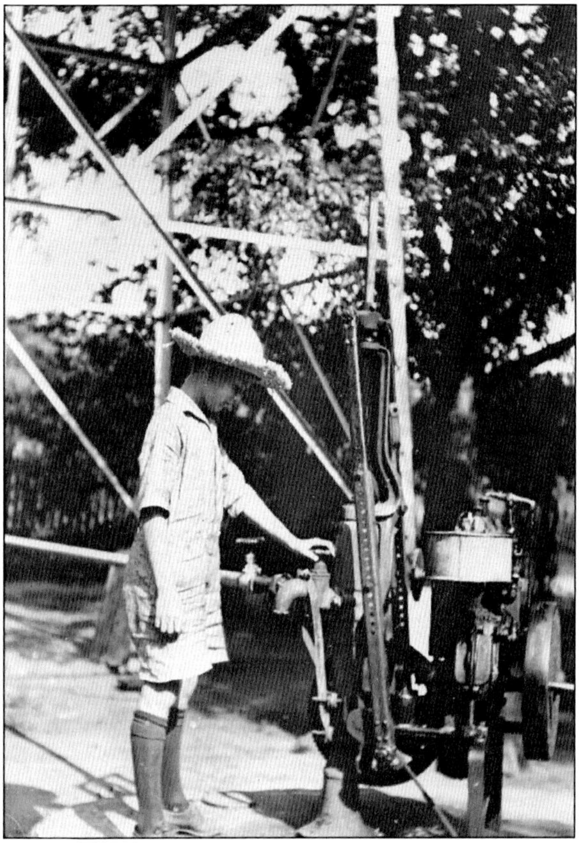

Deep Well Pump. In Cedar Springs, a community deep well pump made life easier for the citizens during 1930. Here, a young child seems fascinated by the workings of the pump. Above the pump was a cypress tank (unseen) that held city water. With pails, jugs, and sometime barrels, water was hauled to homes and business for use in day-to-day living. (Courtesy of Georgia Archives Vanishing Georgia Collection, EAR 61-82.)

Hilton Community Center. Hilton was located near the Chattahoochee River west of Blakely, the county seat of Early County. The post office at Sowhatchee was moved to Hilton. A Methodist church was built there in 1889, and then a Baptist church was built in Hilton. The settlement was named for Elisha Hilton who erected a store there.

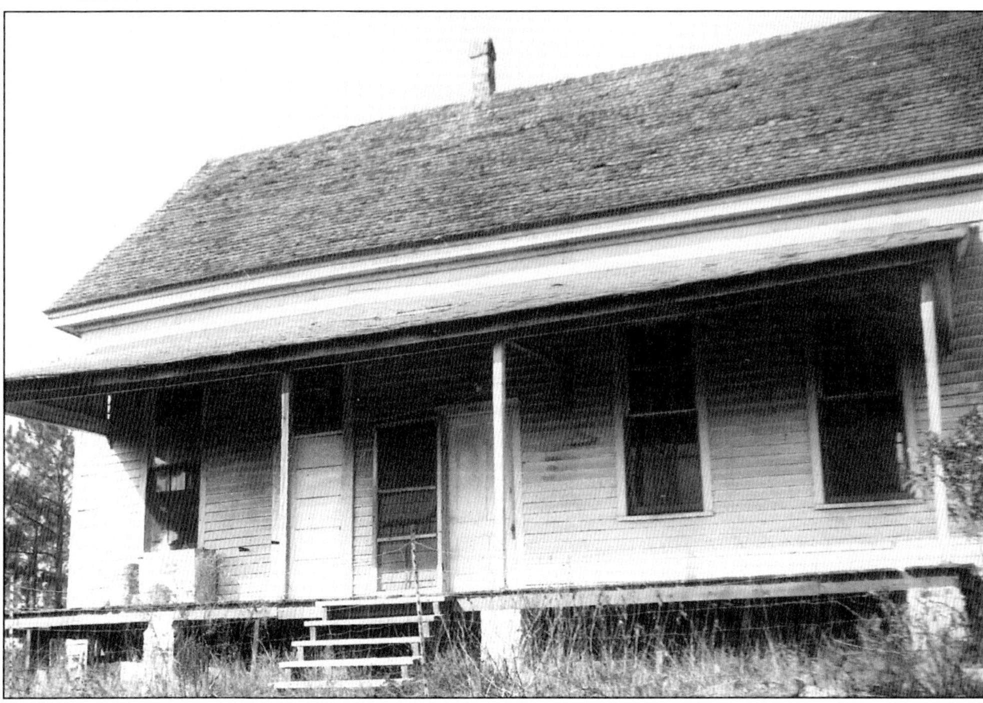

Two

Making a Living

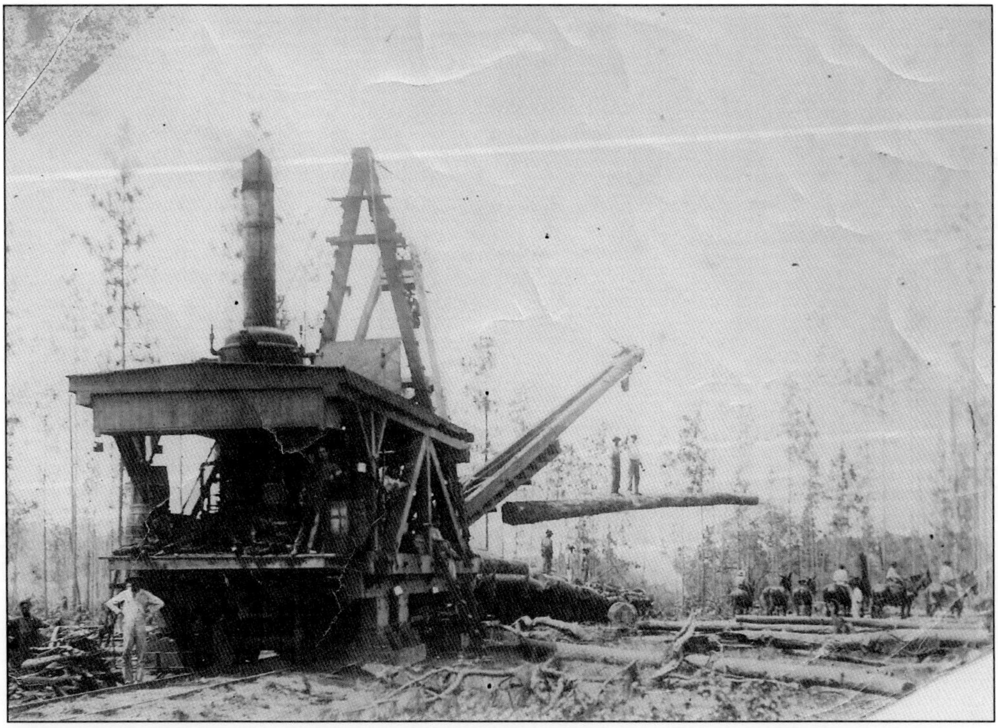

Logging Operation. The lumber business, with its related industries, added to the economic growth of Early County. A logging operation near Jakin supplied trees for sawmills around the area. A "donkey engine," a self-powered steam engine, ran on a rail called a dummy line. It pulled logs with a cable for several hundred yards, lifted the logs, and put them on railcars to be hauled away. After a road from Blakely to Bainbridge was constructed in the mid-1880s, pineland owners began to haul huge square timbers down the road to Bainbridge to be rafted on the Chattahoochee to Apalachicola for shipbuilding.

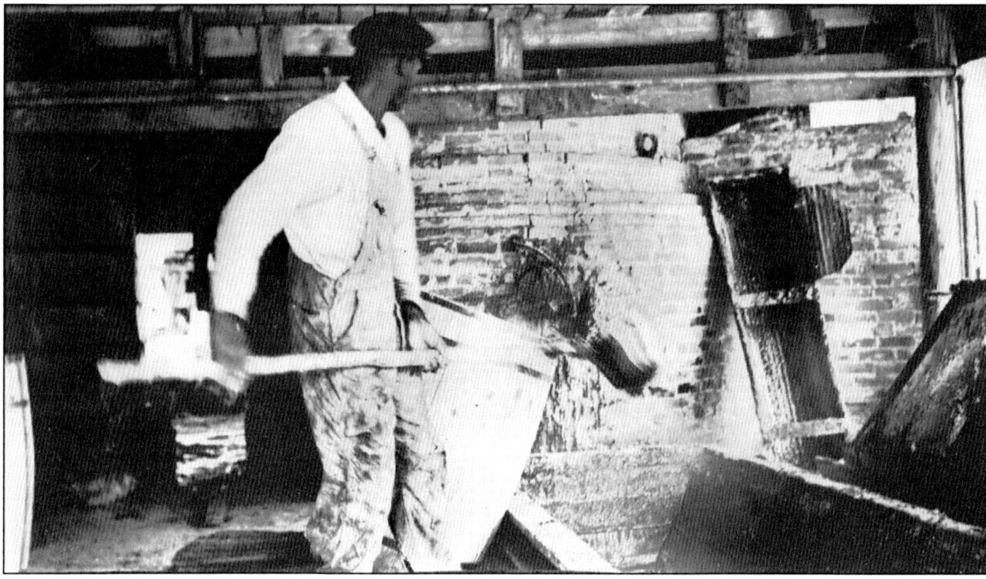

WORKING TURPENTINE. Before the beginning of the 1900s, turpentine stills dotted the countryside in Early County. Workers cut V shapes in longleaf pine trees so that the resin would drain. A trough was placed under the cuts, and the liquid would drain into a turpentine cup or a clay pot. A few weeks later, more cuts were made, and the procedure was repeated. The gum was emptied into a bucket and then into 50-gallon barrels, which were taken to the still. A worker is shown dipping resin in a turpentine still near Cedar Springs in 1938. The second photograph shows the back of the still. (Both, courtesy of Georgia Archives Vanishing Georgia Collection, EAR 57-82 and 55-82.)

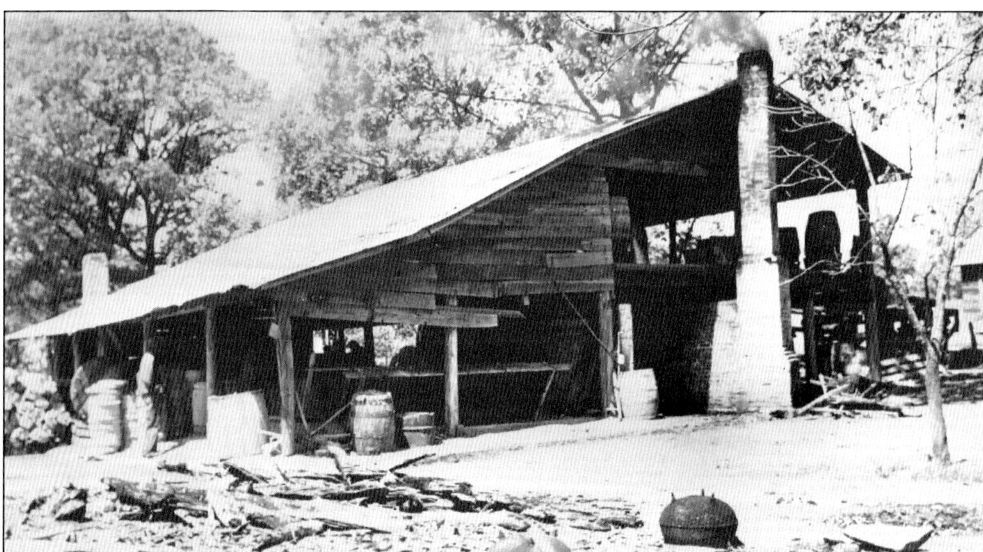

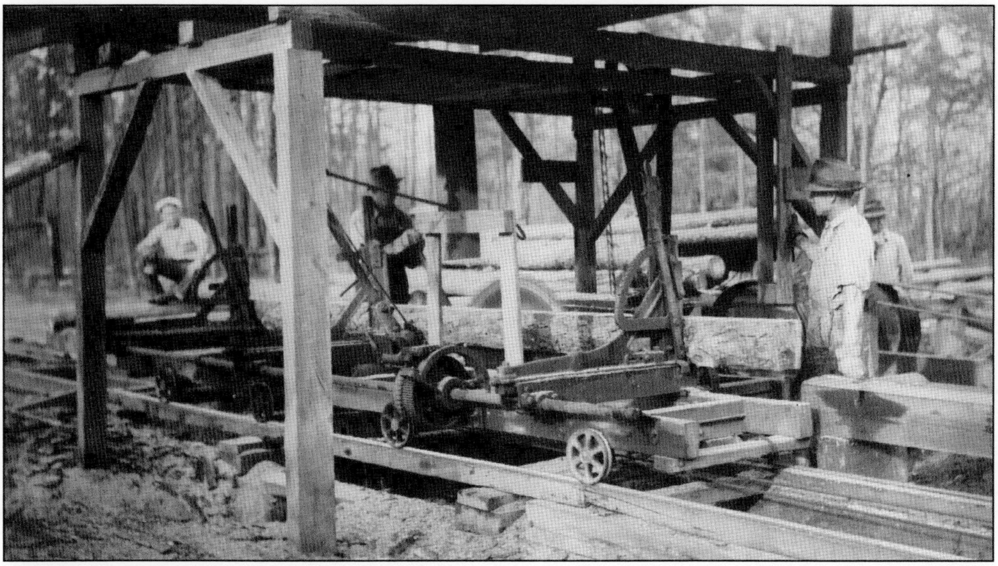

Sawmills. A dangerous, hands-on business, a sawmill prepared wood for shipping and was then used to build homes and businesses. When the train began to run between Albany, Georgia, and Alabama, it opened up a whole new outlet for landowners and loggers. Charlie Baughman's sawmill at Howard's Mill in 1947 was in full operation. (Courtesy of Georgia Archives Vanishing Georgia Collection, EAR 59-82.)

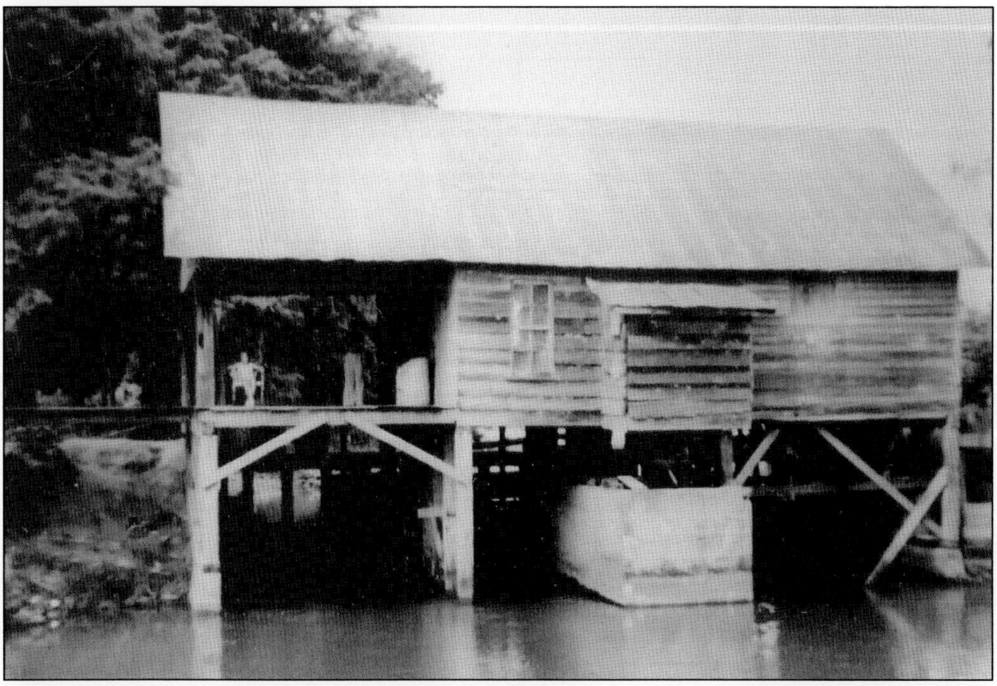

Howard's Mill. Owned and operated by John Howard, Howard's Mill furnished lumber from virgin pine for early homes. Built in the early 1830s between Cedar Springs and Jakin, it ground corn for meal and grits for 135 years with the same 20-inch grindstone. Gates near the front and under the porch opened and closed, controlling the flow of water. The landmark was a favorite gathering place for families to fish, swim, and boat.

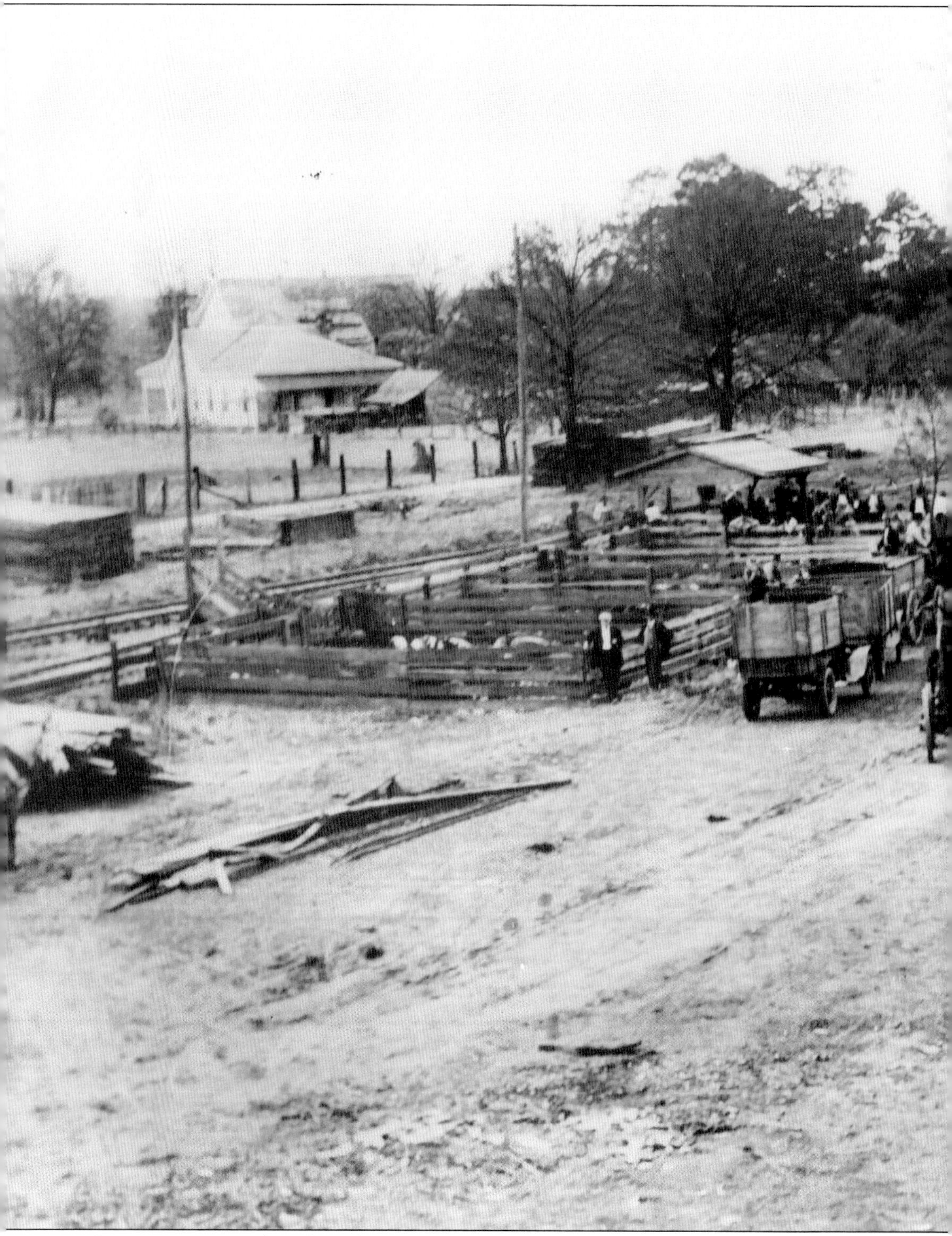

Hogs to Market. When the railroad came into Blakely, it opened up new possibilities for farmers, including loading hogs onto the train to go to market. Wagonloads of hogs were brought to the

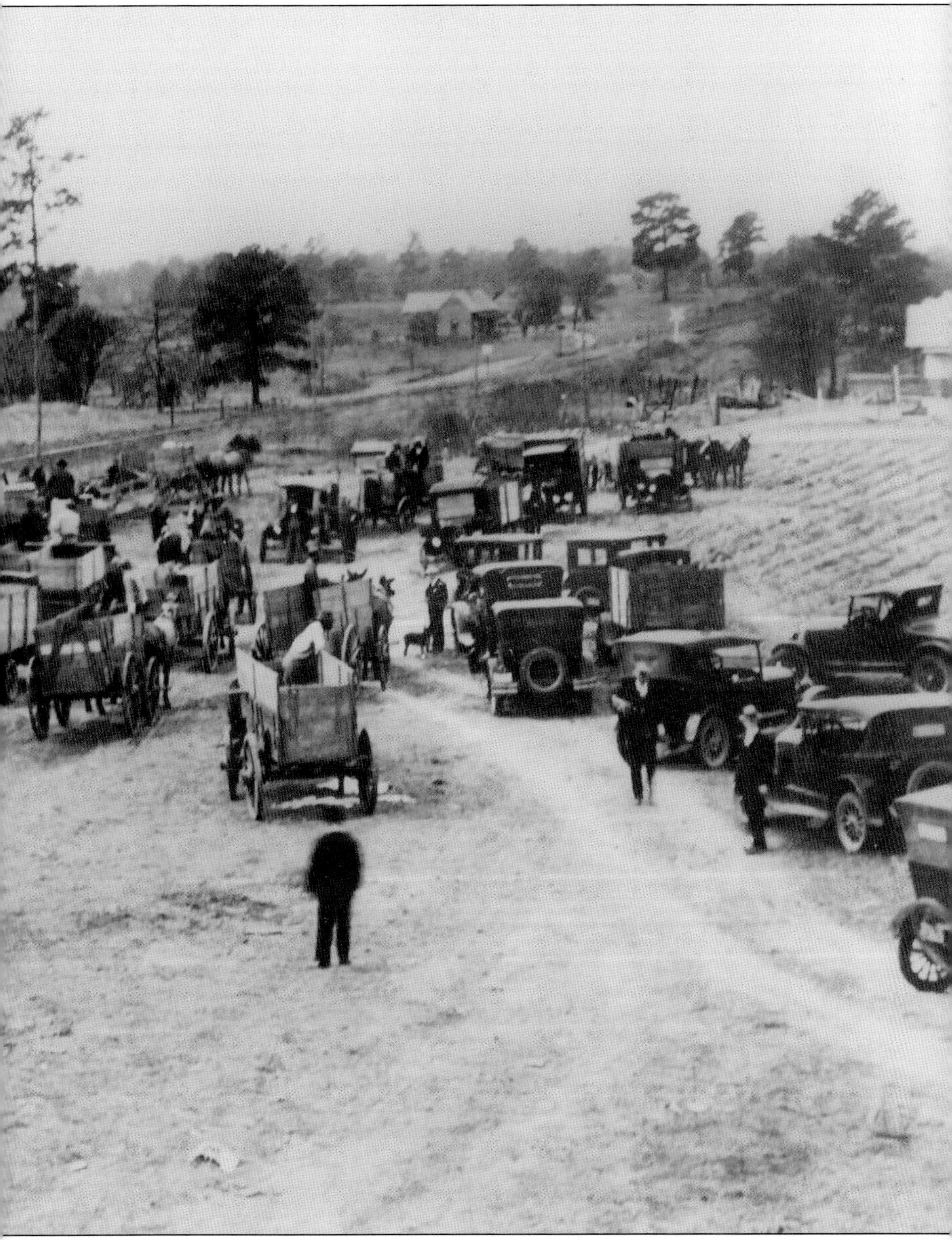

holding pens at Mosely Livestock Yard on Highway 62 west of Blakely. Loading hogs onto the train cars became a common sight.

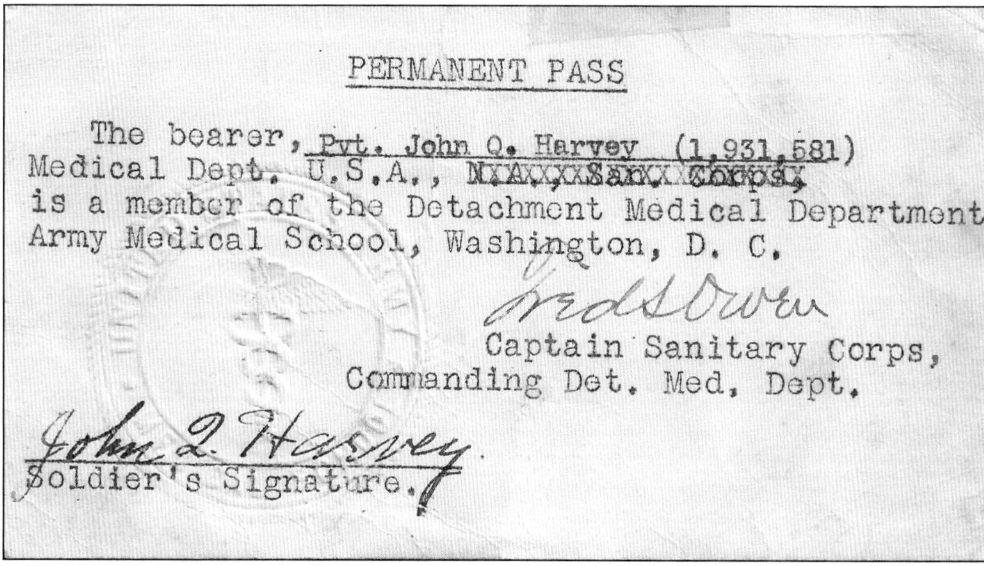

PERMANENT PASS

The bearer, Pvt. John Q. Harvey (1,931,581)
Medical Dept. U.S.A., ~~N.A., Sani. Corps,~~
is a member of the Detachment Medical Department
Army Medical School, Washington, D. C.

Fred Owen
Captain Sanitary Corps,
Commanding Det. Med. Dept.

John Q. Harvey
Soldier's Signature.

World War I Pass and Identification Card. World War I, originally called the "Great War," was a major war centered on Europe that began in the summer of 1914 and lasted until November 1918. It involved all of the world's great powers. J. Quitman Harvey was the rural mail carrier in Jakin and left his job with a substitute on April 12, 1918, to serve in the Army. When he returned after the war, he resumed his route until April 15, 1923. Harvey's "Permanent Pass" indicates he was a member of the medical department in the Army, and his identification card verifies that he was an employee of the US Treasury Department. (Both, courtesy of Virginia Harvey.)

FORM 21

TREASURY DEPARTMENT
WASHINGTON

Sept 3/18
DATE

This is to certify
that John Q. Harvey
is an employee of the U. S. Treasury Department and is entitled to enter the Treasury Building during official hours for the performance of official duty.

O B Allen
Chief Clerk.

NOT TRANSFERABLE.

2—8347

Countersigned:

(Head of Office)

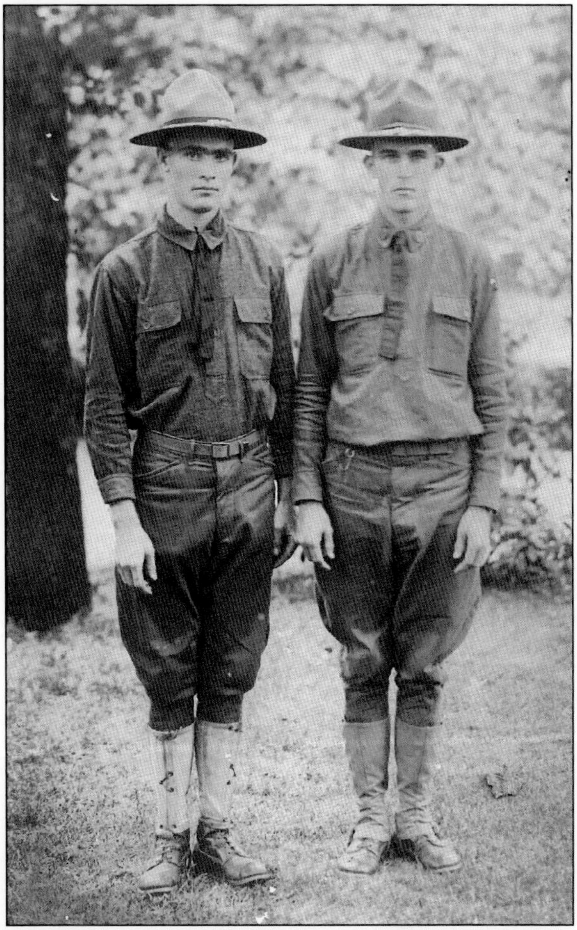

Boys at War. Young men went to war to make the world safe for democracy. Shown here with a friend, Luther Tiberious Robinson, left, is dressed in his World War I uniform. He was born in 1894 in Bluffton, Georgia, to W.R. and Sally Robinson. Those from Early County who gave their lives were Willie Fleetwood Alexander, Thomas F. Hartley, Bertchall Odum, Alba Leon Roberts, Guerry Temples, and Grover C. Willis. (Courtesy of Mr. and Mrs. John L. Harris.)

A Mystery. Discovered in a group of Early County photographs, this original photograph has stumped everyone. The steam-powered tractor with tracks from the 1920s carries what appears to be a large, tubular shape, and more of these tubes seem to have been erected in the background. What is it? What are they doing? And, when did this occur? The following are clues: The brand "TAUY" is on two different pieces of equipment; a handwritten number, "SA 305," is visible; and in the background to the right is a building with "J.B.? LAWS Ford."

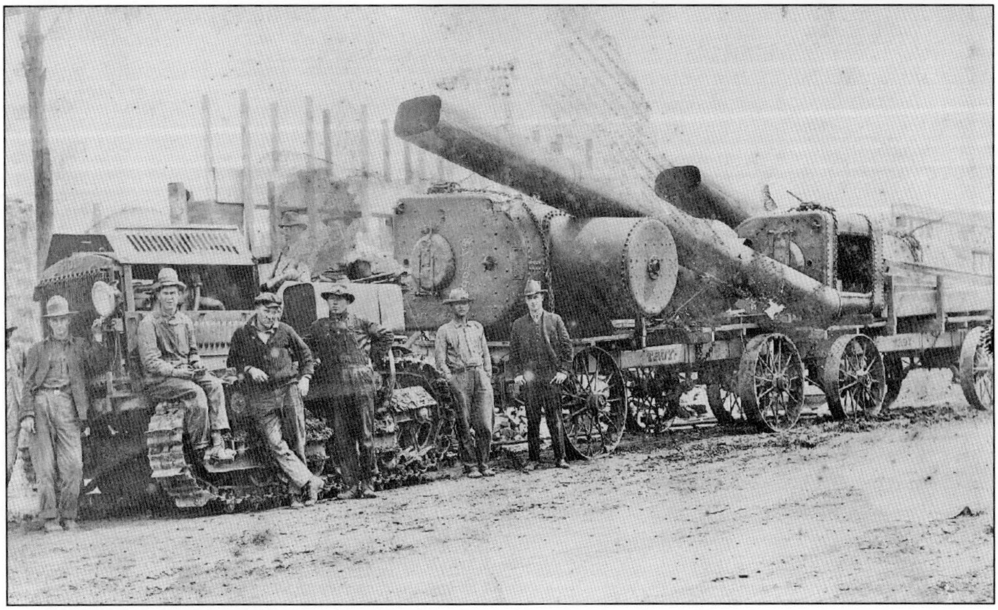

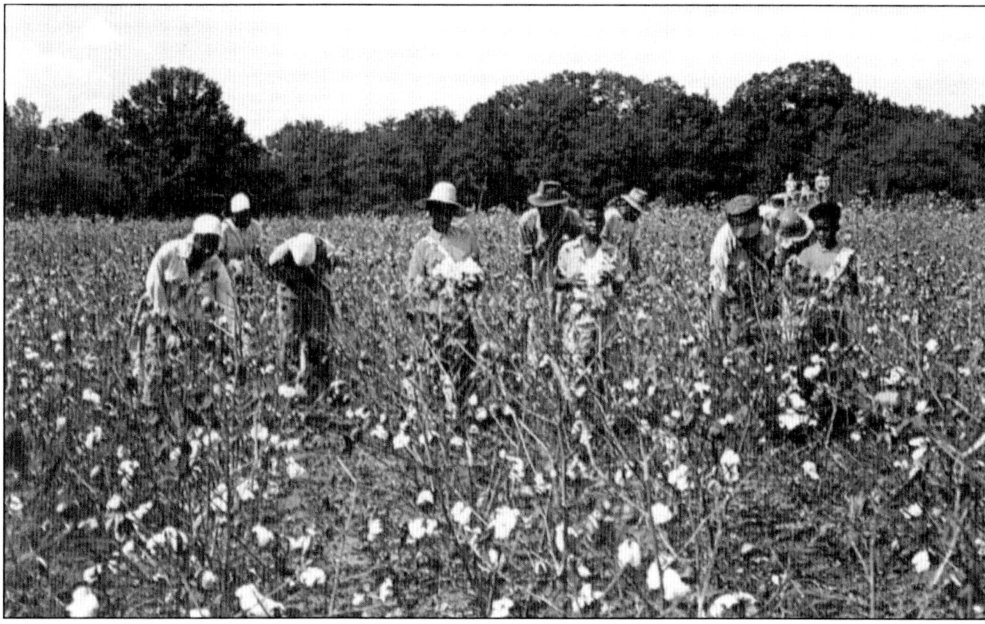

Cotton King. At the end of the Civil War, Blakely primarily remained a market for farmers of the county. Cotton was only 10¢ per pound in 1880 and only 5¢ a pound in 1894. The area survived because citizens extended credit to one another as small stores and offices were established. Dragging the long cotton sacks and painfully pulling the cotton out of the jagged bolls to fill the sacks required a great deal of toughness. (Courtesy of Mrs. Cary Logan.)

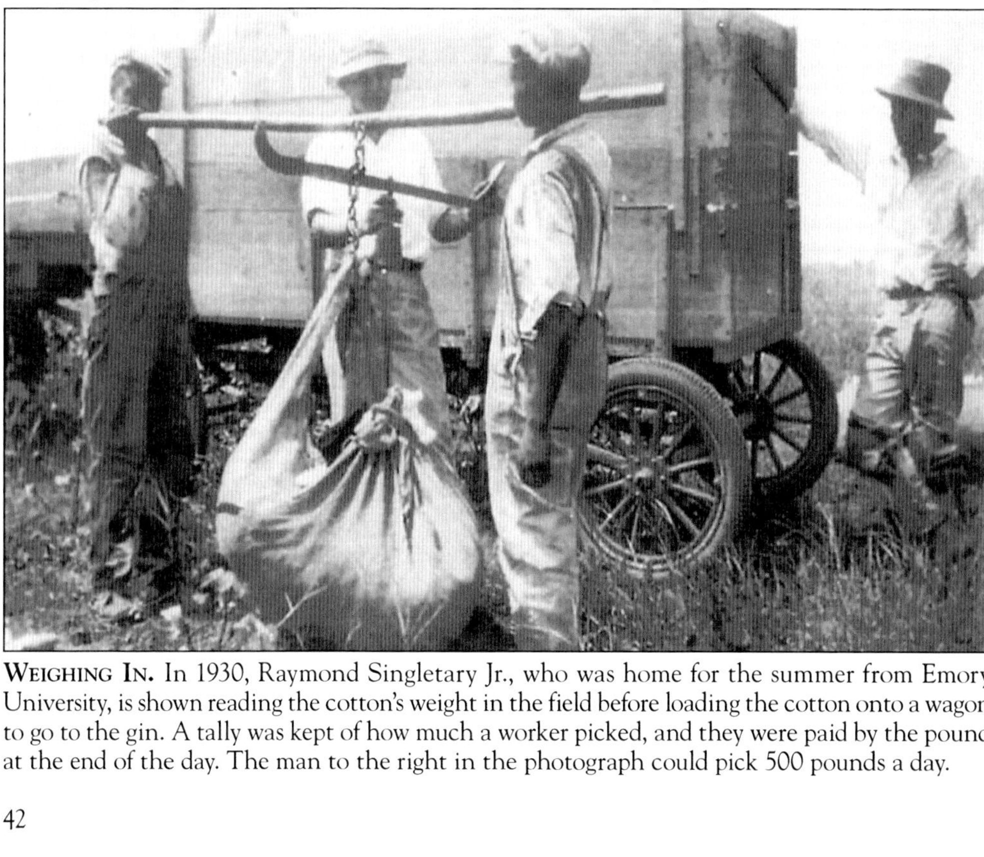

Weighing In. In 1930, Raymond Singletary Jr., who was home for the summer from Emory University, is shown reading the cotton's weight in the field before loading the cotton onto a wagon to go to the gin. A tally was kept of how much a worker picked, and they were paid by the pound at the end of the day. The man to the right in the photograph could pick 500 pounds a day.

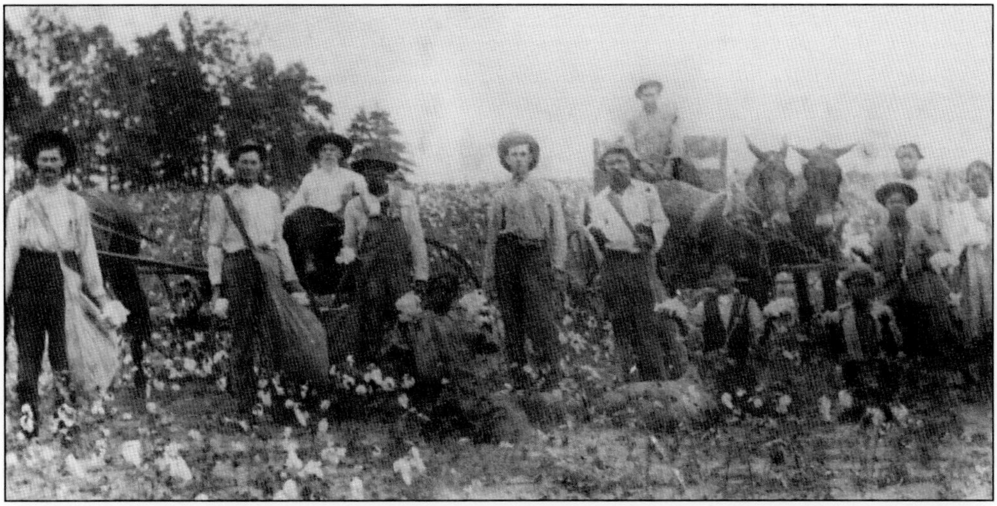

PICKING COTTON. A family affair, everyone pitched in each fall to harvest the cotton grown during the summer. Here, around 1910, family and friends gather to pick the cotton crop. In the group are Oss Arthur, Dalton Pritchett, Mr. ? Arthur (in buggy), Carl Arthur, and Lemen Arthur (in wagon). (Courtesy of Mr. and Mrs. John Pritchett.)

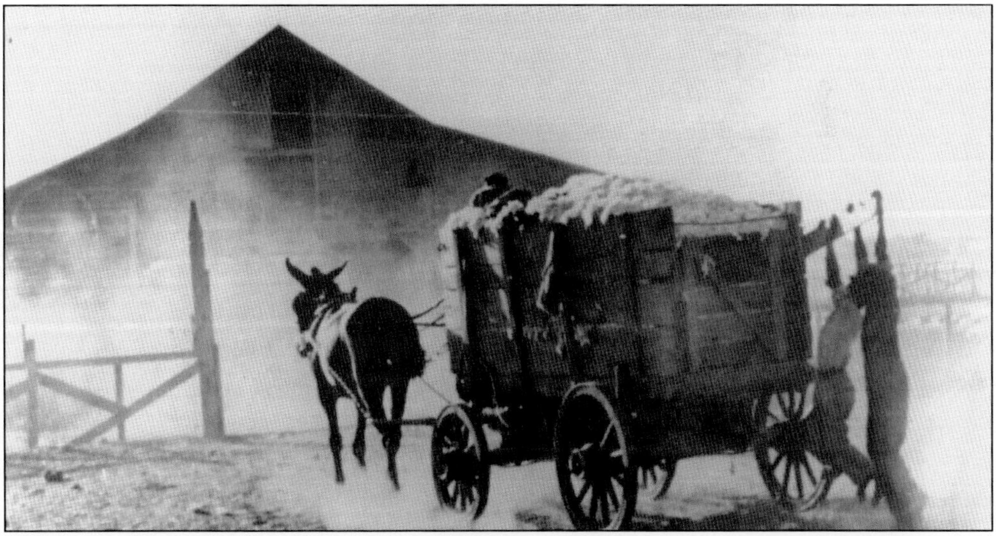

END OF THE DAY. After having traveled south from north Georgia on a mule and wagon in the 1920s, T.H. Owen purchased a farm west of Blakely from a Mr. Bryant. The land originally belonged to Flowers Lumber Company. Upon moving his family to the new farm (his wife, Mary, called it a "rock farm"), he discovered rocks and boulders had to be blasted to clear the way for mule-drawn plows. The dust flies during the drought of 1954–1957, as a wagonload of cotton is rolled into the barn at sunset to protect it from the overnight dew. (Courtesy of the Owen family.)

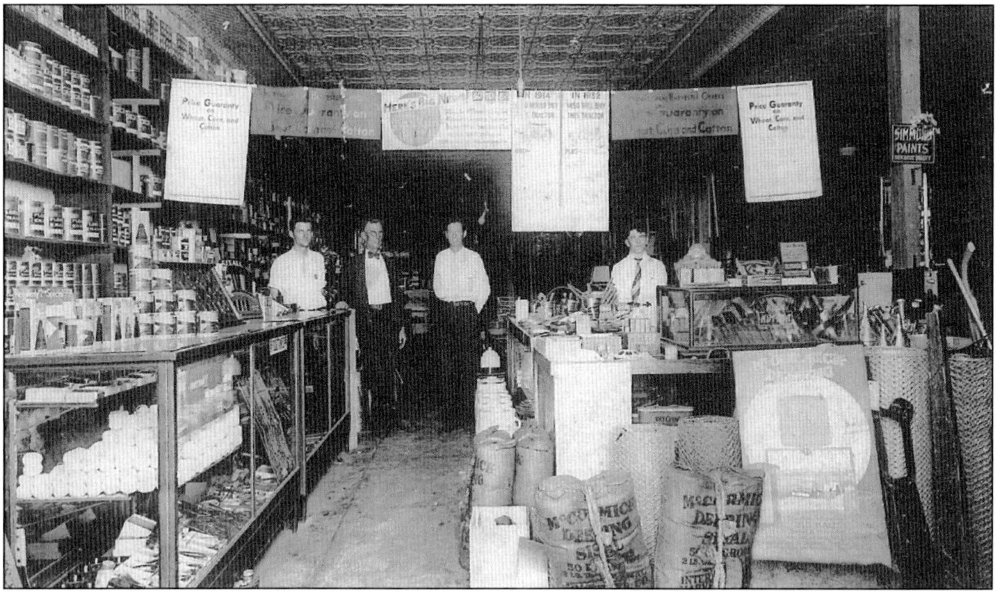

Middleton Hardware Company. In 1932, inside the first Middleton Hardware Company on North Main Street are rolls of wire, cases of knives, and signs that indicate "Price Guarantee for Wheat, Corn, and Cotton." In the store are, from left to right, young Harvey Middleton, unidentified, Thurman Hodges, and Andy Middleton. Less than two blocks off the square, the store was changed into Middleton Implement Company when the second hardware company was built across the street. (Courtesy of Mr. and Mrs. Gene Regan.)

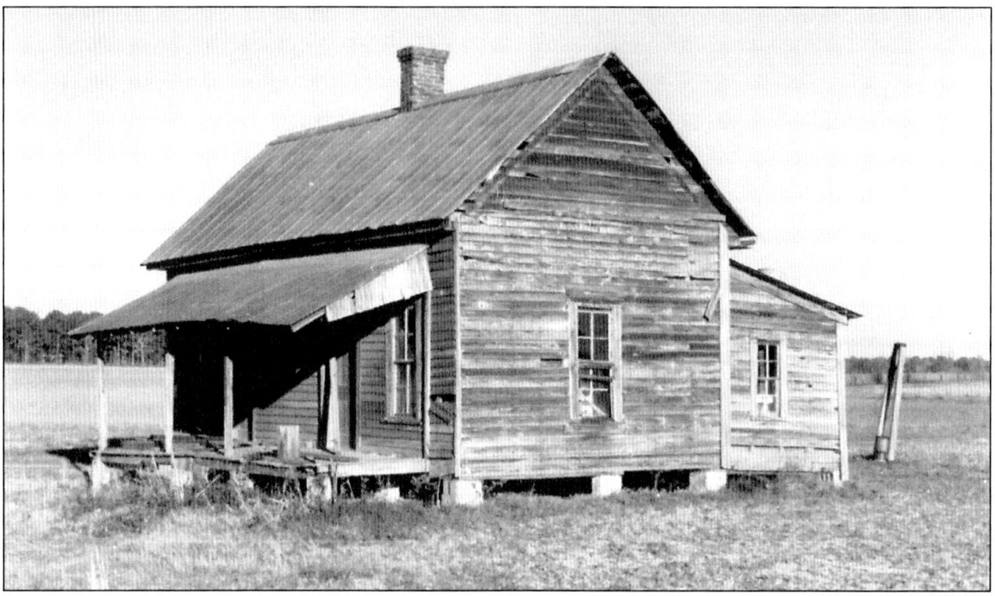

Tenant House. When plantations and large farms were common in the 1930s and 1940s, tenant farmers either worked as field hands in nearby fields or became sharecroppers. A typical tenant house had a fireplace and sometimes a wood stove for heating and for cooking. Iron beds with crude mattresses were common. A tenant house on the Owen farm, located west of Blakely on Chancey Mill Road, is said to be more than 100 years old and was on the land when Flowers Lumber Company owned it. The house was occupied by families who worked for the Owen family.

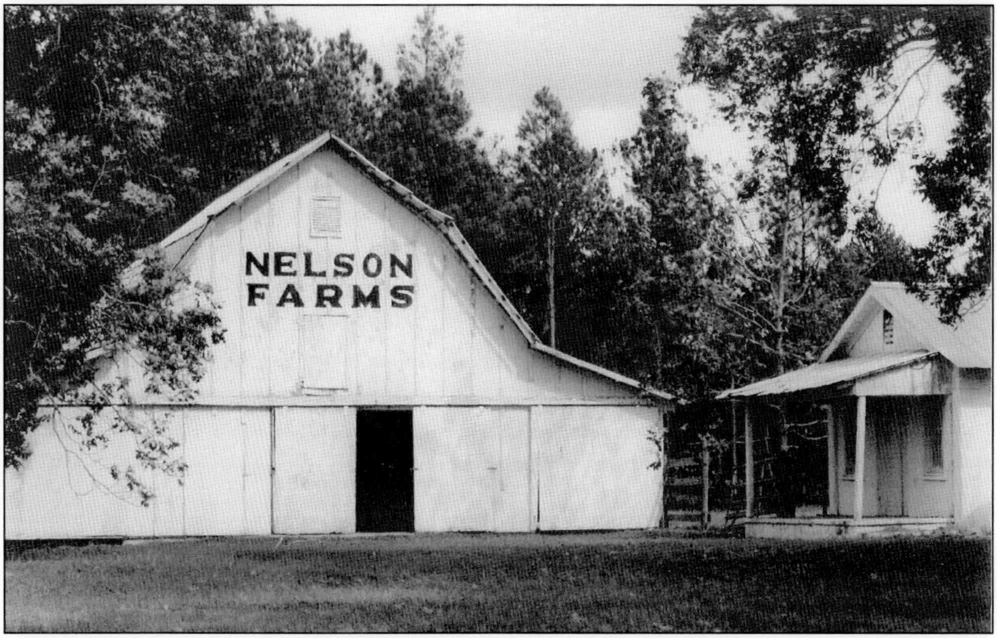

NELSON FARMS. Land along the Chattahoochee River on the western edge of the county at one time comprised large plantations, including those of Jim and Joe Freeman and the Griers. This part of Nelson Farms extends over four miles along River Road from Roaring Branch along the river. The grave of James Alexander, a Revolutionary War soldier, stands alone along this stretch of land.

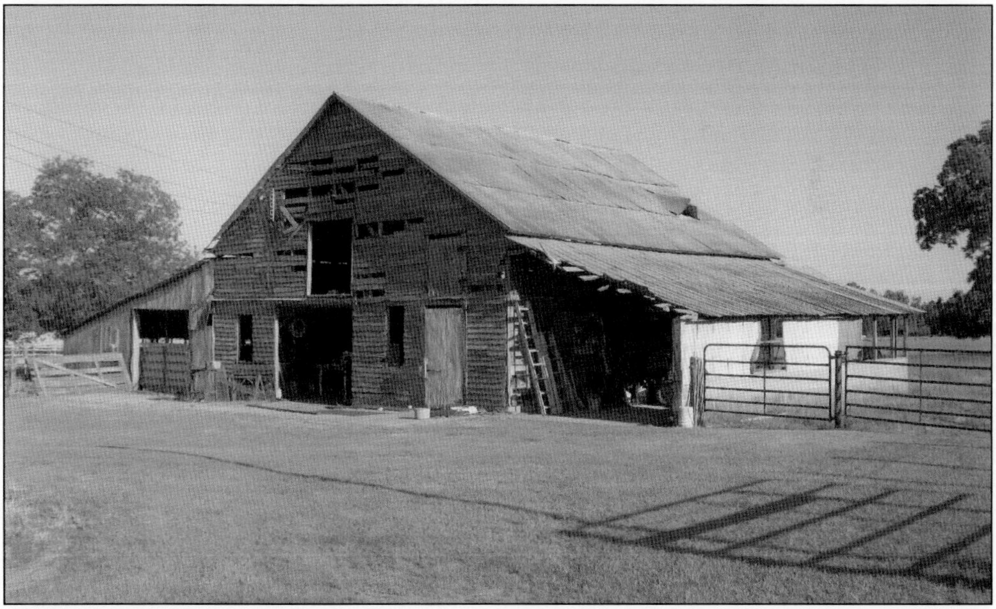

BOWMAN BARN. Photographers roam the roads of the Southern states to find such interesting old buildings as those on country roads in Early County, Georgia. The rusty tin roofs lend themselves to watercolor paintings in sienna, burnt umber, and sky blue. But the nostalgia element, the memories of the day Joe Bowman completed the barn on January 31, 1929, of the sharecroppers that used it, of the farm wagons stored under the "lean-to," and of the corn crib full of corn are all stimulated by this photograph.

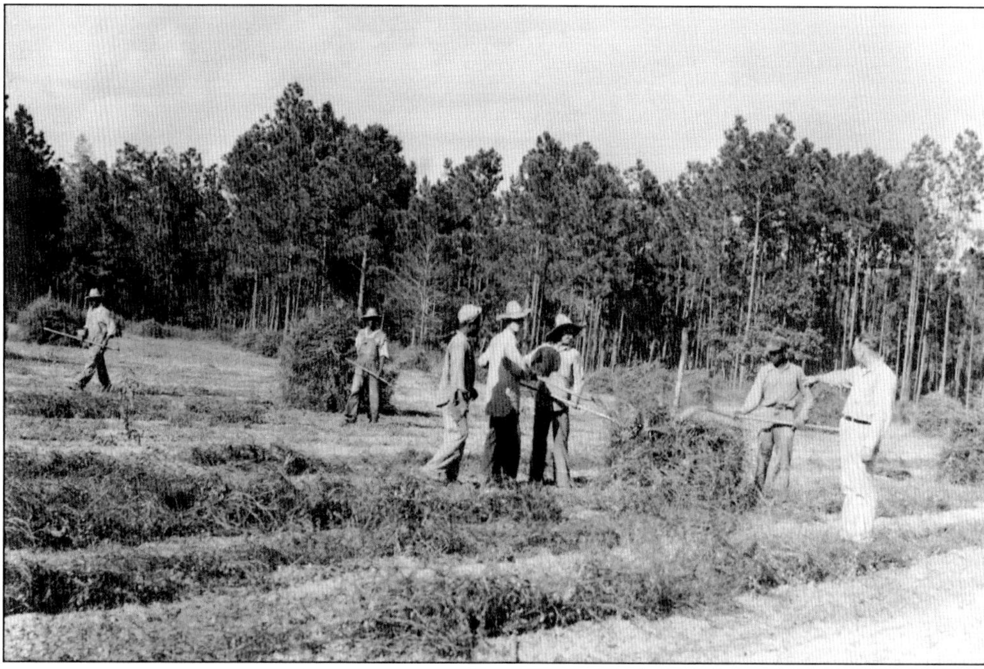

Stacking Peanuts. The soil in Early County has always been greatly suited to the growing of peanuts. After peanuts were planted and matured, they were plowed up with mules, and workers labored hard to stack the peanuts around a center pole (stock) to dry. Drying usually required four to six weeks of good weather. Stacking poles, around which green peanuts were dried, were saved, stored in a barn, and used year after year. In these photographs, the Willis farm operation loads peanut vines into the picker. Long belts ran from a wheel on the tractor to another wheel on the picker. It rolled peanut vines until the nuts separated, leaving only the vines. (Above, courtesy of Georgia Archives, Vanishing Georgia Collection, EAR 30-82; below, courtesy of Mr. and Mrs. John L. Harris.)

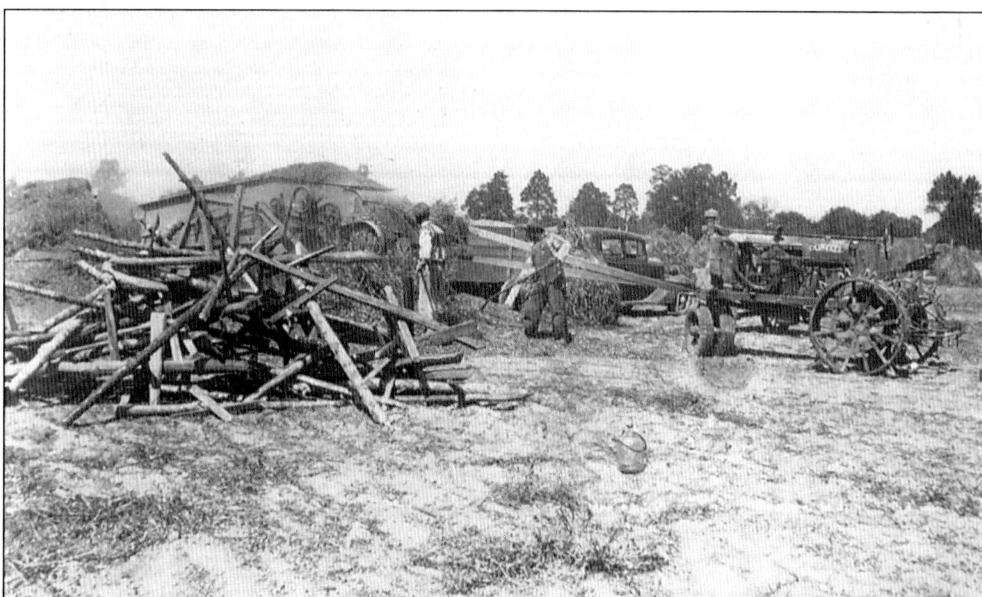

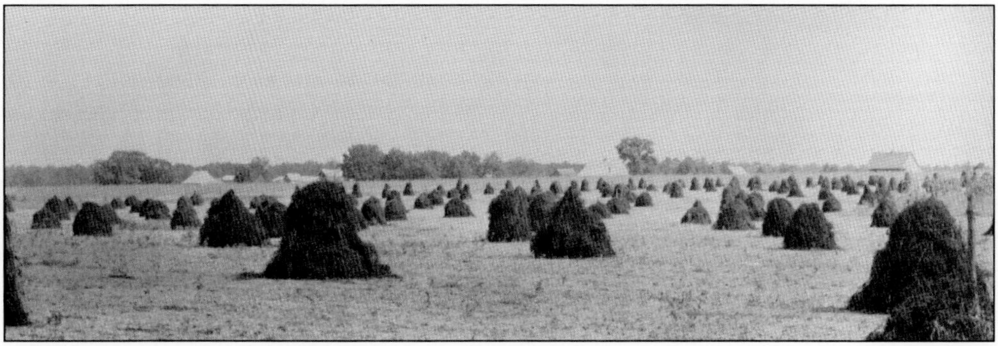

Stacks of Peanuts. Workers, mules, and equipment are gone from the field, and farmers wait for the peanuts to dry. Large barns and farmhouses can be seen in the distance. No doubt they are the property of a local farmer. Baling peanut hay on September 20, 1941, machinery is at work on the Willis farm near Cedar Springs below. The baling crew is on the left, and the picking crew is on the far right. (Both, courtesy of Georgia Archives Vanishing Georgia Collection, EAR 32-82 and 68-82.)

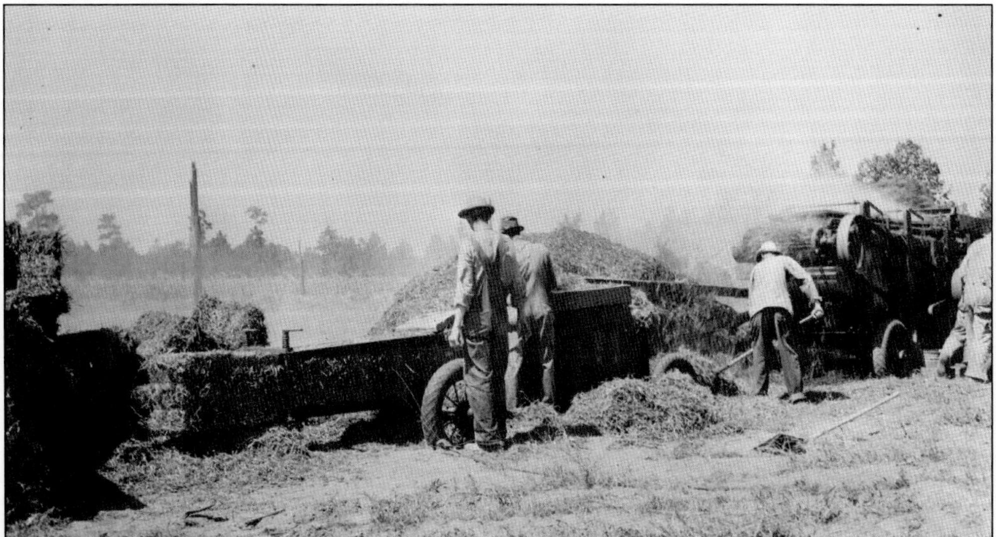

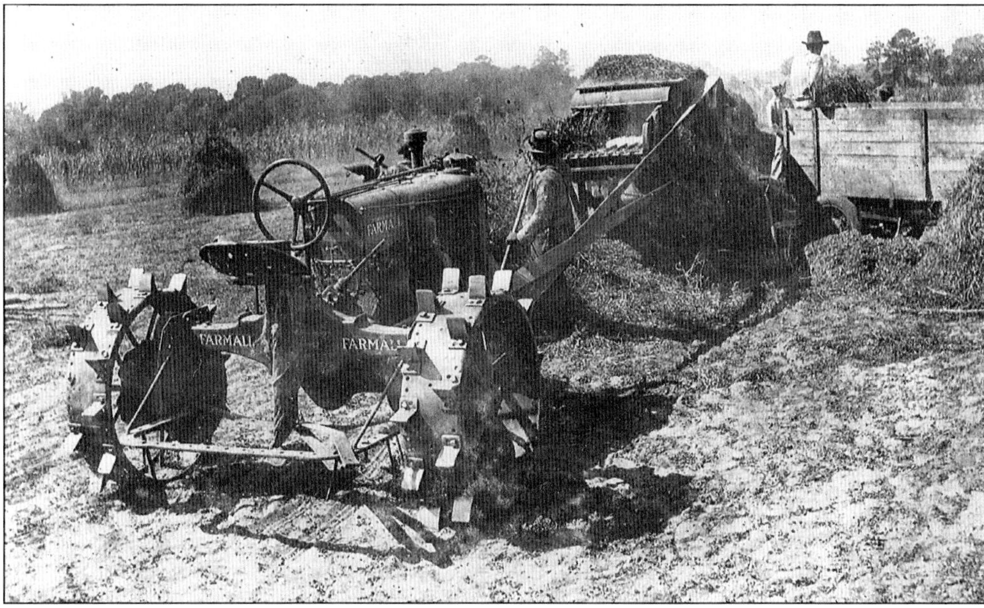

Goobers. Peanuts have been called groundnuts, earthnuts, and ground peas as well as goobers since 1889, when they first became a cash crop. Peanuts have always been known to be nutritious. George Washington Carver (1864–1943) also found more than 200 non-food uses for the peanut. On the Willis farm on Cedar Springs Road, peanuts are removed from the vines (above). The loose nuts are hauled to market, and workers go through the process of creating bales of hay. Workers with heavy oak presses (below) square up the hay into bales, which are stored in barns and used to feed cattle or sold to cattle farmers for the same use. (Both, courtesy of Mr. and Mrs. John L. Harris.)

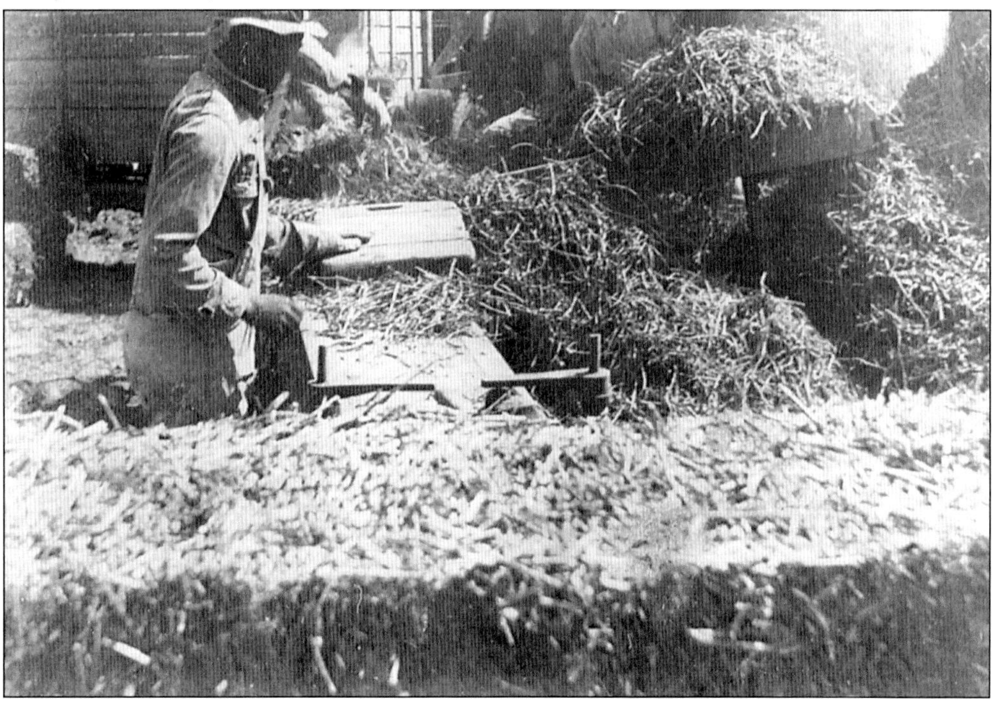

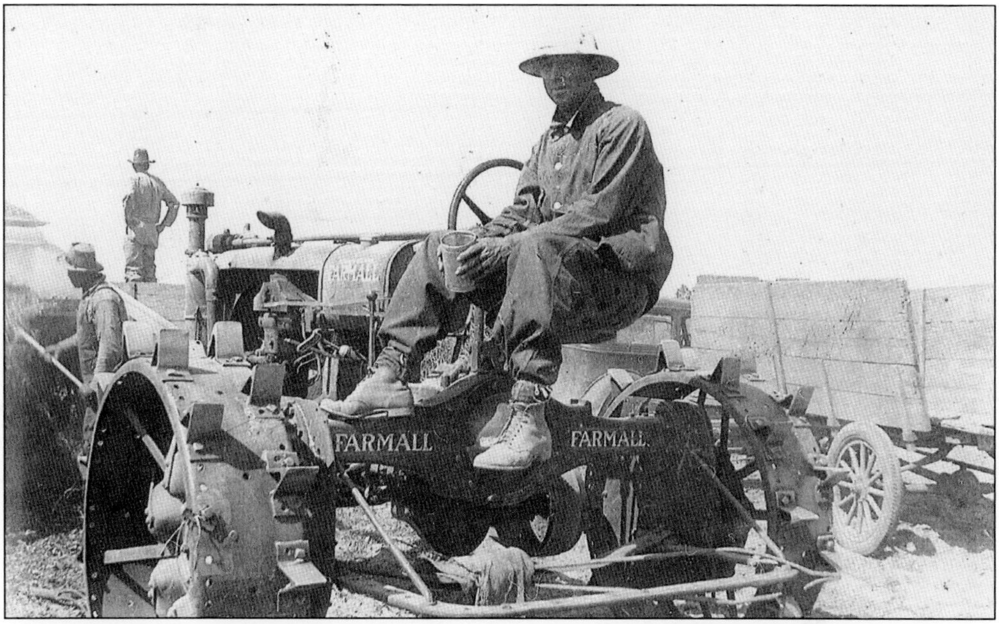

Family Farm. Two miles south of Blakely on the Cedar Springs Highway, the Willis farm was the first farm every year to have its peanuts picked. They had all their own equipment, and after all their peanuts were gathered, they would move on to pick those on other farms. Herbert Foyt called on them to pick his peanuts. Besides farming, Foyt ran a cotton warehouse on Victoria Street, located just off the southwest corner of the square. Next to the warehouse was Allen's Fish House on the corner of Victoria and Cotton Streets. Homer Willis rests atop a 1925–1932 Farmall tractor as he supervises the picking of peanuts. (Courtesy of Mr. and Mrs. John L. Harris.)

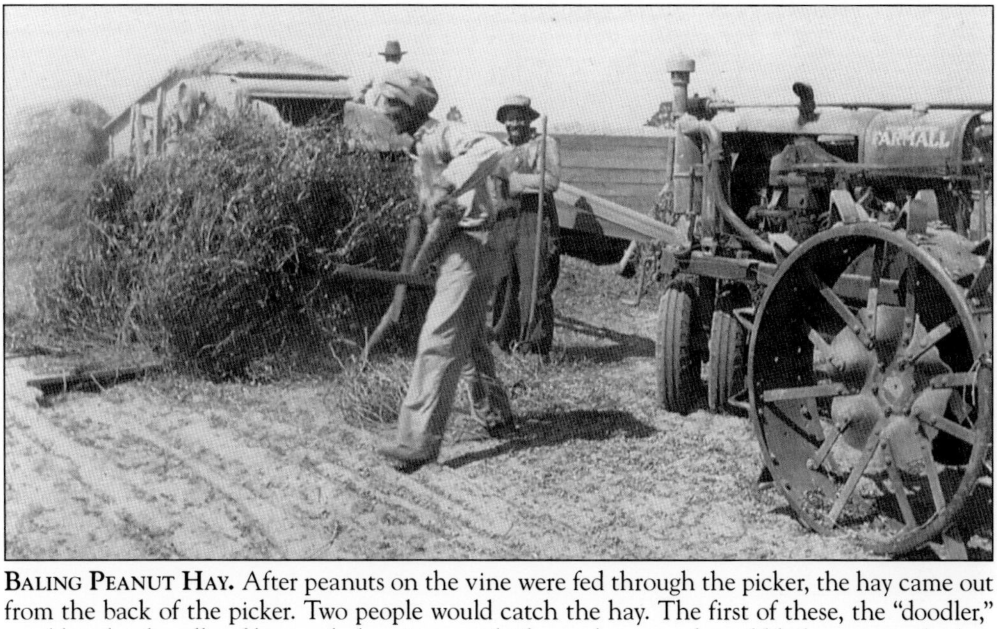

Baling Peanut Hay. After peanuts on the vine were fed through the picker, the hay came out from the back of the picker. Two people would catch the hay. The first of these, the "doodler," would grab a bundle of hay and place it on a platform; the second would help to press the hay into a metal box "form." Square wood hay-presses aided in separating the bales and helped with wiring the bales of hay into a stackable form. (Courtesy of Mr. and Mrs. John L. Harris.)

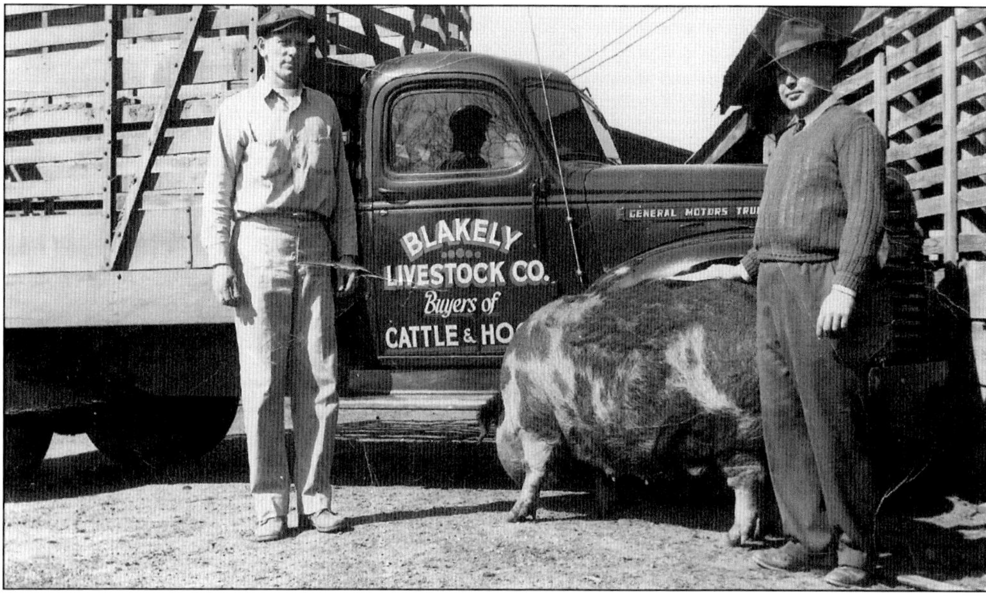

Big Hog. "Red" Pritchett (left), the owner of Blakely Livestock Company, and Raymond Singletary of Singletary Farms look at a big hog before loading it up. At the time, the stockyard was located on Fort Gaines Street across from the Lowery Stone home. (Courtesy of Mr. and Mrs. John Pritchett.)

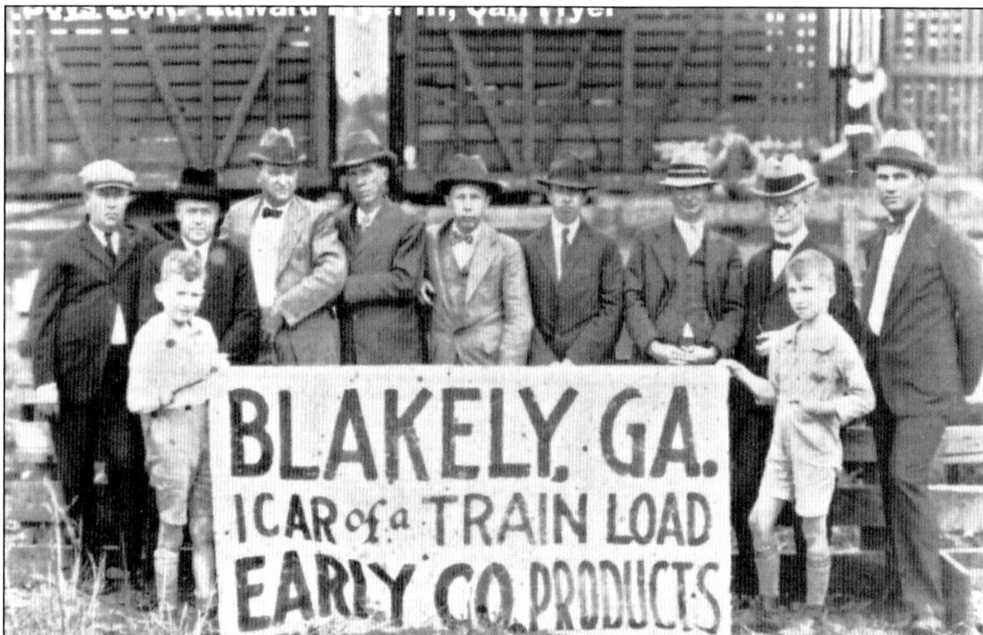

To Market, To Market. By February 1927, the use of the railcars for shipping farm products was in full swing. Proud of their new capabilities for selling crops, Blakely fellows create a sign proclaiming the trainloads of Blakely products. In the photograph are, from left to right, Luther Warrick, Baptist reverend Hantsville, Ed Fryer Jr., Oscar Bridges, school superintendent Graham, J.B. Jones, John Butler, H.B. Ainsworth, Don Bridges, and boys Edward Fryer III and Carl Fryer.

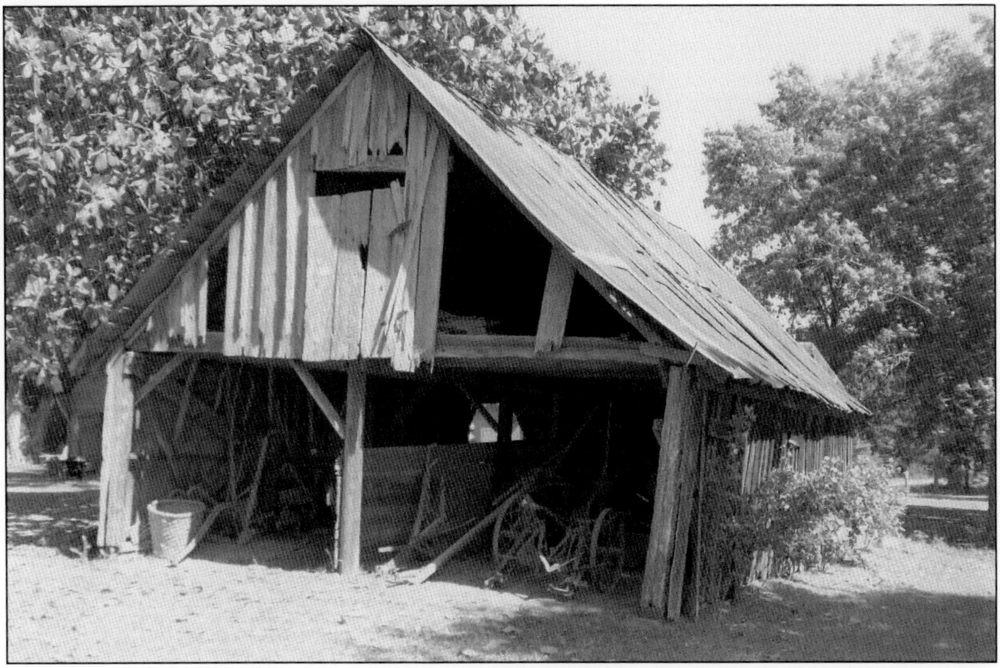

COUNTRY BARN. Standing as a testament to times gone by, a weathered barn still contains the mule-drawn plows and planters once used by farmers. The loft, which once held hay for mules, now contains remnants of that hay, pieces of rocking chairs, an iron cot, quilting poles, and ancient household items. Cotton wagons were once driven under the shelter to keep dry if the weather looked inclement. (Courtesy of the Owen family.)

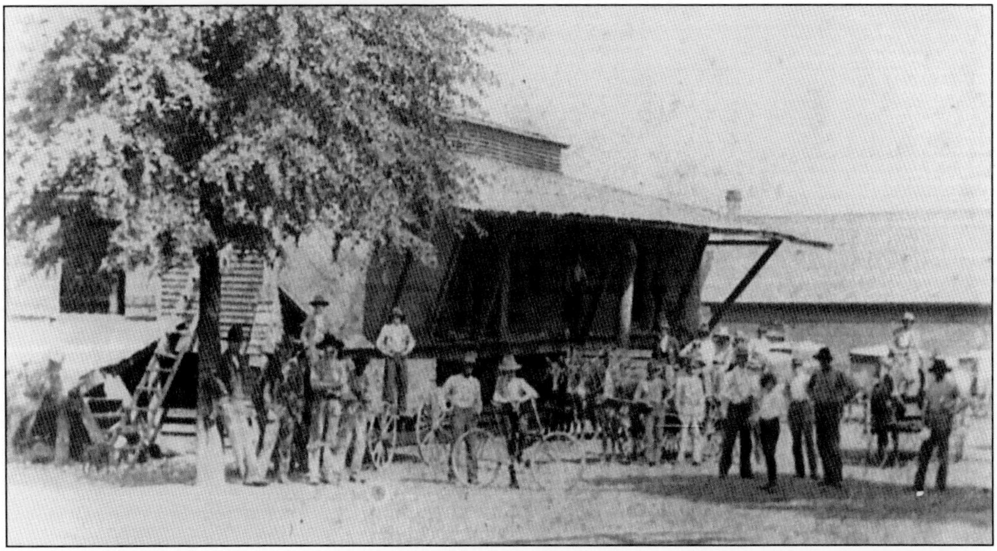

CHANCEY'S GINNERY. John C. Chancey's ginnery, Blakely Ginning Company, was located on Church Street south of Columbia Street. In 1904, it ginned and baled 80 bales of cotton a day. His milling company and steam ginneries used a Winship System and a Munger System (in a separate building) for ginning and baling cotton. Chancey was also a farmer and owned 25 or 30 of the "finest mules anywhere to be found," according to the Early County Historical Society, to help till the soil on his farm.

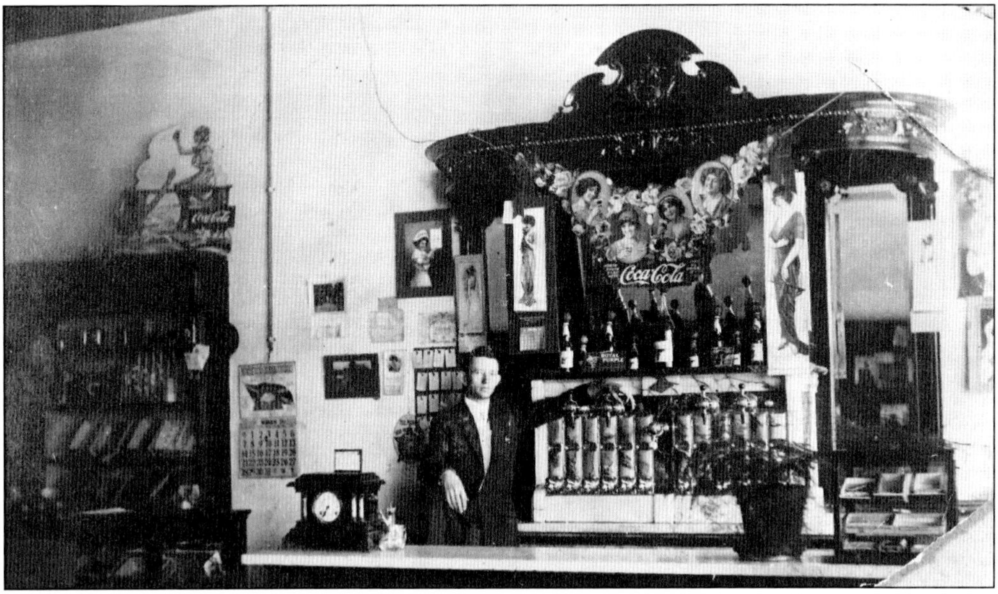

DAMASCUS, KESTLER, OLD TOWN. By any other name, it would still be a small town on Highway 200 in Early County, Georgia. In the 1890s, Dr. P.H. Keaton wanted to build a new town near Damascus on the railroad. The depot continued to be called Damascus, but the town was Kestler. The drugstore in the photograph was in downtown Damascus in the early 1900s. John Wesley Wiley and his partner Johnny Webb owned it. (Courtesy of Georgia Archives Vanishing Georgia Collection, EAR 78-82.)

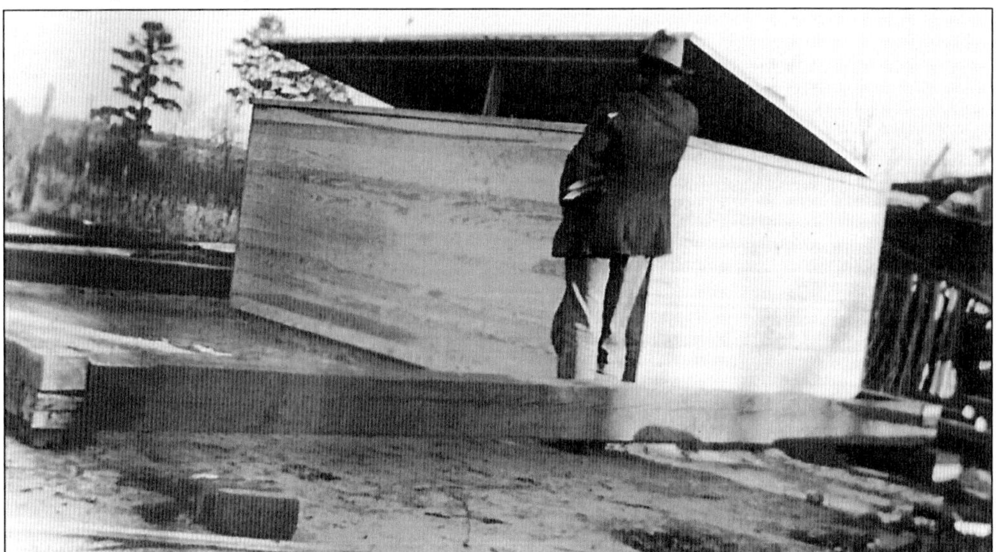

THE ICEHOUSE. Before refrigeration, families had a number of easy ways to extend the use of different foods. A cool, spring-fed creek was used for fruits and some vegetables. Pork was salted, smoked, and hung in a smokehouse. Canning vegetables and fruits was a common undertaking. In the process of building an icehouse in the early 1930s for a country family, John Stokes checks out the box in which large cubes of ice would be placed to create a cool icebox. Connected to pulleys, the lid on the heavy wood box could be lifted to give access to the interior. (Courtesy of the Owen family.)

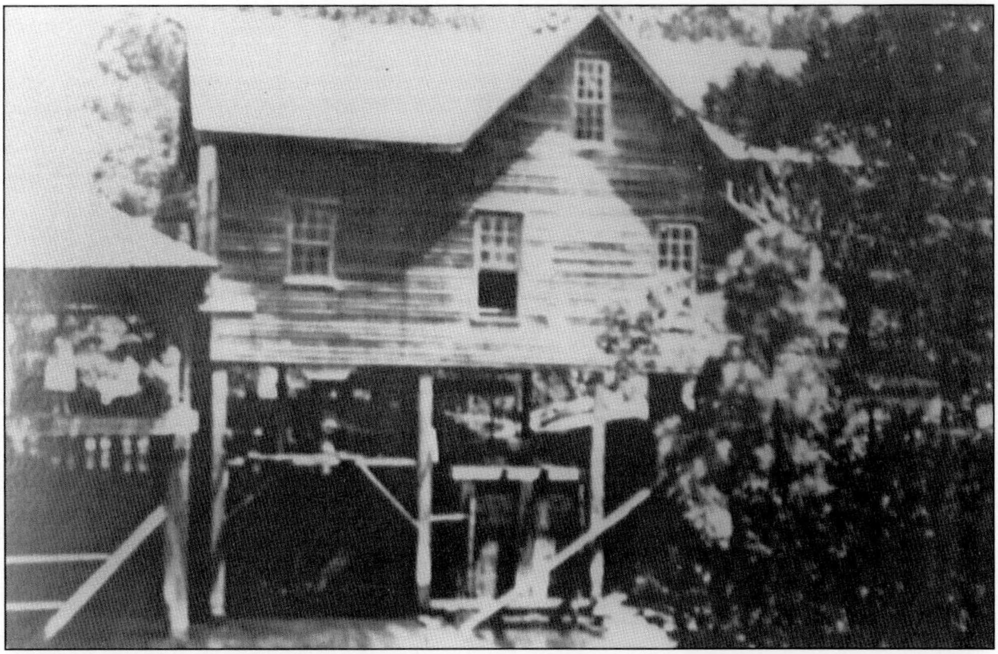

Sheffield's Mill. Located just off Cedar Springs Road south of Blakely, Sheffield's Mill was established around 1820. A swimming area provided summer entertainment for local children and adults. The Fourth of July brought crowds of people with their picnics, watermelons, and games to play. Years later, the mill burned to the ground.

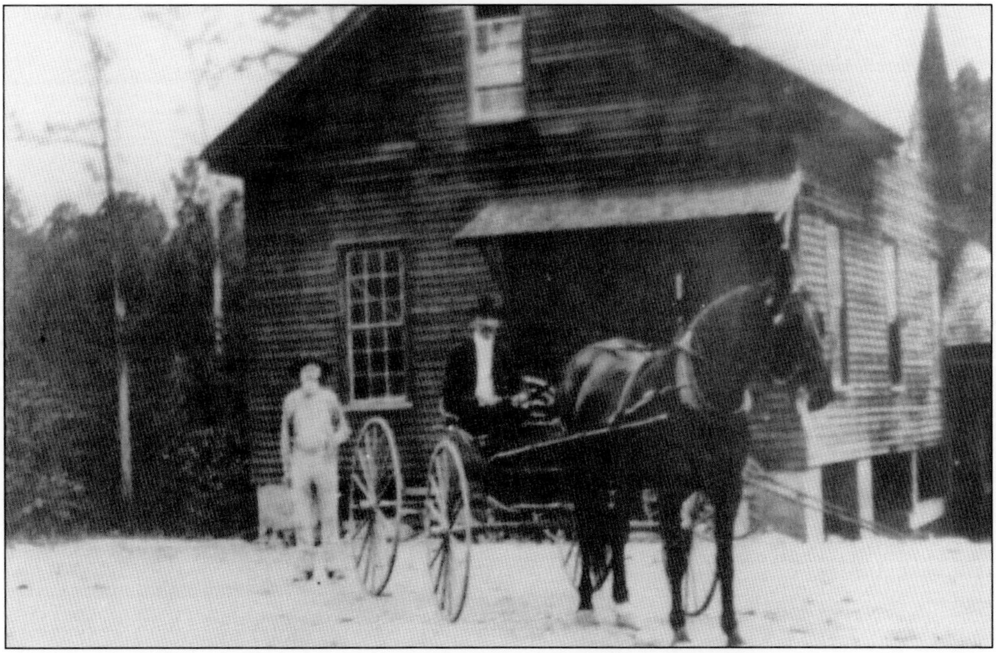

Eat My Grits. The word "grits" is most likely derived from the German term *grutze* and the Italian *gruzzi*, which mean coarsely ground corn. However, grinding corn for meal and grits was not the only purpose of Sheffield's Mill. A water wheel and a covered bridge made a picturesque sight. Year-round, families spread their quilts on the grass for picnicking and naps for the children.

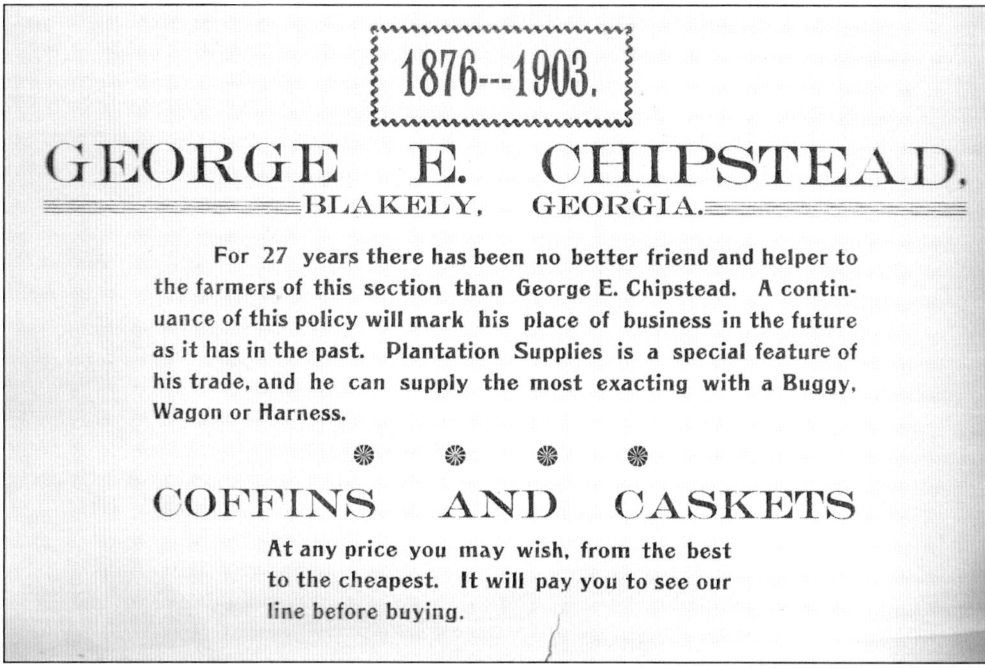

1876---1903.

GEORGE E. CHIPSTEAD,

BLAKELY, GEORGIA.

For 27 years there has been no better friend and helper to the farmers of this section than George E. Chipstead. A continuance of this policy will mark his place of business in the future as it has in the past. Plantation Supplies is a special feature of his trade, and he can supply the most exacting with a Buggy, Wagon or Harness.

COFFINS AND CASKETS

At any price you may wish, from the best to the cheapest. It will pay you to see our line before buying.

CHIPSTEAD ADVERTISEMENT. George E. Chipstead's advertisement in the *Blakely Reporter* in 1903 indicated that his place of business had been selling coffins, caskets, and plantation supplies, such as buggies, wagons, and harnesses, for 27 years. Since 1876, Chipstead's in Blakely had offered to the public "any price you may wish, from the best to the cheapest." Mrs. Chipstead tended the store on the west side of the square and kept her sewing machine there to use in making clothing for her family. It is said that the Chipstead name is nearly extinct, and the family seeks to find the name in phone books wherever they go.

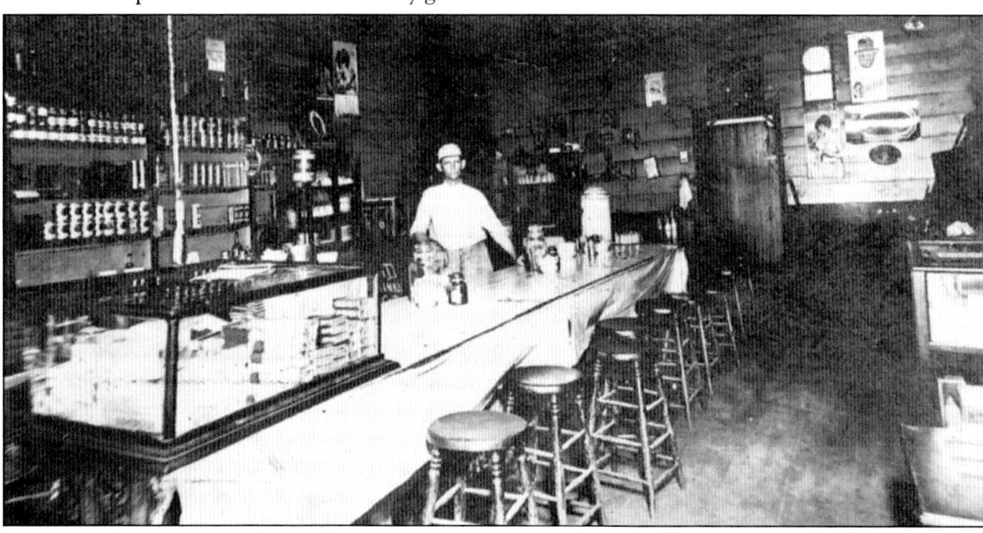

WILLIAMS RESTAURANT. Across the street from the train depot, Williams Restaurant was especially busy when the train pulled into the station. Citizens came early to meet the train at mid-morning and to visit with neighbors over lunch. Many times the passengers, who came in on the train from Alabama and Albany at 6:15 p.m., would be hungry enough to cross the street to the restaurant rather than wait for the evening meal at the hotels around town.

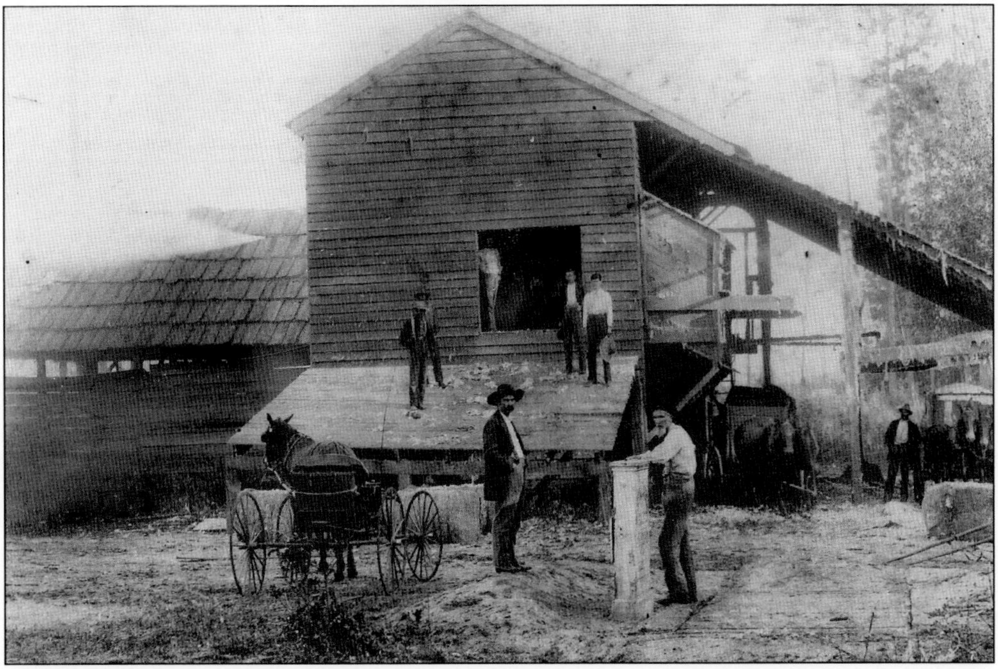

COTTON WAREHOUSE. Built in 1905 on North Main Street, this cotton warehouse was owned by Dr. C.S. Middleton and Thomas Barton Harris. On the inside of the warehouse, below, Harris stands ready to serve farmers and buyers as part of the Early County agricultural community. The turn-of-the-century photograph above shows Thomas Bartow Harris, in the dark jacket in the middle by the buggy, and his workers running the operation of Harris Cotton Gin. (Both, courtesy of Mr. and Mrs. Gene Regan.)

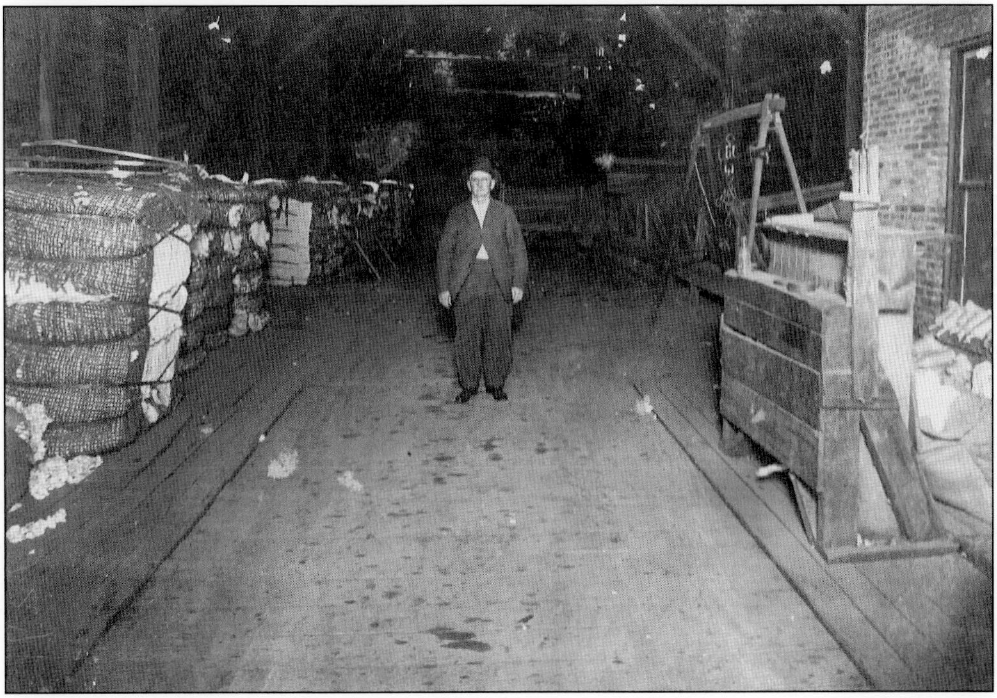

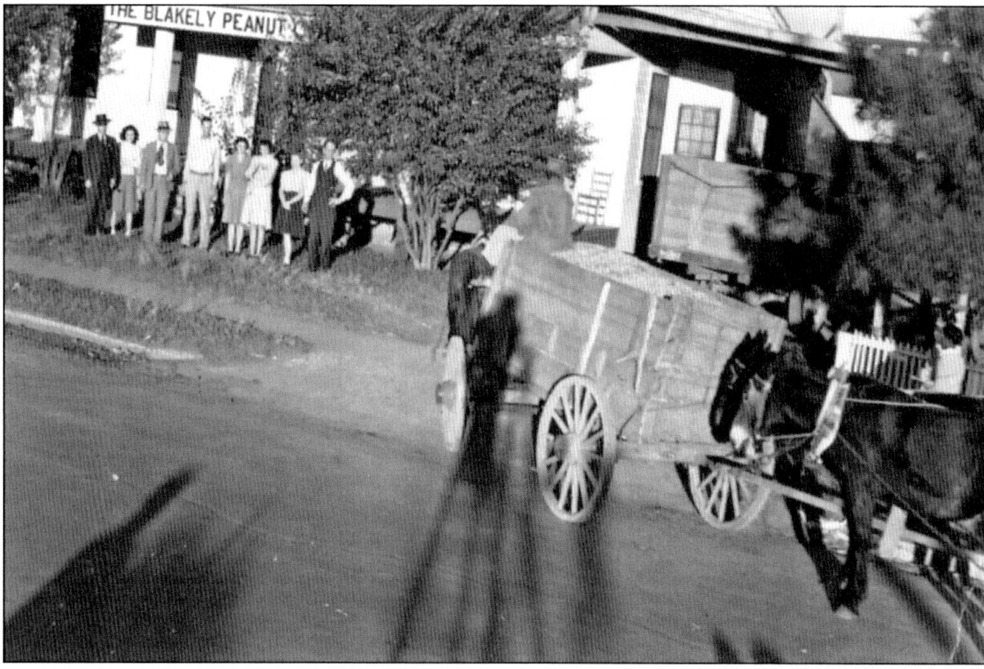

Moving On. The workers and owners of Blakely Peanut Company gather to watch the last load of peanuts come through the North Main Street receiving area. Located in a building that was originally the Dudley McDowell home, it was necessary for the growing company to find larger facilities.

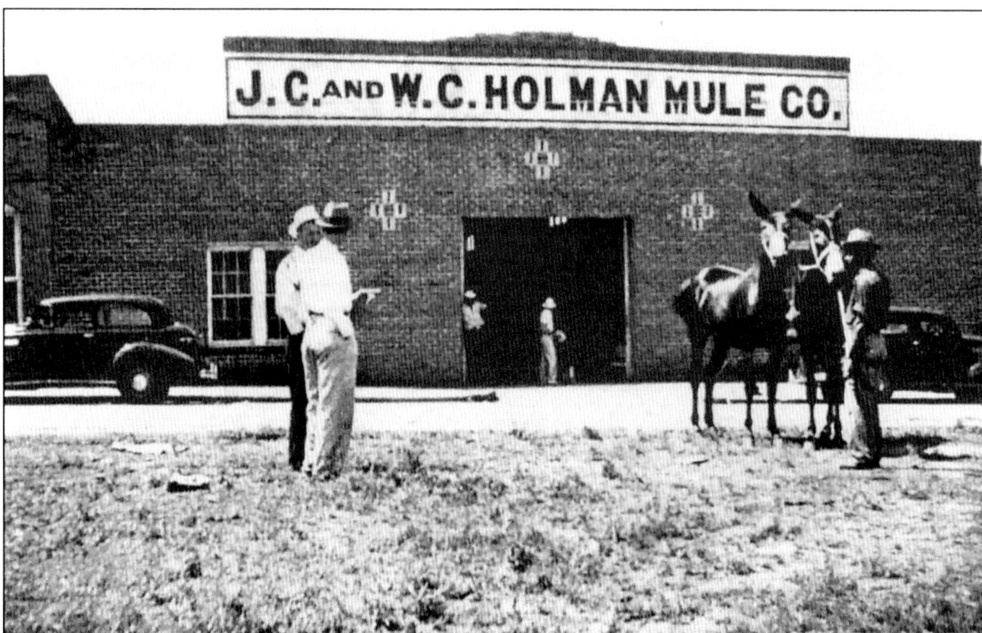

Holman Mule Company. Built in 1913 by Grady Holman Sr. and Grady Holman Jr., the building had a central vehicle door with twin windows. On River Street, it is said that there is a faded sign that says, "McM . . . Co." over the doorway.

Three

Square Society

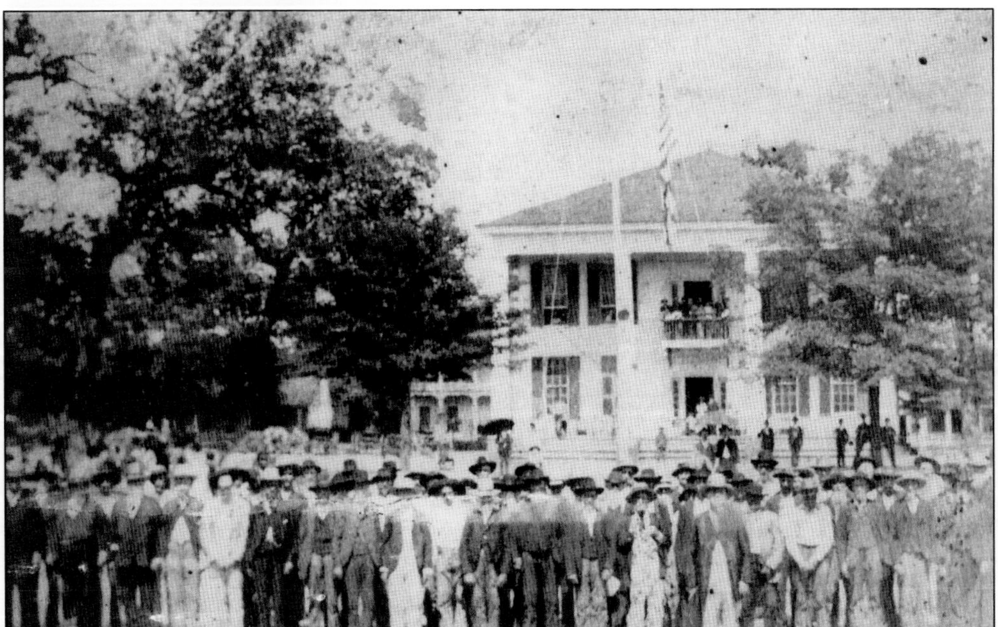

Soldiers of War. Erected in May 1861, a wooden Confederate flagpole stands behind a group of Civil War soldiers gathered for a reunion. Facing west, the Early County Courthouse in the background was the third courthouse to be built (1858). The flagpole, erected just before the Civil War, was 100 feet tall and was made from a pine tree from south of Blakely. It is currently the only Confederate flagpole still standing in the United States. The old Livingston Hotel can be seen behind the courthouse on the east side of the square.

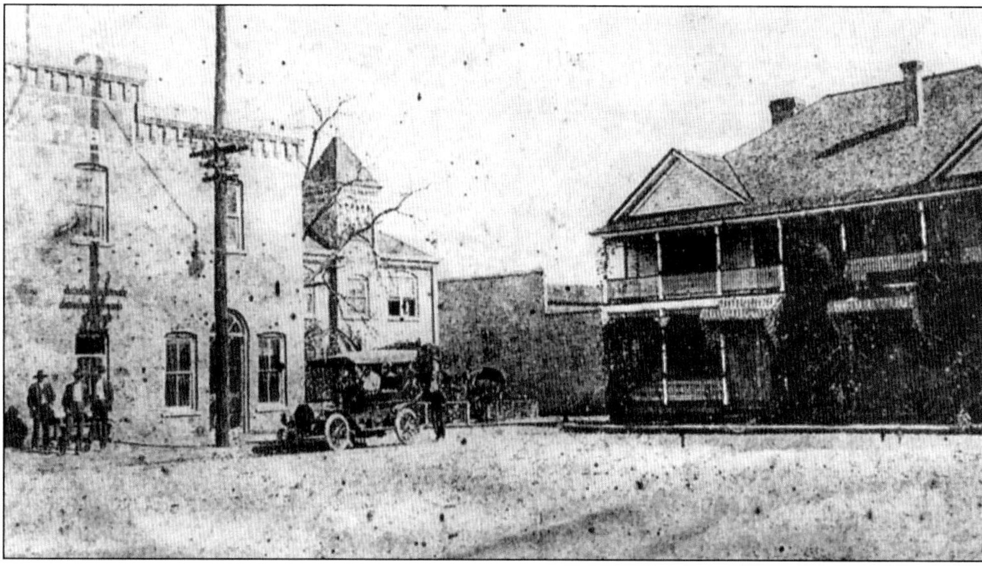

Faded Memories. This newspaper clipping from the turn of the century shows the northeast corner of Court Square. Visible to the left is the two-story jail with a tower. The jail was the second in Blakely. The first was on the site of the old Chipstead barn, which was on the south side of College Street. To the right of the jail, across the corner, is the elegant Hotel Thompson.

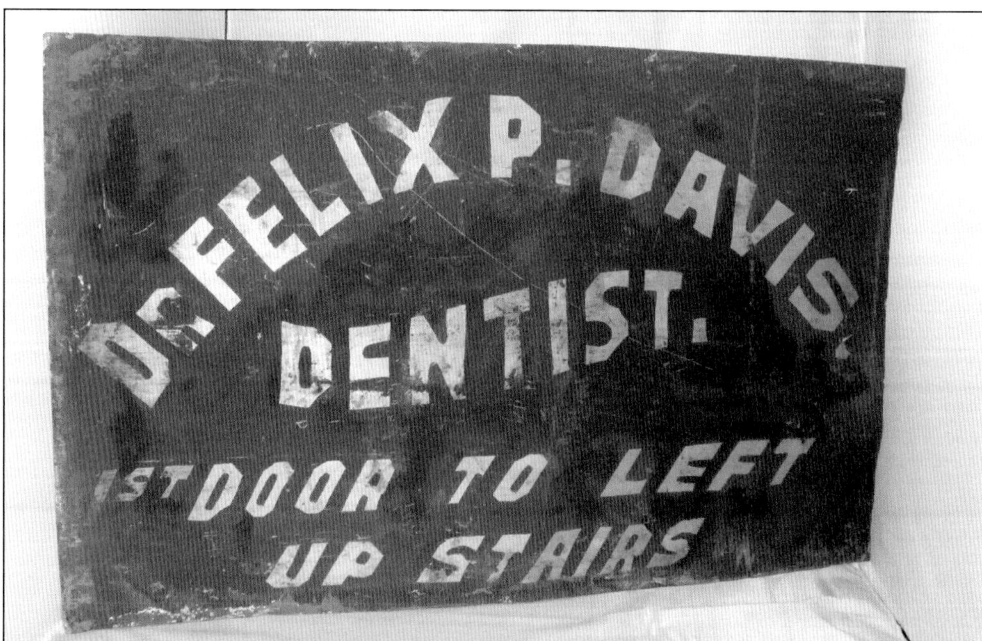

Up the Stairs. By the sidewalk on the brick wall, this metal sign indicated that in the early 1900s, Dr. Felix Davis's dentist office was located up the stairs. On the west side of the square in 1904, A.G. Powell erected the building that housed the opera house on the second floor. Offices of Dr. C.P. Whitehead, Dr. Clarence Alexander, Lowery Stone Sr., and D.H. McDowell were on the second floor. Also, a billiard parlor, a restaurant, and Murdock grocery were located there. (Courtesy of Felix Davis III.)

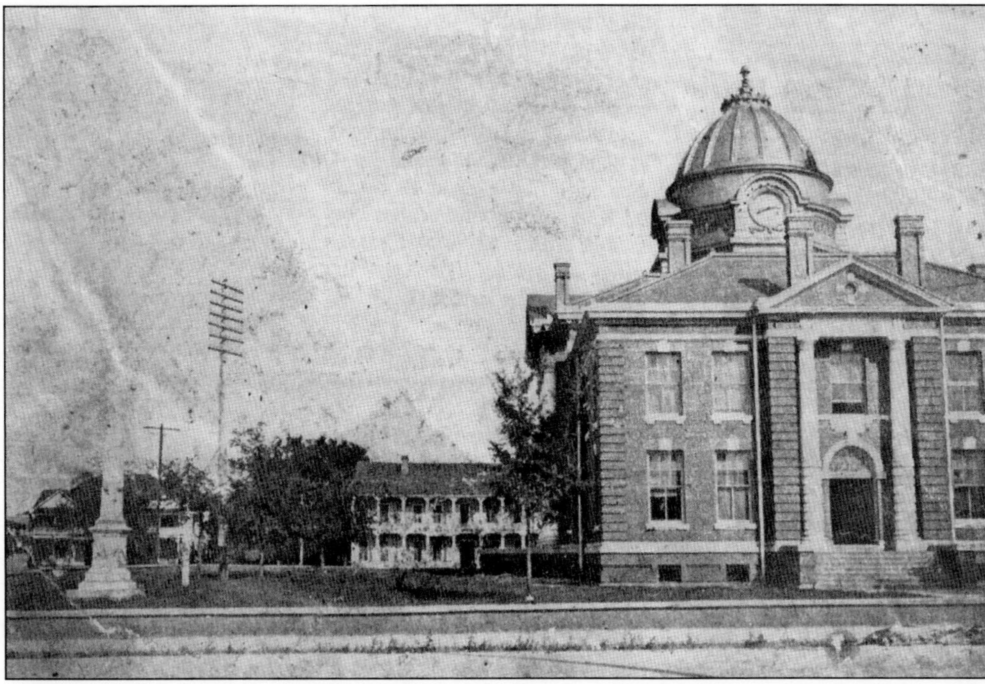

LIVINGSTON HOUSE. A rare glimpse of the old hotel comes from the *Early County News* archives. In the last two decades of the 19th century (1884), times were tight. Horses sold for $5 each, and Blakely hoped for a railroad connection from Albany to Dothan. Mary Livingston, a popular innkeeper from Arlington, moved her place of business to the square in Blakely. It was said that she "kept customers well-fed and furnished comfortable beds" at the Livingston House. "Splendidly Furnished, $2 per day," reads the advertisement. T.C. Dismukes ran the hotel.

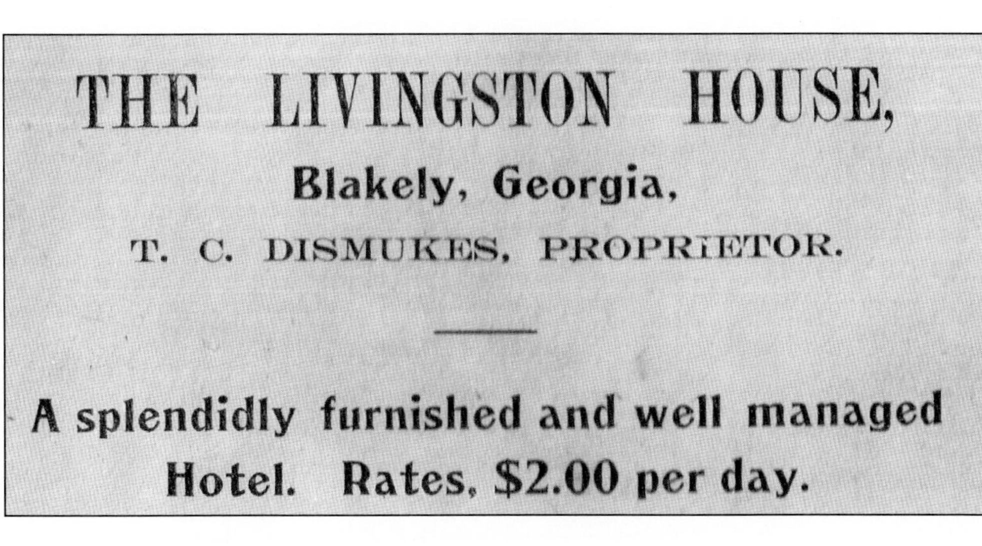

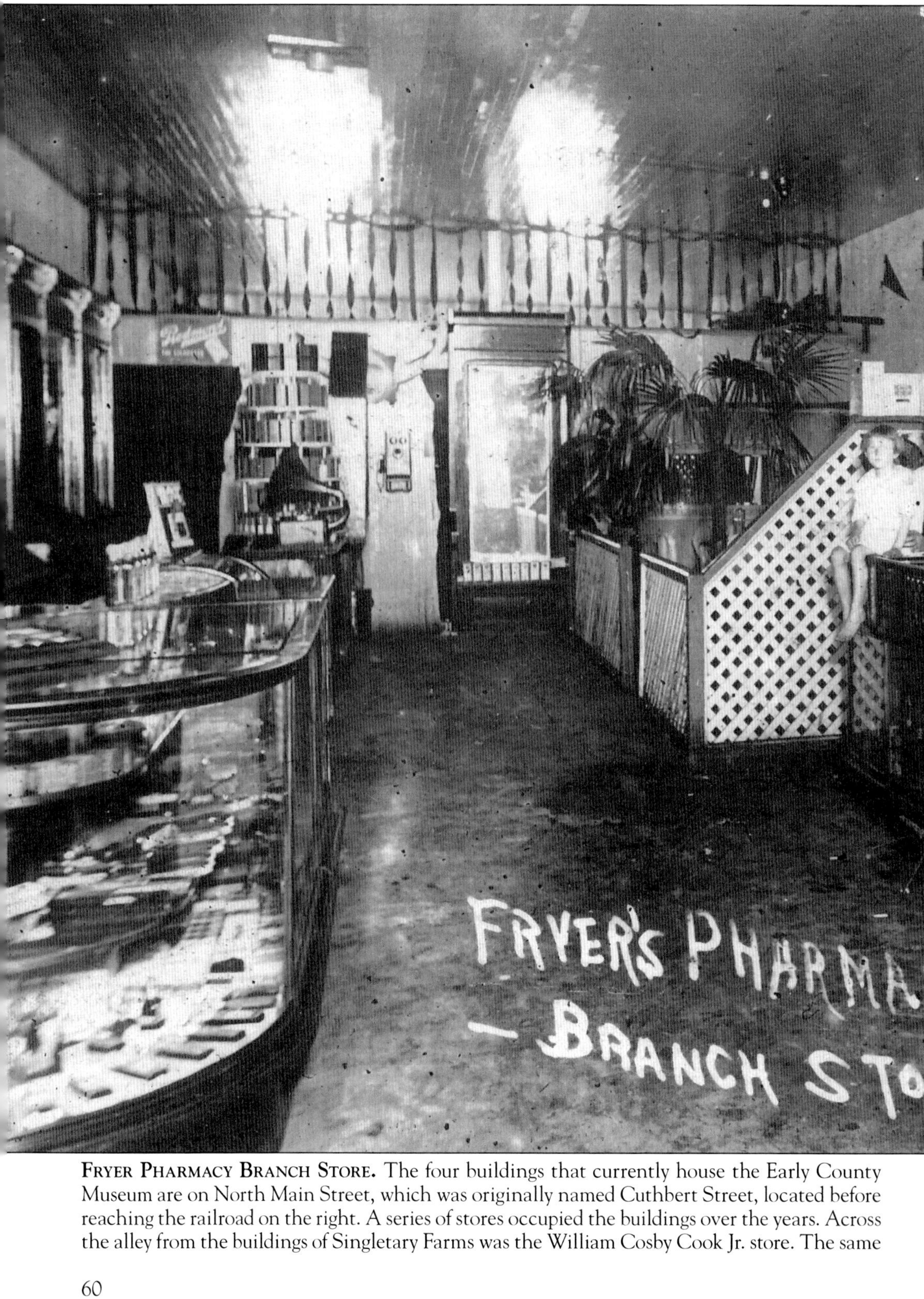

FRYER PHARMACY BRANCH STORE. The four buildings that currently house the Early County Museum are on North Main Street, which was originally named Cuthbert Street, located before reaching the railroad on the right. A series of stores occupied the buildings over the years. Across the alley from the buildings of Singletary Farms was the William Cosby Cook Jr. store. The same

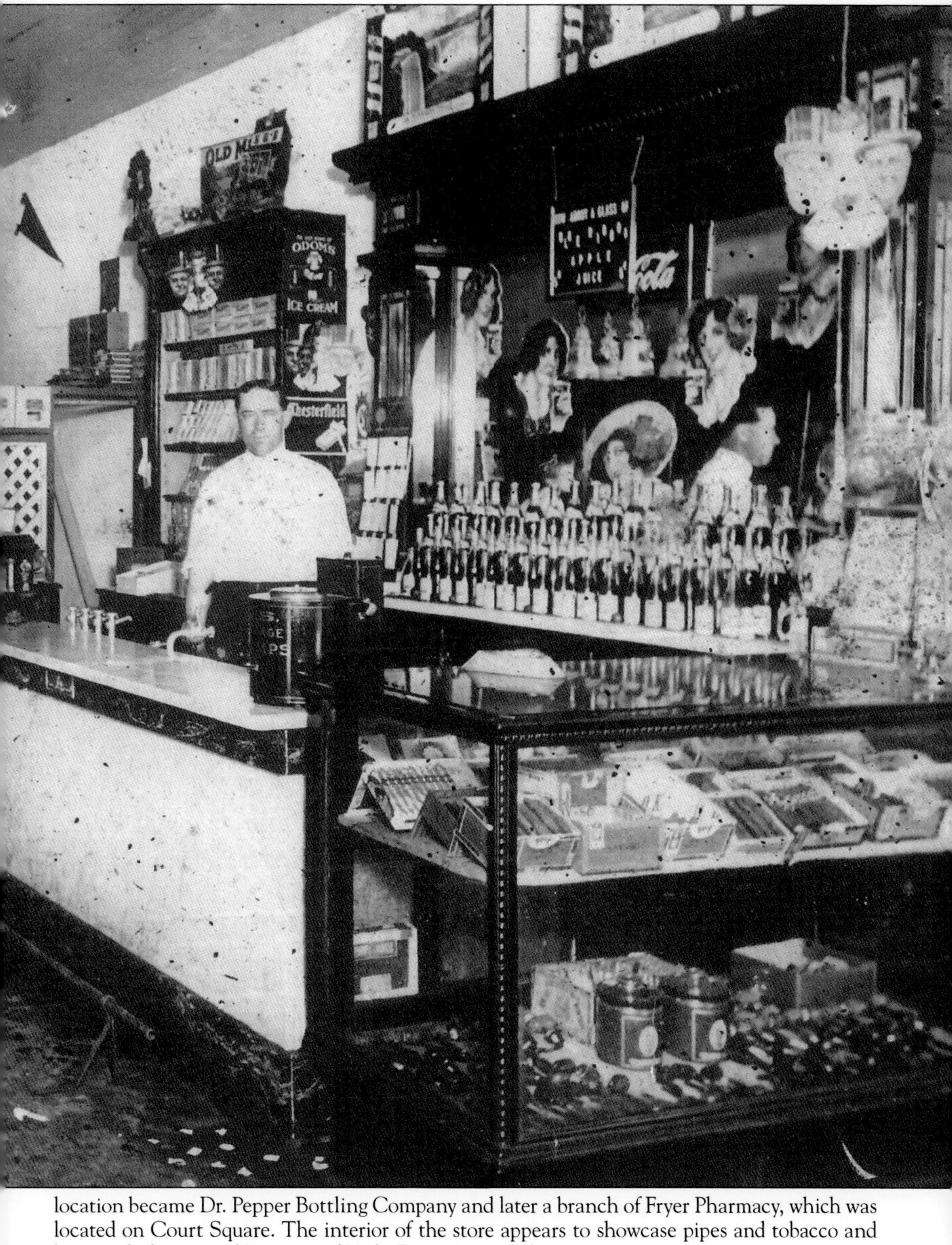

location became Dr. Pepper Bottling Company and later a branch of Fryer Pharmacy, which was located on Court Square. The interior of the store appears to showcase pipes and tobacco and has a soda fountain. (Courtesy of Vicki Fryer Kornegay.)

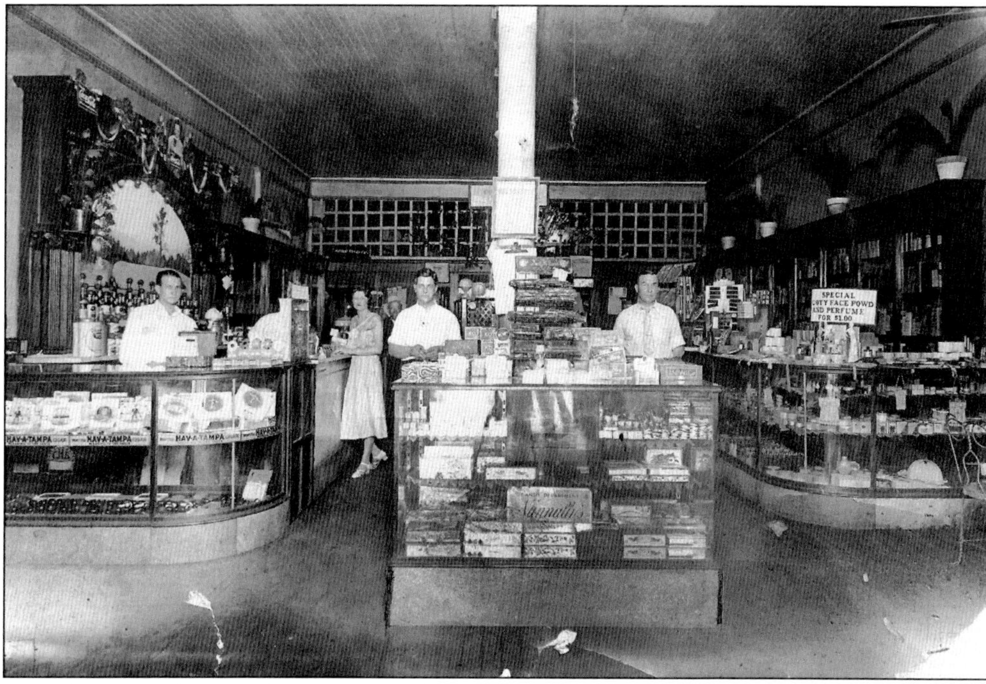

Fryer's on the Square. Rare photographs of Fryer's Pharmacy on the west side of Court Square show the display cases that housed everything from HavaTampa cigars to toiletries and writing implements. The pharmacy was in the same location on the square for 70 years. Edward Fryer was the first owner; his brother Lewis Fryer Sr. joined him and eventually bought Ed's part. Lewis Fryer was the eventual owner. The pharmacy, which dispensed medications, was located in the rear. (Both, courtesy of Vicki Fryer Kornegay.)

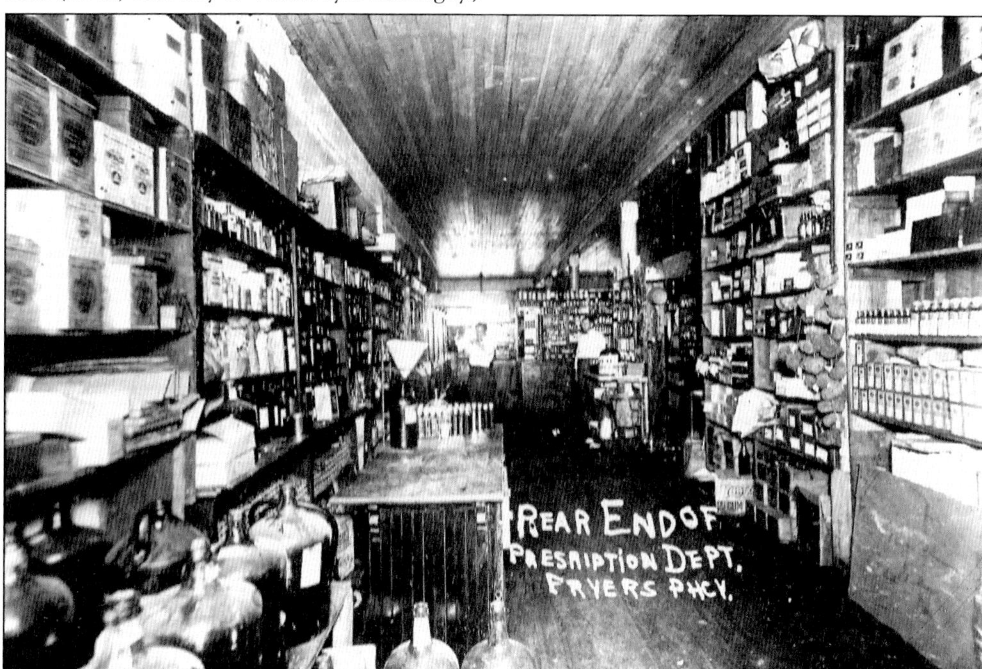

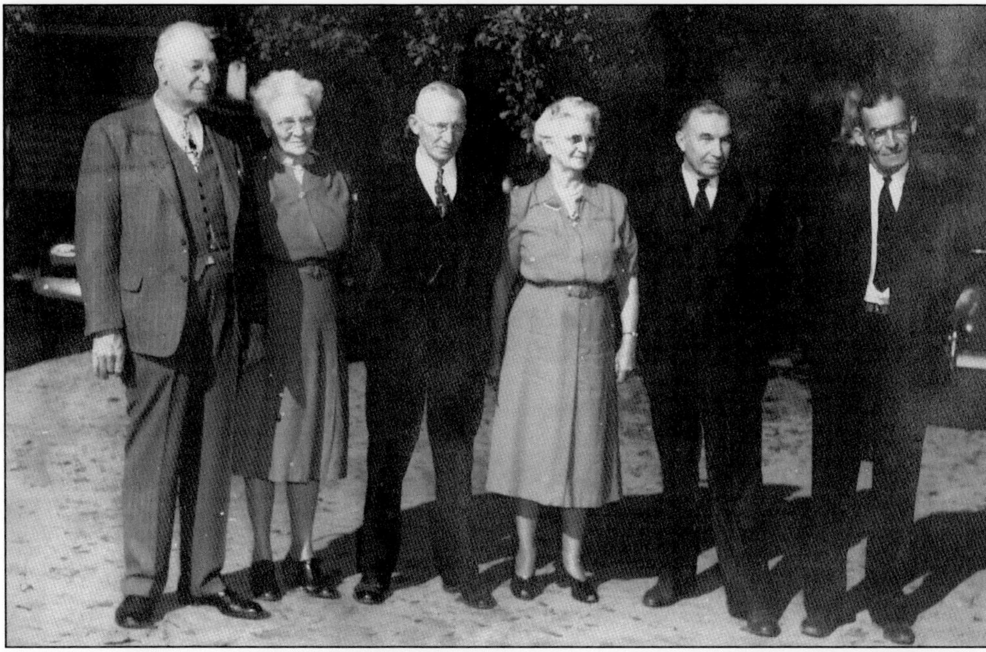

The Fryer Family. In 1947, the Fryer family was heavily involved in Early County and the Blakely community. Owning property and businesses and serving as public officials, they were integrated into many aspects of the area. Likely at a family reunion, the E.L. Fryer family is shown in this rare photograph. Those pictured are, from left to right, E.L. Fryer Jr., Mable Fryer Underwood, H.C. Fryer, Ellene Tarver, L.B. Fryer, and C.S. Fryer. H.C. Fryer was Blakely's postmaster and was appointed in 1874 by President Grant. (Courtesy of Vicki Fryer Kornegay.)

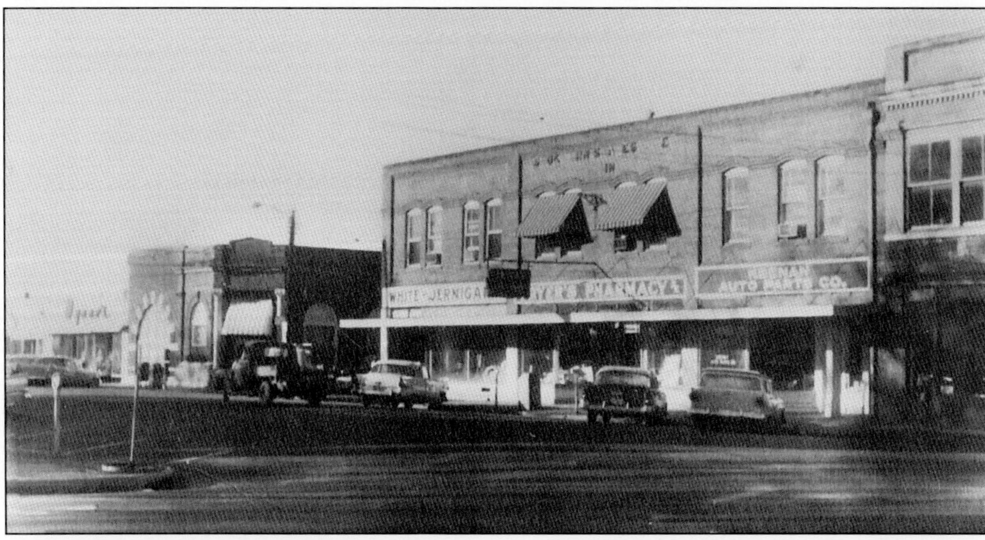

Square West. An old faded photograph shows the buildings on the west side of the square in Blakely. At one time, the west side of the square housed stores, such as New York Smith's Merchandise, built in 1910; J.B. Tarver Furniture Company; Walter Jordan's Grocery; A&P store; and Keenan's. Also, Fryer's Pharmacy was located on this busy block. The store on the east corner of River Street and Court Square housed J.C. Chancey Merchandise, D.M. Wade's business, and White Jernigan.

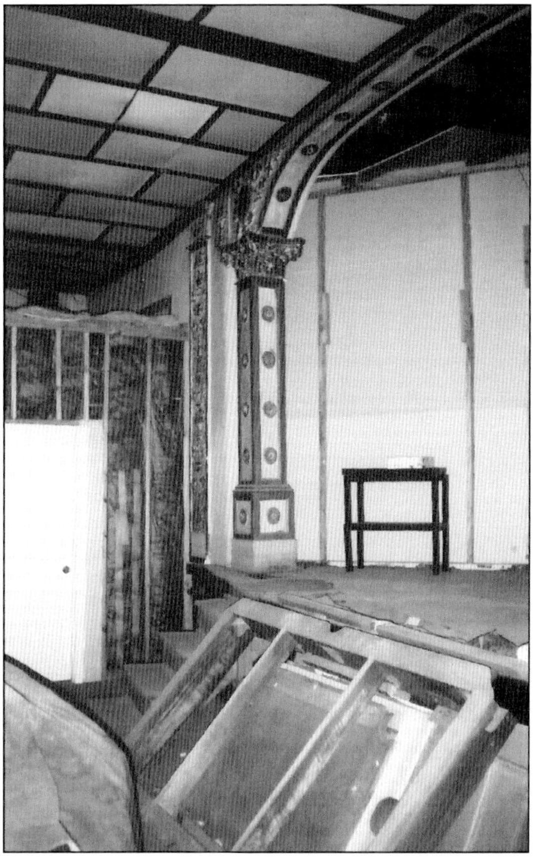

The Opera House. The "opera house" upstairs over Collier Insurance never had an opera performance. The elegance of the building, with its decorative ceilings and Corinthian capitals, is still evident. The stage and dressing rooms are located in the front. Remnants of sets and backdrops are still present. Erected by A.G. Powell in 1904, the building had a third floor with dressing rooms and a balcony, but after fire destroyed the top floor, it was not replaced. Seating 750 people, the opera house was used for numerous plays and other literary events.

Bank of Early. In the late 1950s, the Bank of Early occupied the building at the corner of River Street and Court Square. It was granted a charter in April 1941. Parked outside the bank is Mrs. Roscoe Roger (Olga)'s 1957 or 1958 Oldsmobile. Sanborn insurance maps show that in 1906 a bank was located on the corner of River Street and Court Square. In 1912, the same space was labeled "First National Bank." The 1920 maps continued to show that First National Bank occupied the same space.

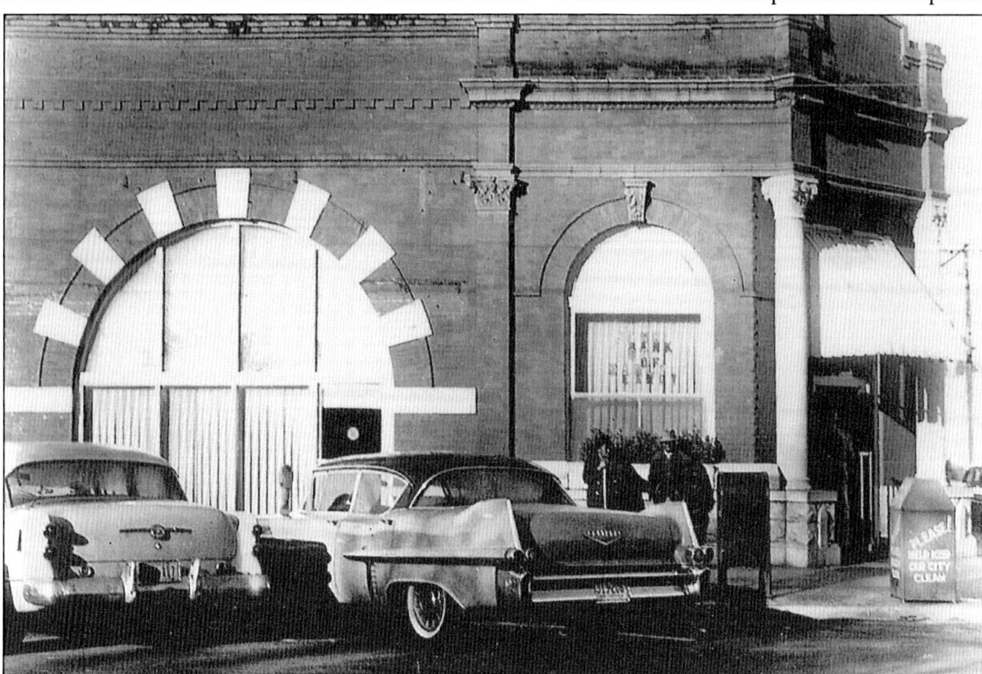

Masonic Lodge. Built in 1893 by Wade Powell for a telephone building, the Magnolia Lodge, Order of the Eastern Star, was located just off the square on River Street. Occupying space to the west on the same block was Holman Surveying Company, which was built in the 1890s. Both buildings are still occupied.

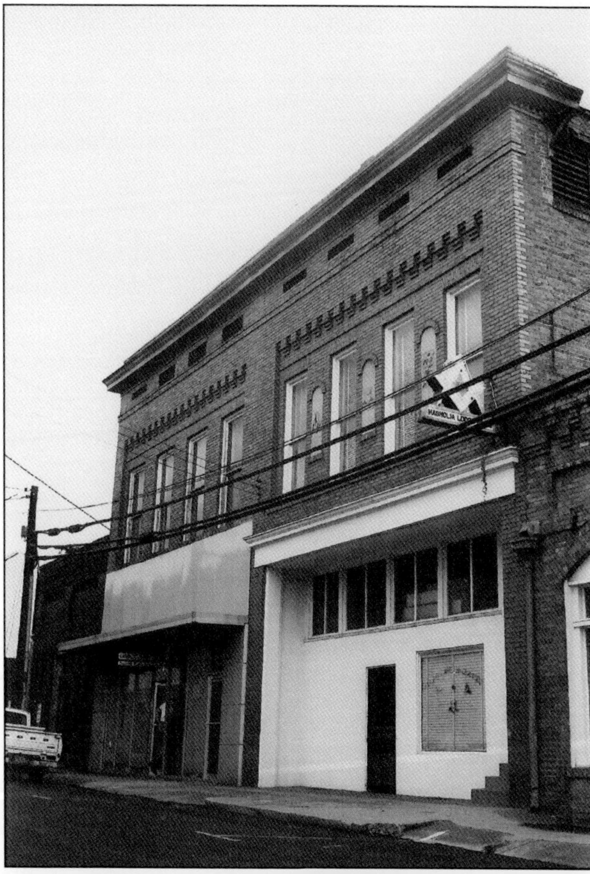

A Postcard from Hattie. A 1911 postcard to Douglas Harvey of Jakin, Georgia, from B.D. Harvey and Hattie Mae Chancy reads, "Do you recognize a single person in this group? I think it is a very poor picture. What do you think? Hope to see you real soon. H.M.C." The unidentified group gathered in front of the Confederate monument on the downtown square in Blakely.

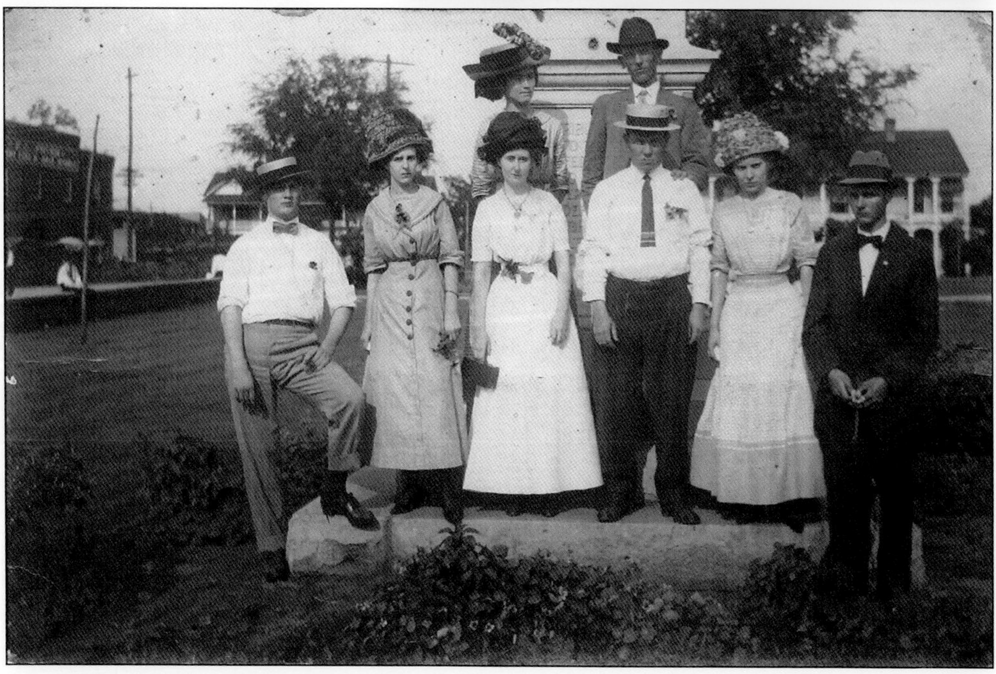

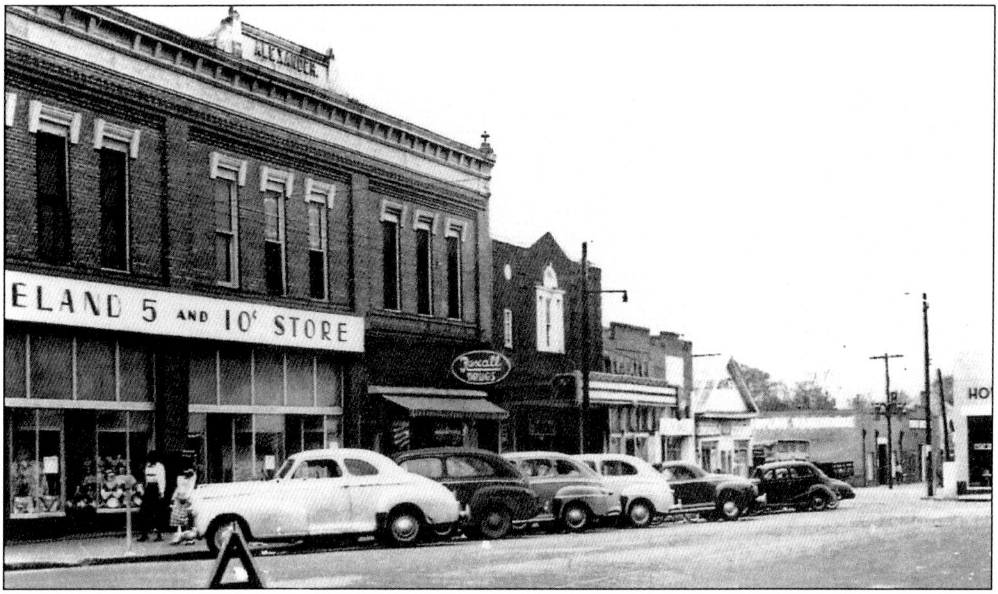

SQUARE SOUTH. Wyatt Alexander built the two-story building at the corner of Court Square and South Main Street in 1904. Peters Rexall Drugs was built at the same time. J.C. Peters built the Blakely Theater, with the pointed roofline and a marquee, in 1936. It stands tall with memories of Saturday afternoons with 10¢ movies and Tarzan and Cheeta on the screen. The white frame building at the far end of the block is the oldest store in Blakely. George Chipstead brought in the frame building from his farm in the late 1890s.

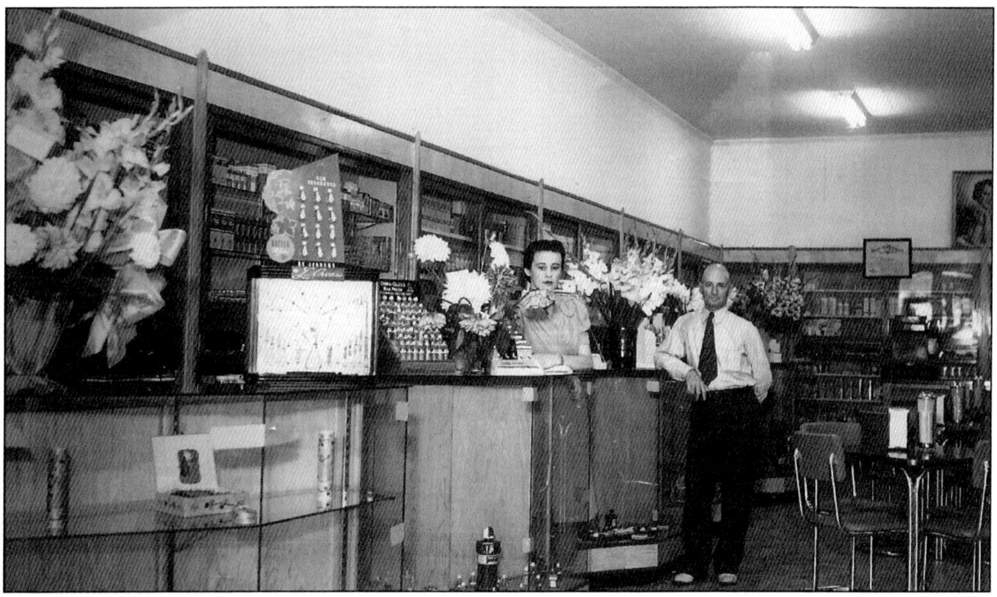

PETERS REXALL DRUGS. Moving to Blakely in 1930, Joseph "Pete" Clyde Peters and his wife, Kathleen Dunn Peters, brought in two pharmacists, Lizzie King and husband Frank, from around Cairo, Georgia. They built Peters Rexall Drugs, where Tom Sawyer had a dry goods store on the square in Blakely. Tables were set up in the center of the drugstore to accommodate the girls who worked at stores around the square. They would come for coffee breaks at 10:00 a.m. and 3:00 p.m. during the workweek. (Courtesy of Mr. and Mrs. Billy Peters.)

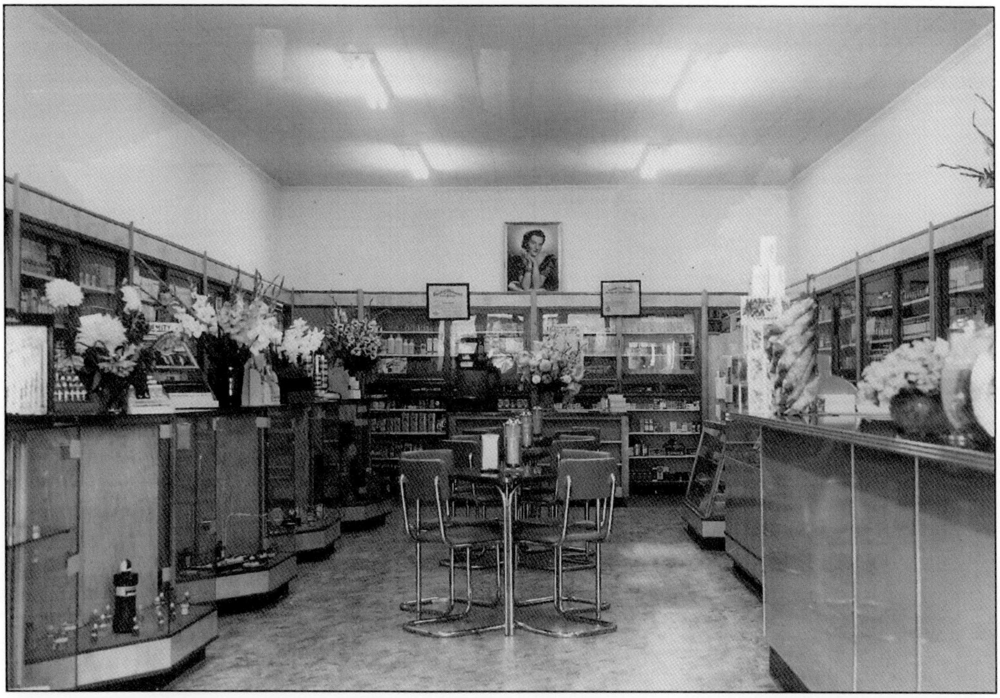

Sunday Good Times. Young and old would come to the soda fountain in Peters Drugs to purchase all flavors of the delicious Supreme Ice Cream, which was produced in Dothan, Alabama. Lizzie, the pharmacist, however, refused to serve two different flavors stacked on the same cone. People of all ages would come in to be served by Maynard Mock (center) and other clerks in the store, especially on Sundays. Regular customers were Mary and Grady Holman Sr. and Col. Lowery and Ann Stone. (Both, courtesy of Mr. and Mrs. Billy Peters.)

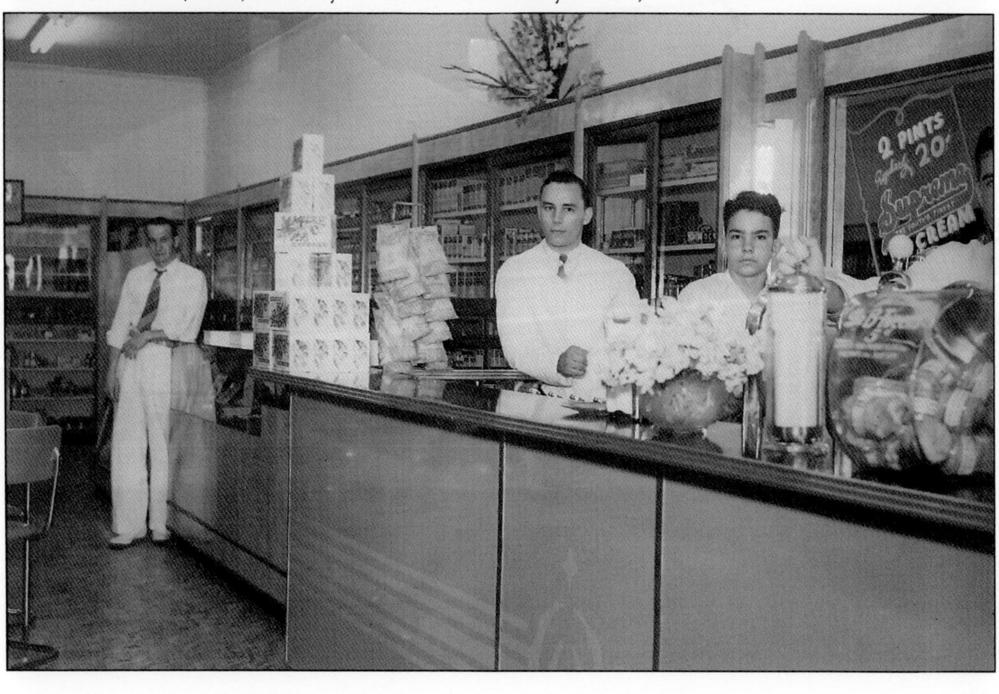

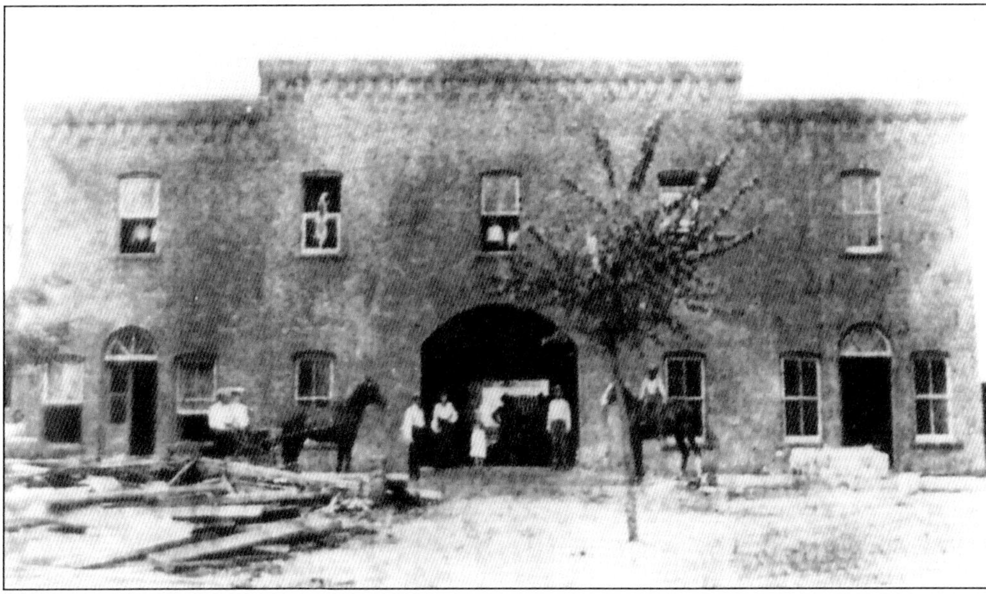

Fryer Livery. E.L. Fryer Sr. concentrated his several businesses under one roof at his livery stable. The livery, located on the north side of the square, took up most of the lower floors. On the second floor, he sold buggies, wagons, and harnesses. He also conducted an undertaking business and stocked coffins and caskets. Horses and buggies were rented by townspeople for rides around town or the countryside. Bars over openings at the rear, found on the east wall of the building today, are evidence that horses were kept there 100 years ago.

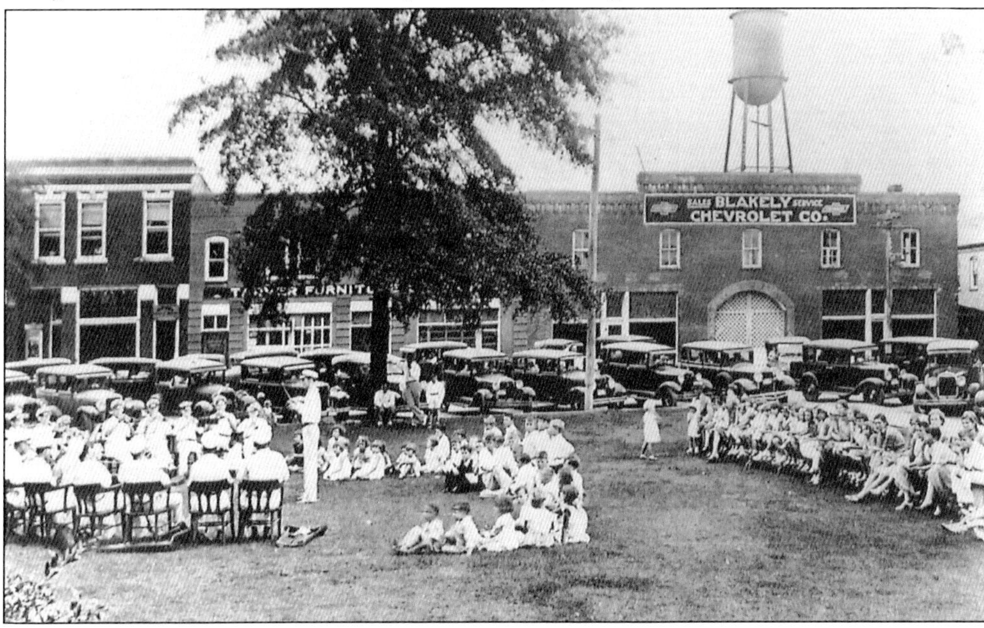

Concert on the Square. Music lovers of Early County and the surrounding area gathered every Sunday afternoon to hear the Peanut Band present outstanding music. The band set up its instruments on the courthouse lawn across from First State Bank at the corner of North Main Street and Court Square. On the same block can be seen Tarver Furniture and Blakely Chevrolet Company, which was where Fryer Livery was located years earlier.

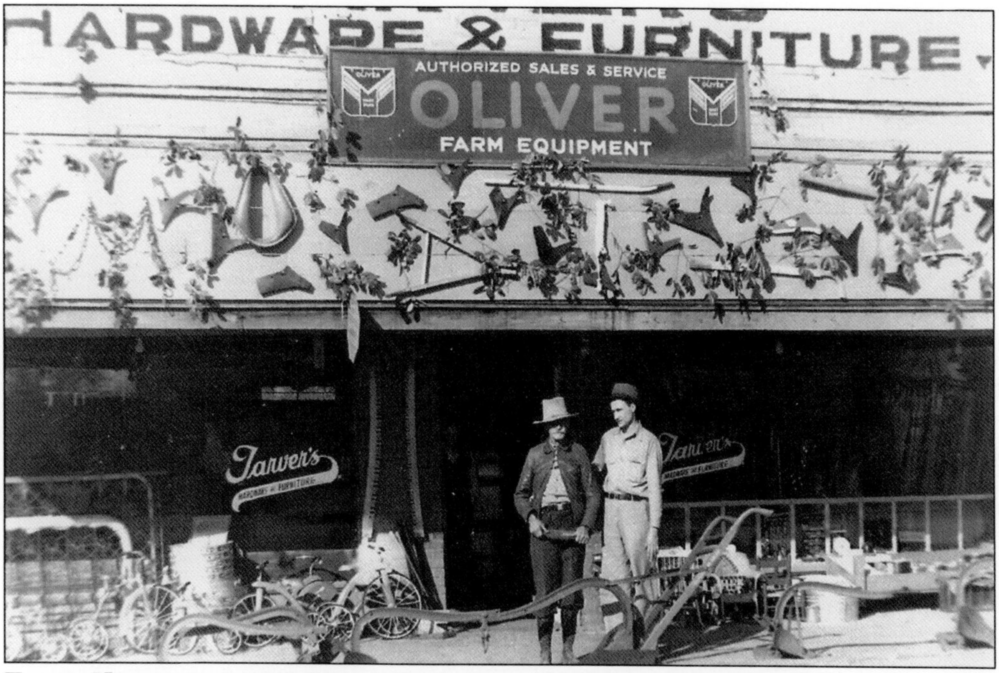

TARVER HARDWARE. In 1937, Tarver's Hardware and Furniture Store was located on the northeast corner of the square, where Fryer's Livery had been located in years prior. Pictured in front of the store are owner J.B. Tarver (left) and employee Bill Houston.

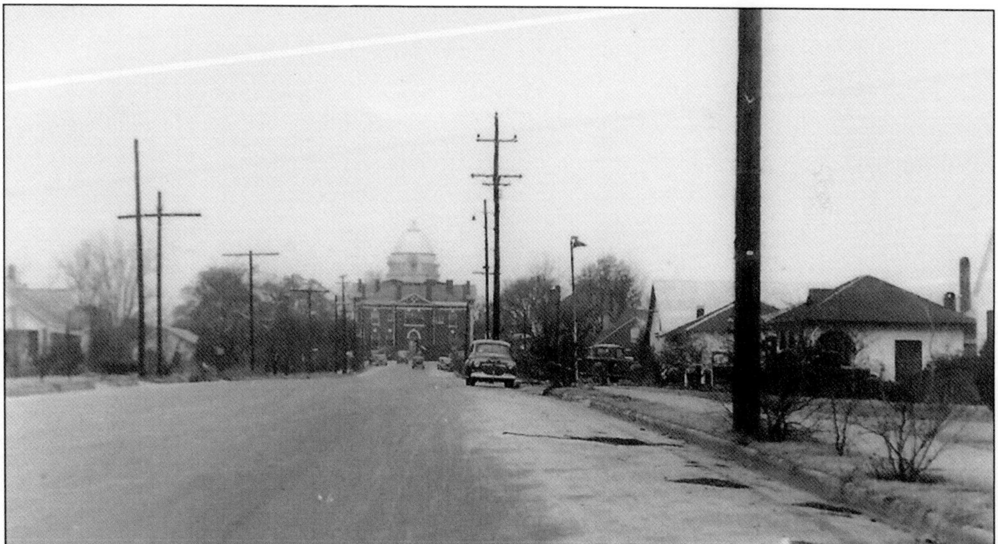

SWAMPS TO THE EAST. In the early days of the 1900s, when the "Grand Ole Lady" was built, the woods extended in all directions. It has been said that the east side of the majestic courthouse does not have columns like the other three sides because there was nothing to the east of the square except swamps. There was not even a road heading east to Arlington and beyond. Dr. Jack Standifer, a leading physician and citizen, once contributed this jingle about Early County clay roads: "The roads are not passable, not even jackassable. And those who would travel 'em, must get down and gravel 'em."

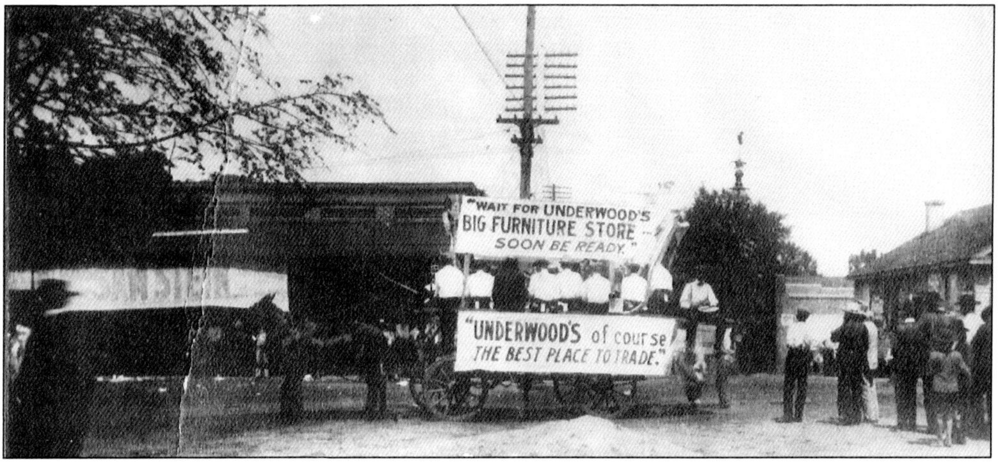

BAND ON A WAGON. The streets around the square in 1905–1906 were dirt. The concert band rides a mule-drawn wagon around the north side of the square displaying signs advertising "Underwood's of Course." The brick building on the left was at one time Hall Drug Company. The wooden structure across the street on the east corner is approximately where First State Bank was constructed. Notice the hanging street lamp is visible just above the trees.

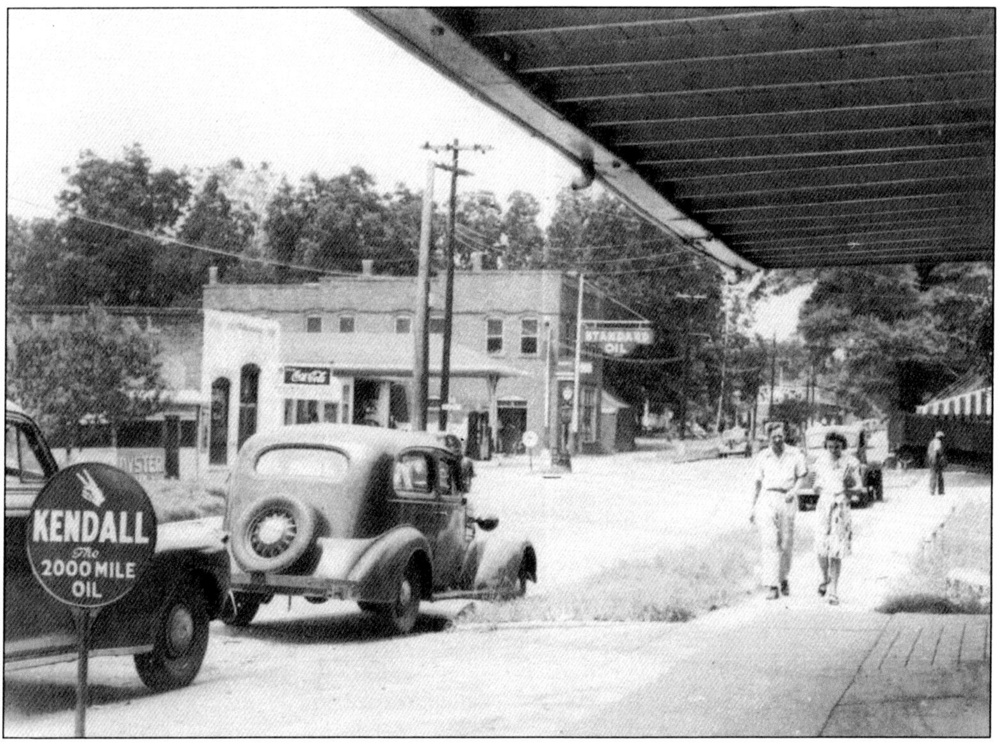

A STROLL ON THE SQUARE. Perhaps out for an afternoon stroll, Hubert Farr and Bessie Loyless enter the square from North Main Street. Across the street is the Oyster Bar, with Knighton's Place (with the Coca-Cola sign) next to it. Across Powell Avenue from Knighton's is Howard Davenport's Standard Oil station. The awning behind the couple covers the entrance to the Middleton Warehouse, which bought, sold, and stored cotton.

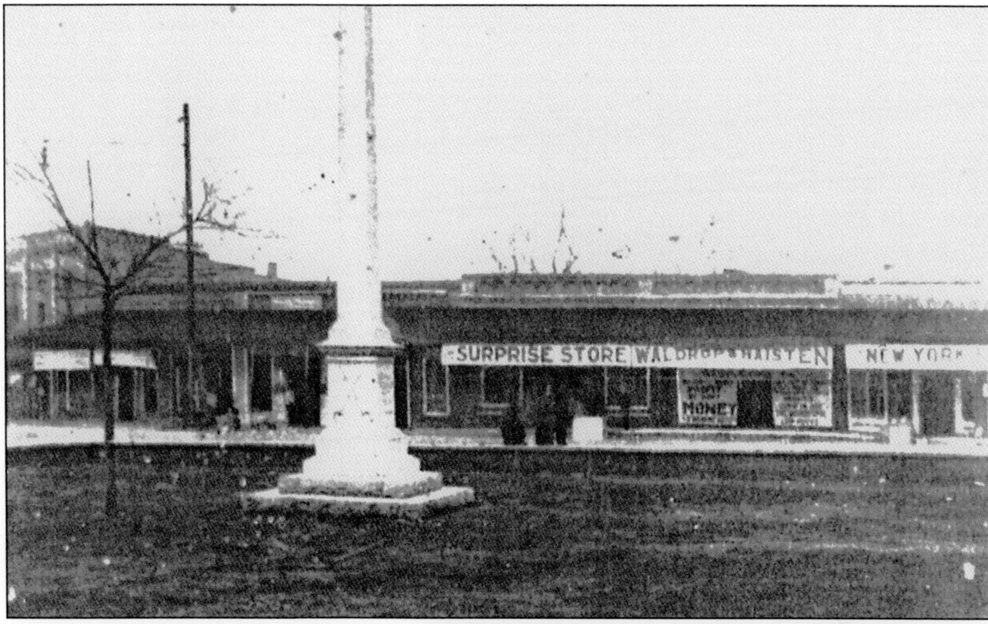

NORTH SIDE. In Blakely on the eastern end of the north side of Court Square, there were a number of stores in 1903: the New York Store, the Surprise Store, the Racket Store, and Sam Stein with the Baltimore Bargain Store. Moving pictures were invented in 1894, but it was 1909 before Blakely's first silent movie theater, the Pictorium, was opened. Located on South Main Street just off the square, it evolved into the Cozy Theatre in 1929 with W.C. "Booty" Cox as owner. Just off the square on College Street, the Cozy is the only two-story building in the photograph. Later, the silent movies were moved to the opera house on the square.

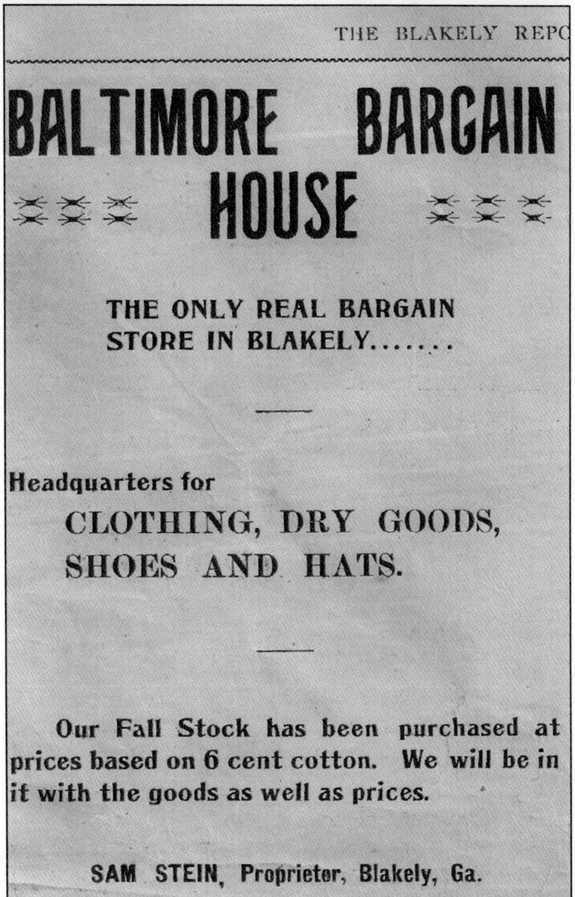
THE BLAKELY REPC

BALTIMORE BARGAIN HOUSE

THE ONLY REAL BARGAIN STORE IN BLAKELY.......

Headquarters for

CLOTHING, DRY GOODS, SHOES AND HATS.

Our Fall Stock has been purchased at prices based on 6 cent cotton. We will be in it with the goods as well as prices.

SAM STEIN, Proprietor, Blakely, Ga.

"BALTIMORE BARGAINS." "THE ONLY REAL BARGAIN STORE IN BLAKELY," reads the advertisement from the September 3, 1903, issue of the *Blakely Reporter*. Located on the north side of the square in Blakely, the store sold clothing, dry goods, shoes, and hats. Sam Stein was the proprietor and advertised that the fall stock had been purchased at prices based on 6¢ cotton.

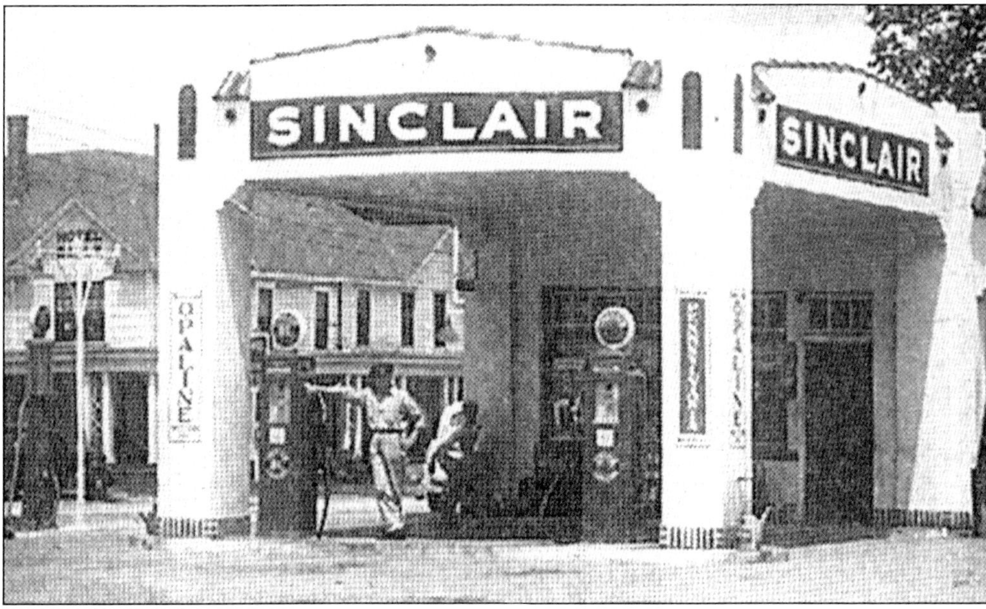

SINCLAIR STATION. A 1930s photograph of the Owen Sinclair station on the south corner of Magnolia Street and Court Square pictures a hotel in the background. In the early 1900s, Hotel Thompson and the Livingston House were on the east side of Court Square. The Hotel Thompson was later moved to the "back of the lot" to make way for city hall. Sanborn insurance maps in 1906 indicate that the hotel in the location in the picture was called the San Juan; it was called the Brown Hotel in 1912 and the Merchant's Hotel in 1920. (Courtesy of the Owen family.)

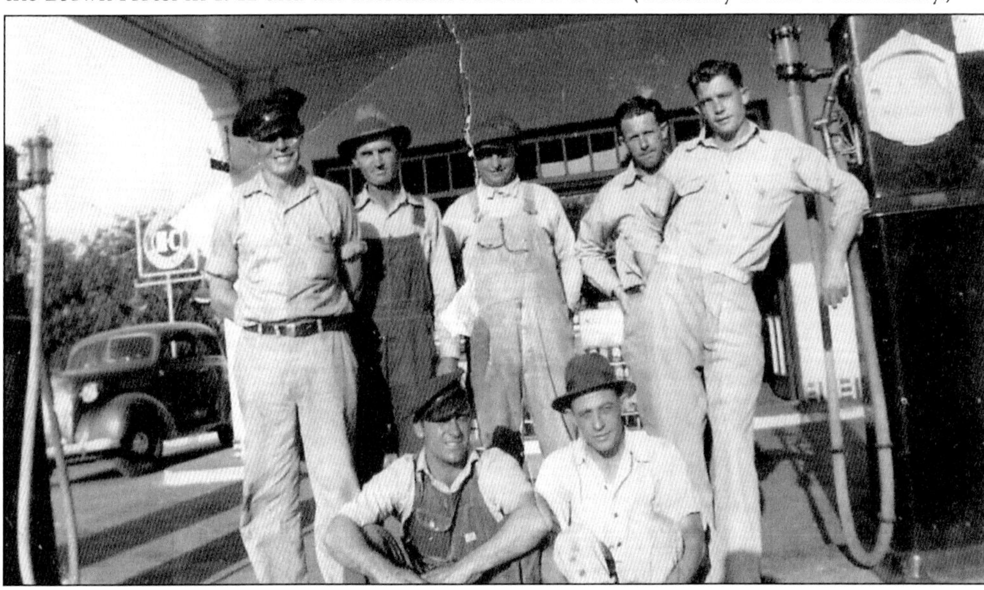

OWEN BOYS. The Sinclair service station was located on the east side of the square. It was operated for a number of years by the Owen brothers, Tommy and twins Sam and Joe. It was also the Trailways bus station. The bus traveled from Albany in the east to Blakely and then across the Chattahoochee River to Dothan, Alabama. It would wait three hours and retrace its route back to Albany. Another bus ran north and south from Bainbridge to Columbus. The Owens operated the station until about 1950, when they left to return to farming. (Courtesy of the Owen family.)

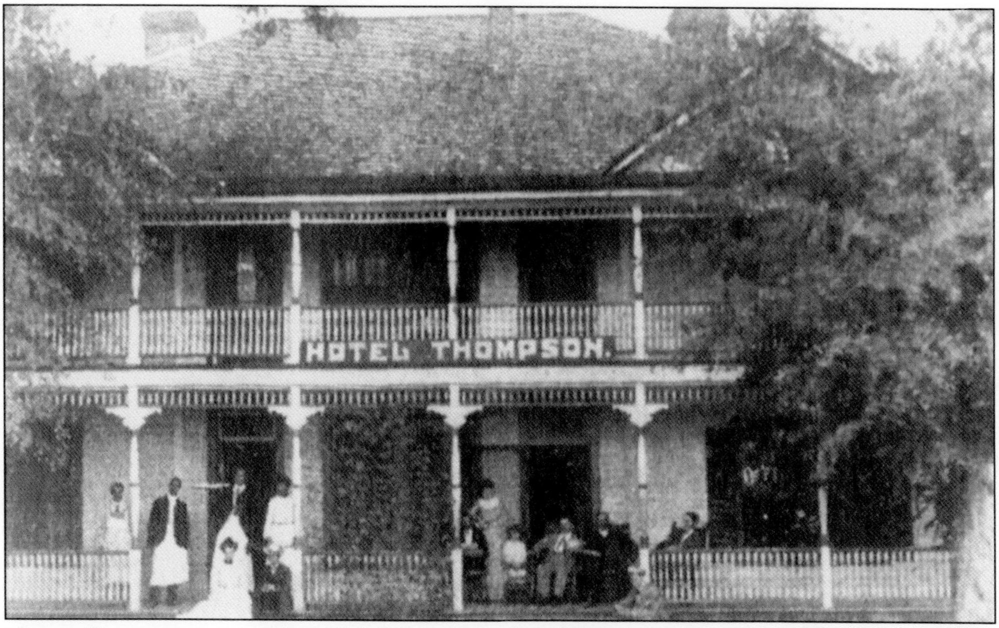

HOTEL THOMPSON. A bustling Blakely in the early 1900s required large hotels to accommodate visitors from the countryside and other towns in the area for special events. The two-story Hotel Thompson, with its elegant verandas on both floors, was an attractive place in the days before air-conditioning. Located on the east side of the square, it was the scene of business deals, family gatherings, and lodging for out-of-town guests. It rivaled the Livingston House next door in attracting guests. The hotel was later bought by members of the city council and moved to the back of the lot to make room for a new building, city hall.

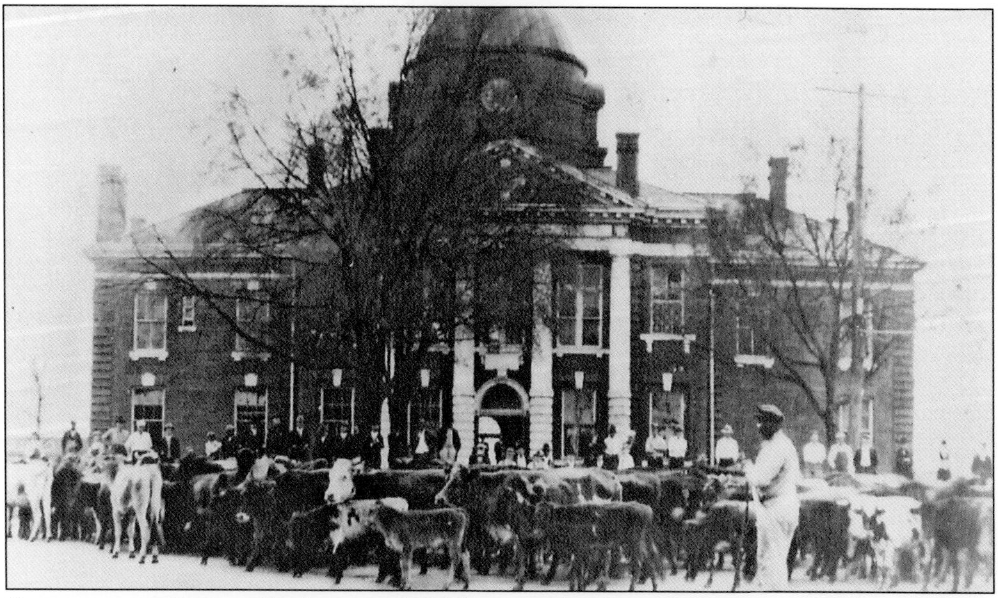

CATTLE ON THE SQUARE. Singletary and Middleton cattle take to the streets around the courthouse on the square in Blakely. New possibilities opened up with the arrival of a rail system in the town, creating opportunities to ship cattle far and wide. Cattle are driven around the square, the shortest distance to the railroad on North Main Street.

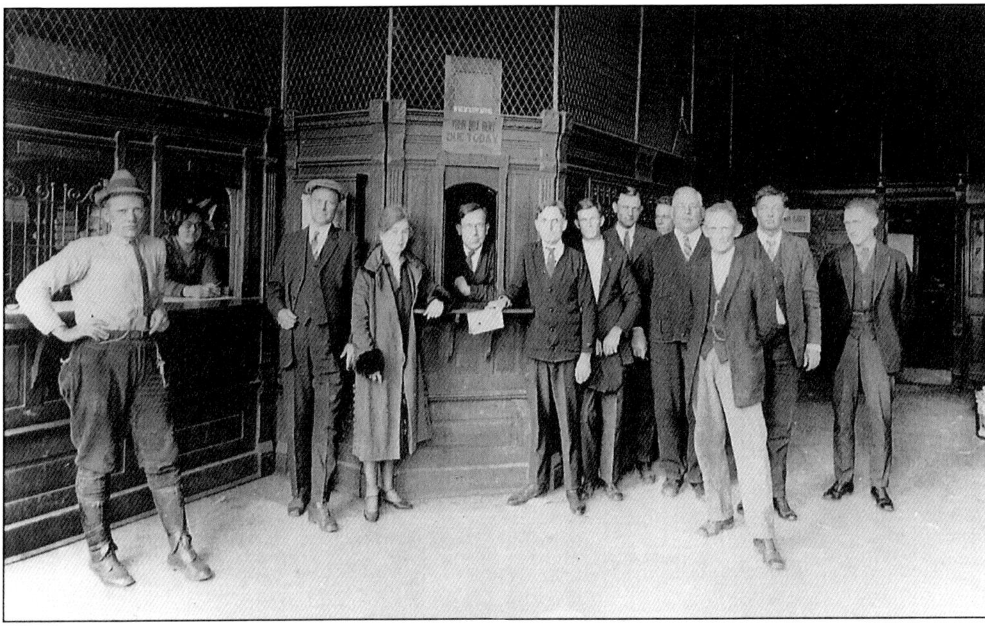

NEITHER RAIN NOR SNOW. Just off the square on South Main Street, the 1918–1920 US post office in Blakely is representative of the beautiful, polished-oak interiors so popular in the early 1900s and before. In the photograph are, from left to right, Mack Strickland, Mrs. Gatewood Freeman (Nettie), Ralph Hobbs Sr., Mrs. Lawrence Rambo, Gatewood Freeman, Chipstead Grubbs, Welborne Balkcom, Dewey Jones, Clayton Stevens, Mann ?, Hill Buchannon, ? Spence, and Lester Camp. The posted sign reads, "YOUR BOX RENT DUE TODAY."

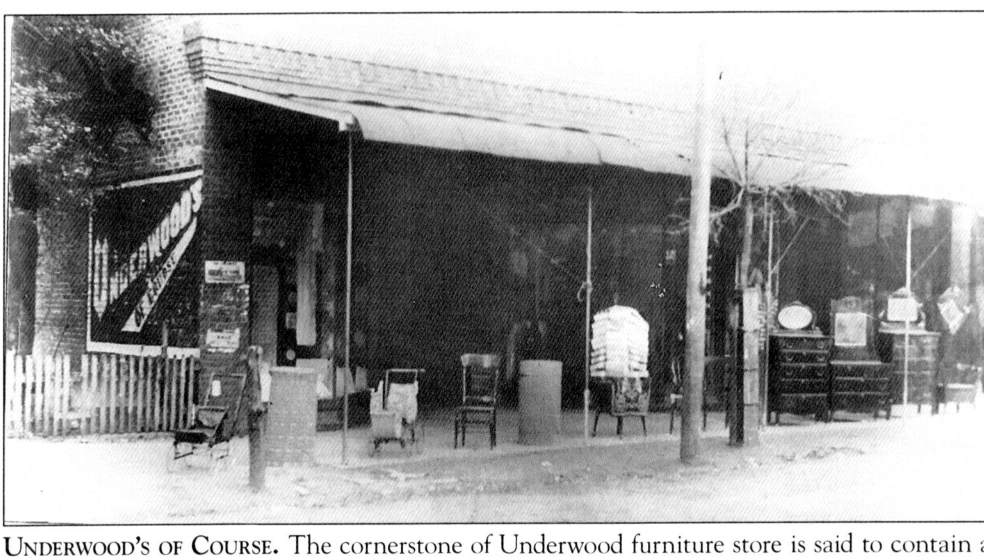

UNDERWOOD'S OF COURSE. The cornerstone of Underwood furniture store is said to contain a crypt, which contains articles and documents of the time. The items were placed there by two-year-old Tom Underwood when the building was erected in 1903. The furniture store sold all kinds of bedroom and living room furniture, as well as such items as baby carriages.

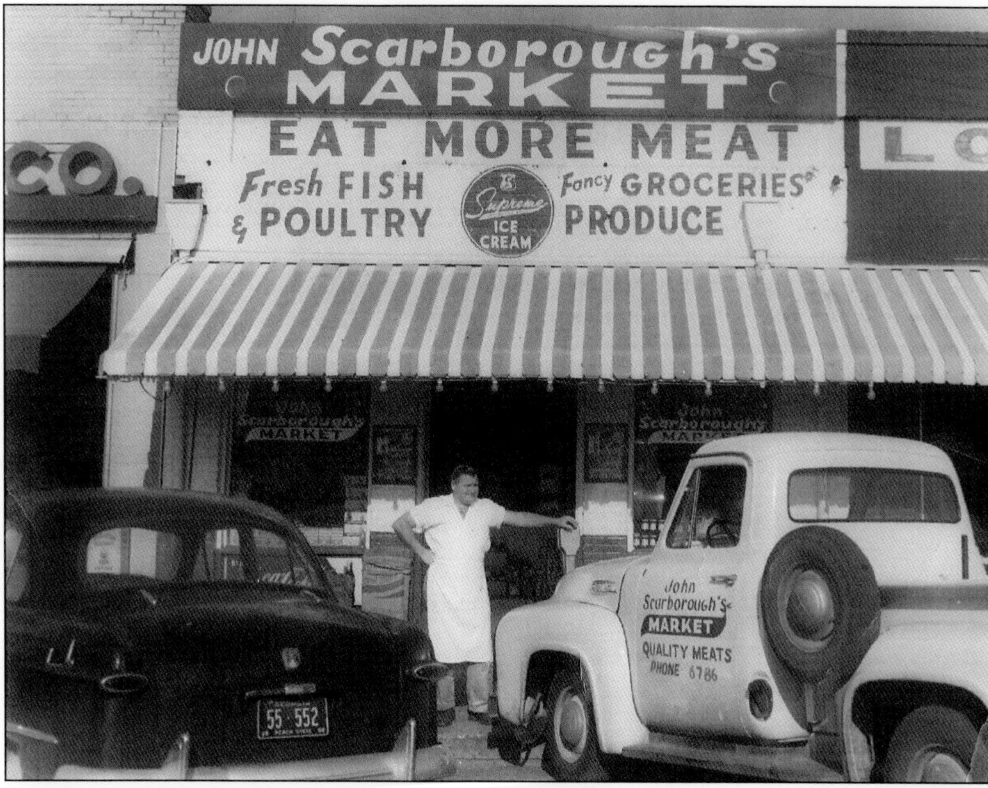

SCARBOROUGH'S ON THE SQUARE. On the west side of the square, John Scarborough bought the Langford store from Lawrence Lane and began to sell meats and groceries. It was a time when housewives could pick out a cut of meat and watch as the butcher cut and wrapped it in white butcher paper. John accepted phoned orders, and helpers delivered home orders on a scooter. In 1968, a fire destroyed the store, a pool hall, and another store next door. Scarborough went to work in Albany but returned to Blakely later to continue his profession at the IGA grocery store. (Courtesy of Johnny Scarborough.)

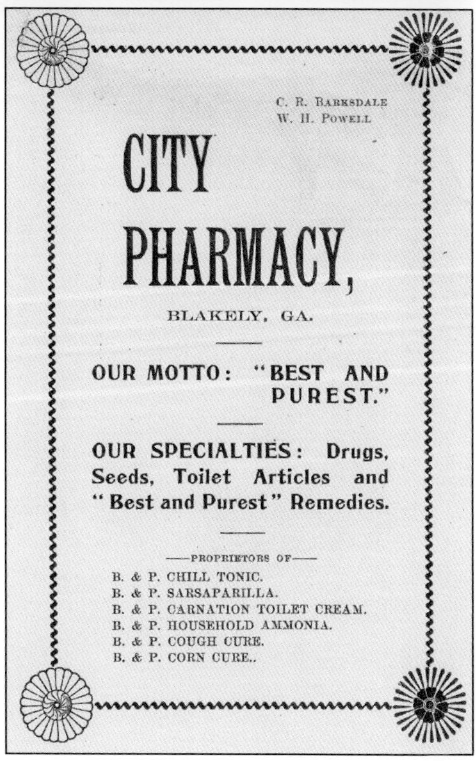

CITY PHARMACY ADVERTISEMENT. Operated by C.R. Barksdale and W.H. Powell, the City Pharmacy had at the top of its list of products for sale Chill Tonic (probably Groves brand). At that time, pharmacists usually mixed their own prescription drugs. Their motto was the "Best and Purest."

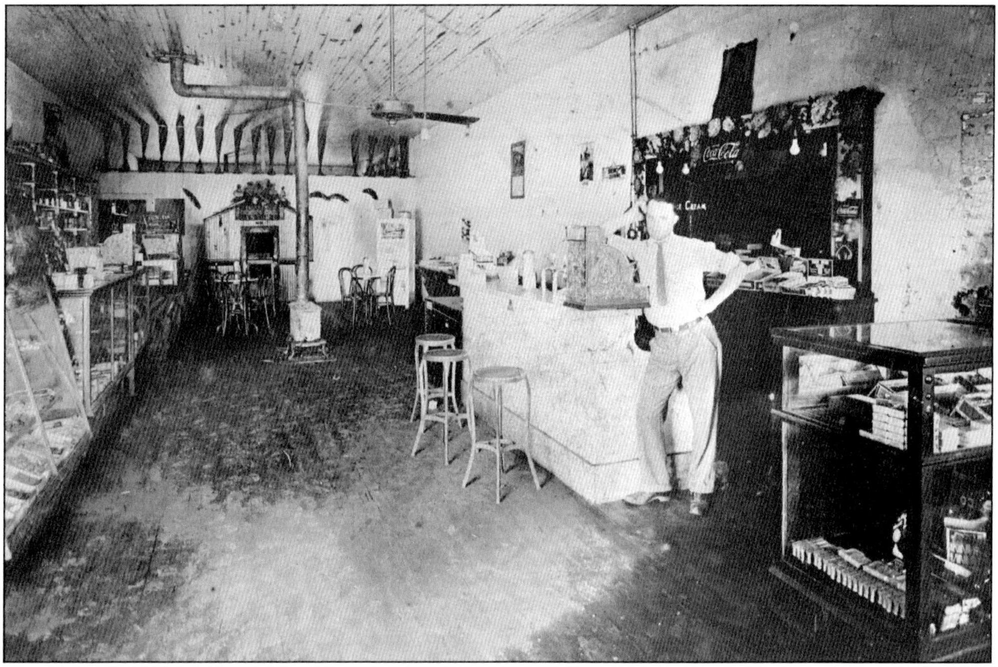

Hall Drugs. Inside Hall Drug Company on the north side of Court Square in the late 1920s and early 1930s, Robert "Bob" Duncan Hall stands ready to assist a customer. Formerly Acme Drugs, insurance maps verify that it was there in 1906. Other tenants in the building were Walter Thomas, Lee Howell (1914–1917), R. Claude Howell (1917–1950), and Carly "Red" Bell and Robert D. Hall (1950–1956). (Courtesy of Georgia Archives Vanishing Georgia Collection, EAR 18-82)

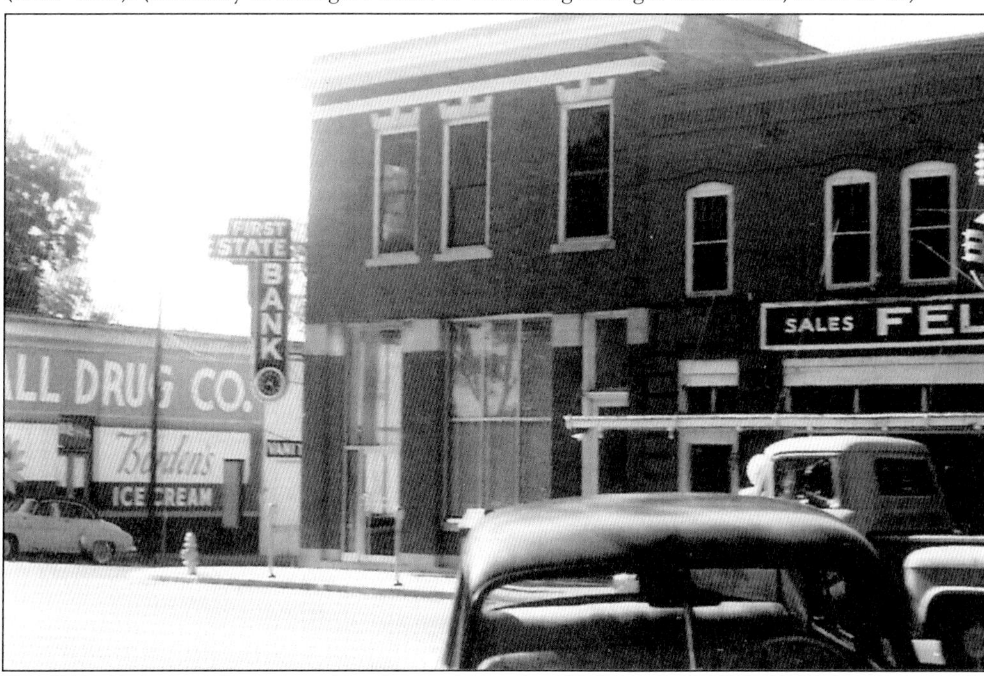

On the Corner. Hall Drugs was located on the west corner of North Main Street and the square. Across the corner was the two-story First State Bank Building.

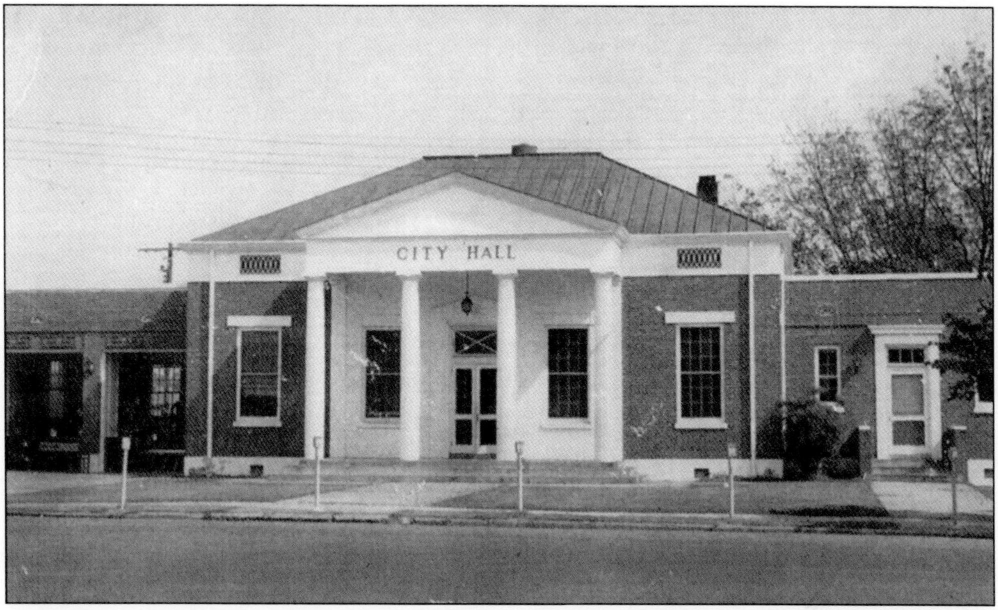

City Hall. A postcard of Blakely City Hall shows the bay where fire trucks were kept between calls. Later, after the turn of the century, the building was renovated, and the fire department was moved to bigger quarters on Magnolia Street.

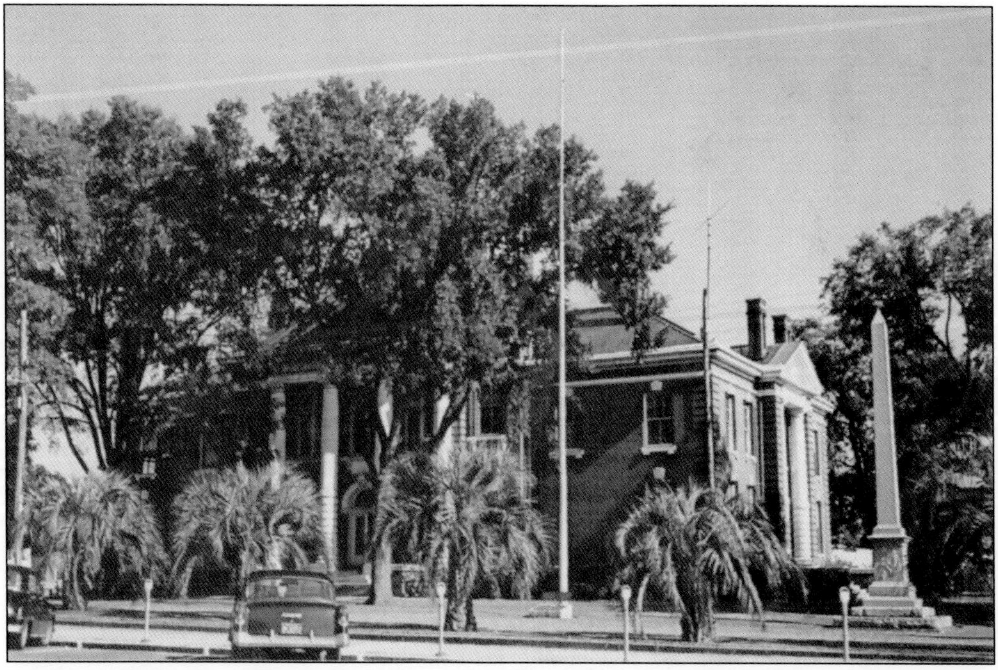

The "Lady" Had Palm Trees. With the arrival of the 20th century, Early County citizens wanted a newer and more commodious brick structure for their courthouse. W.T. Jay of Shellman, Georgia, was the lowest bidder ($50,000) among five others that were received and opened on October 11, 1904. The "Grand Ole Lady," in addition to being a source of pride for the county, has since that time been the background for numerous activities for Blakely and Early County.

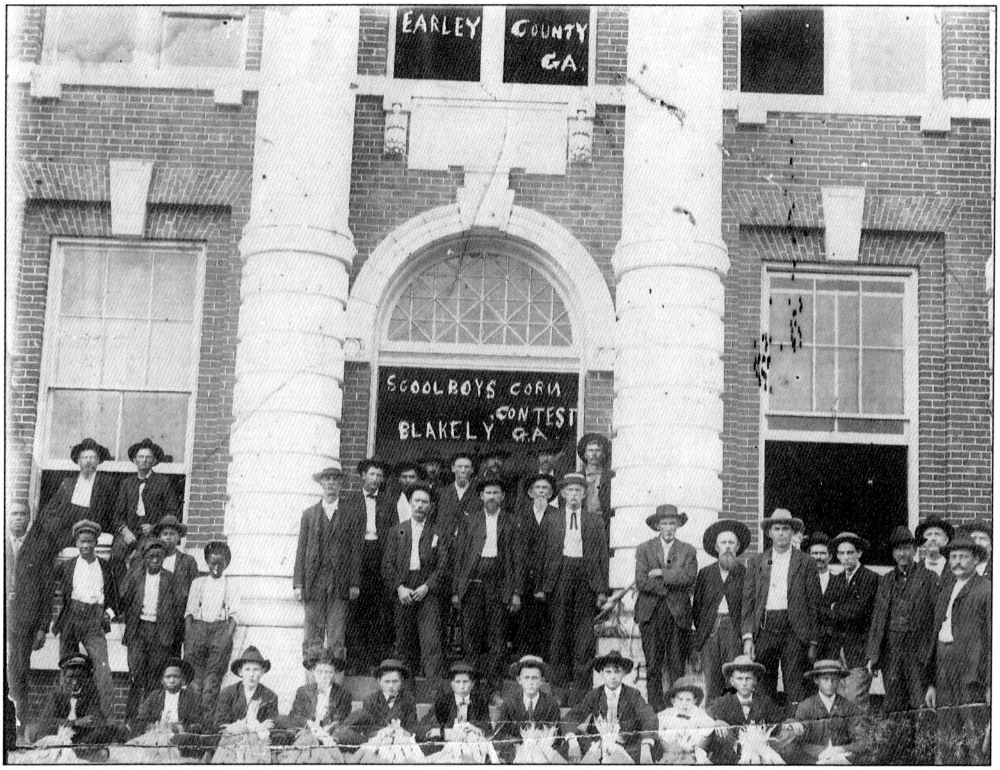

Boys Corn Contest. A forerunner of the 4-H Club, this group of boys from around the area displays the corn from their crops on the steps of the courthouse, competing for prizes. Grown-ups look on. In the window are J.B. "Dude" Chancey (left) and Brown Mosely. Other men in the photograph are Wallace W. Harvey, with his father, T.E. Harvey; Bart Hayes; and John Mosely of Cedar Springs. Notice the misspelled words written on the photograph.

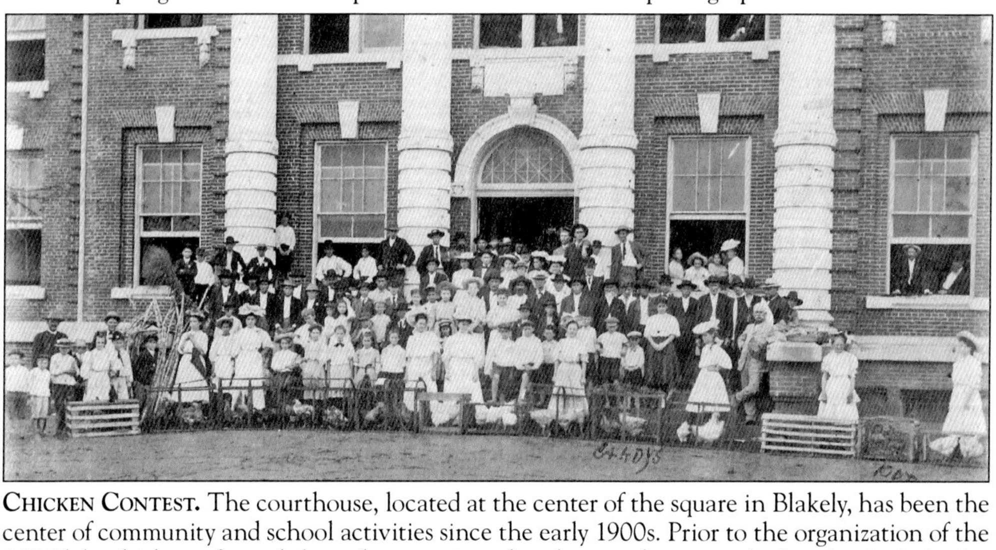

Chicken Contest. The courthouse, located at the center of the square in Blakely, has been the center of community and school activities since the early 1900s. Prior to the organization of the 4-H Club, which was formed about the same time that the courthouse was built, schoolgirls display their prize chickens. The 4-H movement encouraged practical hands-on experiences and taught young people leadership skills. Notice the oak coops that were used to carry the chickens.

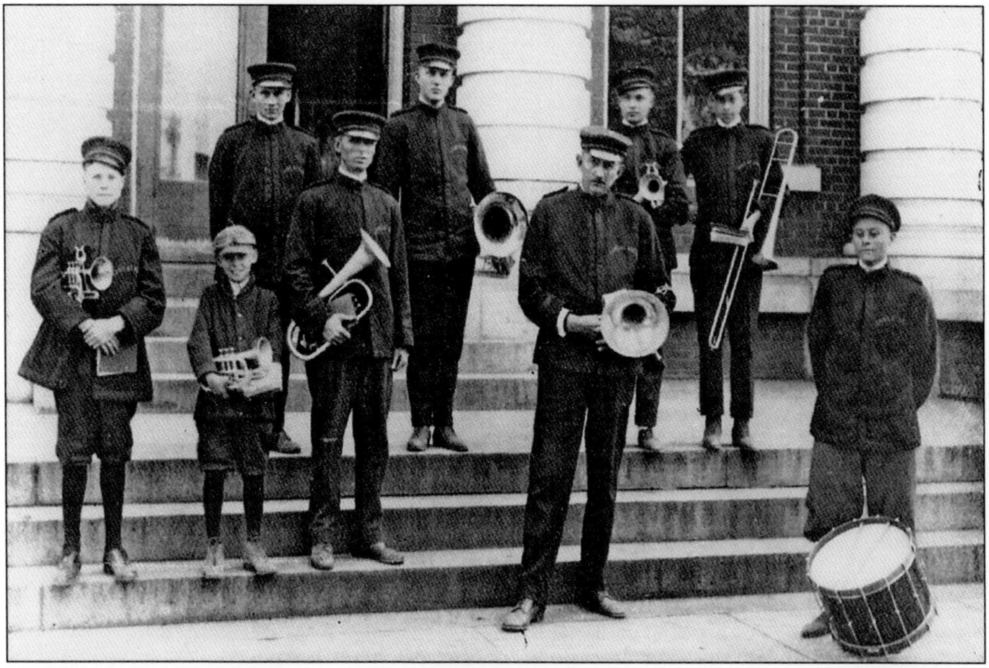

1917 Blakely Concert Band. A group of Blakely musicians gathered up old instruments from barns and attics and even bought three horns for $10 from a traveling tent show. They practiced upstairs in the Alexander Building on the square and had a limited concert at the opera house above Fryer's Pharmacy. Band members are, from left to right, (first row) John Underwood Jr., W.F. "Pete" Underwood, John Underwood Sr., Dennis Wade, and Claude Beasley; (second row) Early Beasley, Clifton Jernigan, Tom Underwood, and Bascomb DuBose.

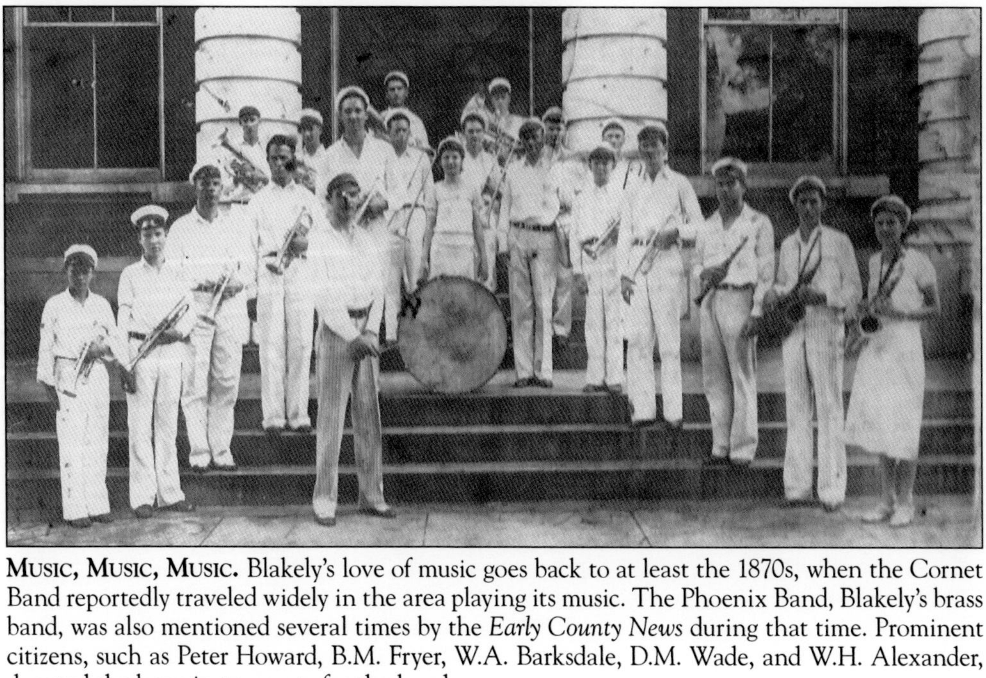

Music, Music, Music. Blakely's love of music goes back to at least the 1870s, when the Cornet Band reportedly traveled widely in the area playing its music. The Phoenix Band, Blakely's brass band, was also mentioned several times by the *Early County News* during that time. Prominent citizens, such as Peter Howard, B.M. Fryer, W.A. Barksdale, D.M. Wade, and W.H. Alexander, donated the brass instruments for the band.

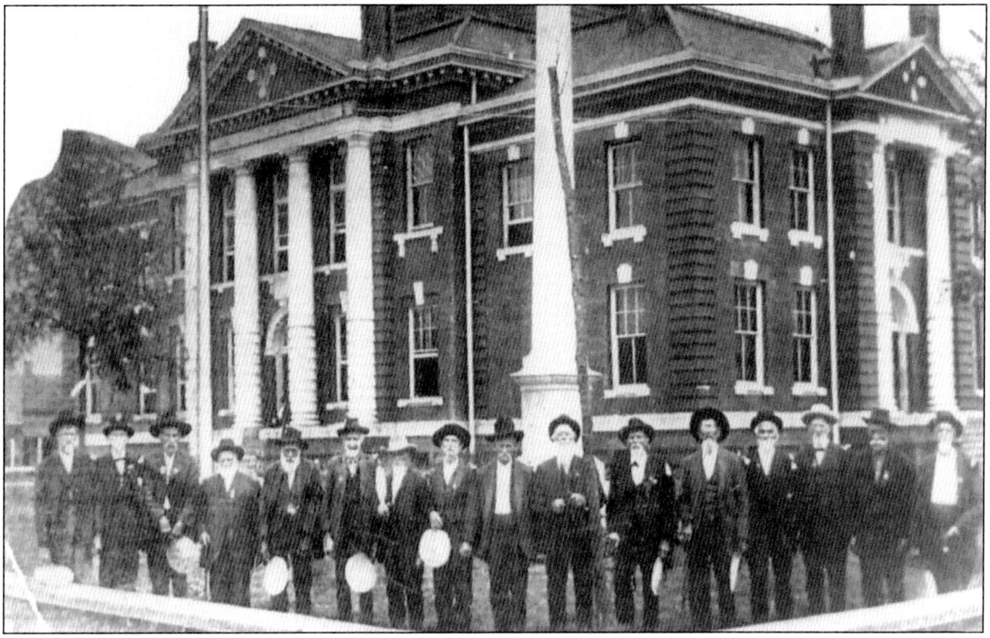

Vets on the Square. The courthouse was always the center of interest. The beautiful brick structure with a generous use of marble replaced a wooden, two-story building with columns. Not averse to change, the citadel of law and order had swapped the cold fireplaces of winter and the heat of summer for modern heat and air-conditioning. It was not surprising that Court Square, with the majestic courthouse, was the site year after year for the reunion of veterans of the Civil War.

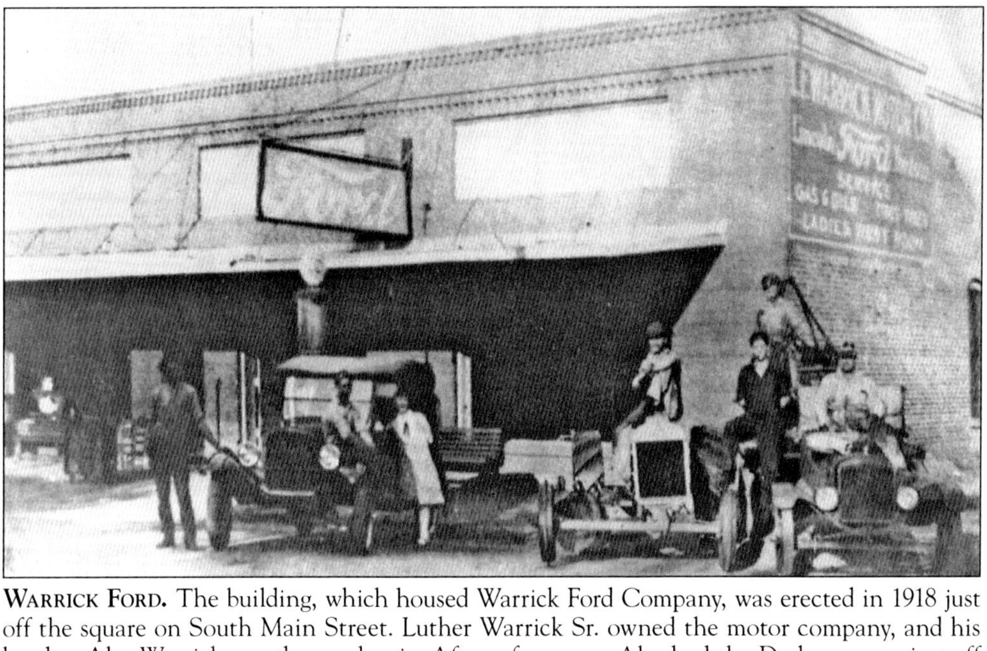

Warrick Ford. The building, which housed Warrick Ford Company, was erected in 1918 just off the square on South Main Street. Luther Warrick Sr. owned the motor company, and his brother Alto Warrick was the mechanic. After a few years, Alto had the Dodge agency just off the square, which was downstairs at the Masonic lodge. The business was across the street from the jail and next door to Holman Mule Barn.

Four

Country Living

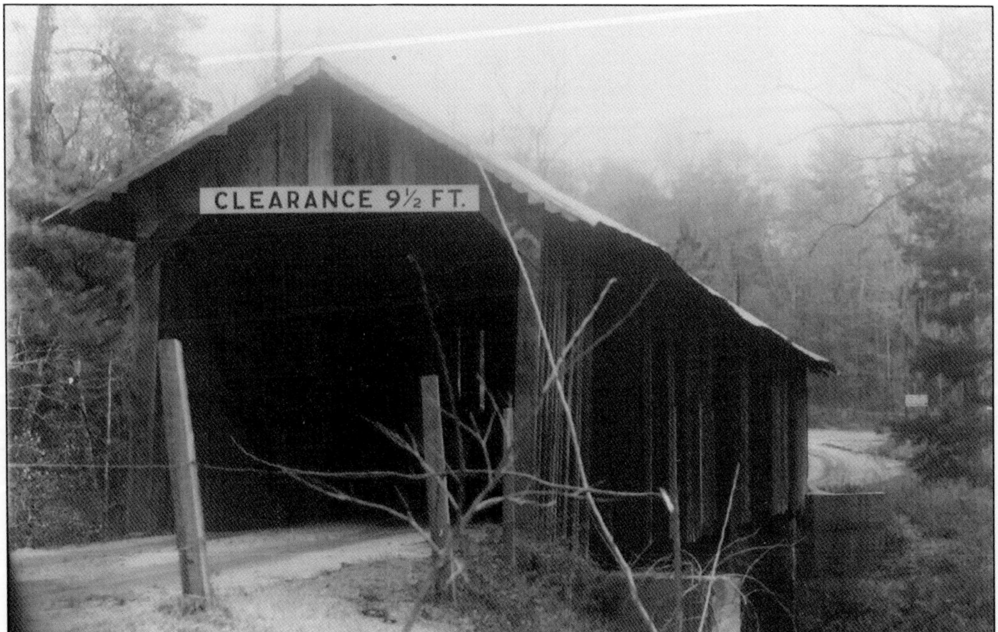

Coheelee Creek Covered Bridge. Spanning Coheelee Creek in Early County, nine miles West of Blakely, the county seat, is the southernmost covered bridge in the United States. Built in 1891, the 121-foot bridge was erected at McDonald's Ford for a price of $491 by J.W. Baughman and 36 workers. The wood bridge still stands today and is a great tourist attraction for the area.

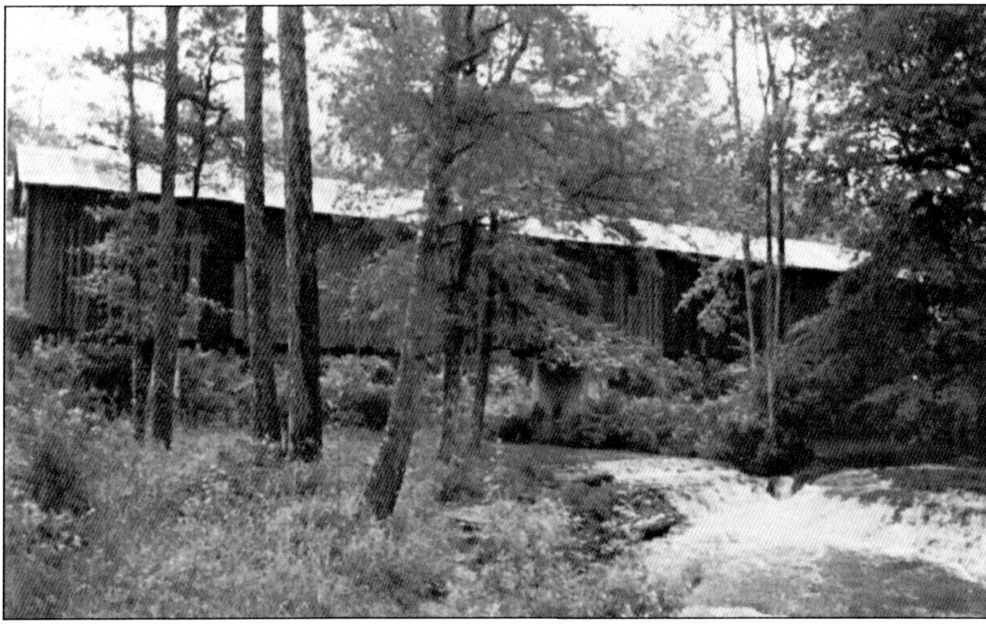

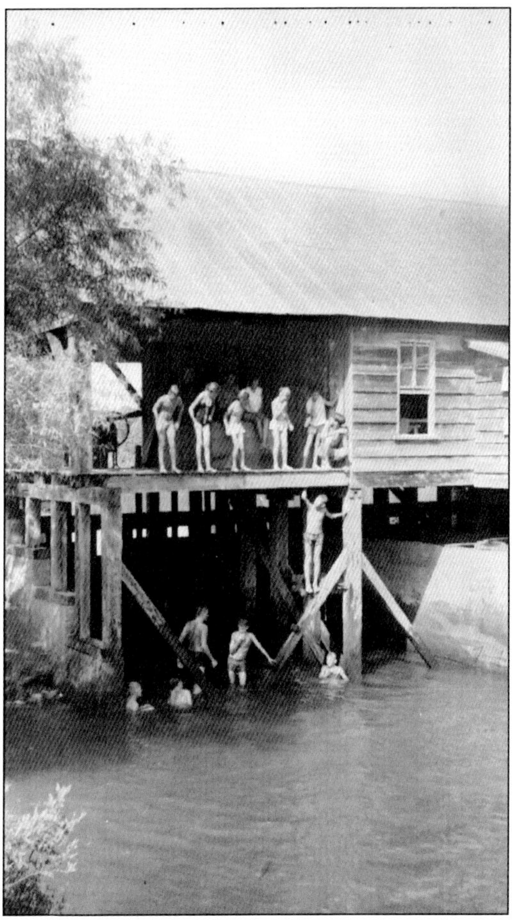

The Covered Bridge. A rambling, narrow tributary of the Chattahoochee River, Coheelee Creek originates about five miles from Blakely and flows south and east to join the river two miles north of Hilton. Spanned by Coheelee Creek Covered Bridge, the creek creates a series of spectacular waterfalls, a rarity in South Georgia, before it spills into the river a couple of miles downstream.

Howard's Mill. Originating in the early 1830s between Cedar Springs and Jakin, Howard's Mill ground corn for meal and grits for 135 years. Families gathered at the mill to fish in the pond and swim in the deep pool. Children learned to swim at the mill and daringly jumped from the front porch into the mill pond while moms and dads had corn ground into meal for cornbread and grits for the breakfast menu.

The Pounds Family. In the Cuba community, a young family proudly poses with its young son for a rare photograph. The board-and-batten exterior walls of the home were the rule for the time. Homes were built off the ground to prevent decay of the untreated wood and to allow for circulation on hot summer days. In the picture are, from left to right, Buddy Jack Pounds, Willie Pounds, and Mattie Pounds. (Courtesy of Mr. and Mrs. Phillip Moore.)

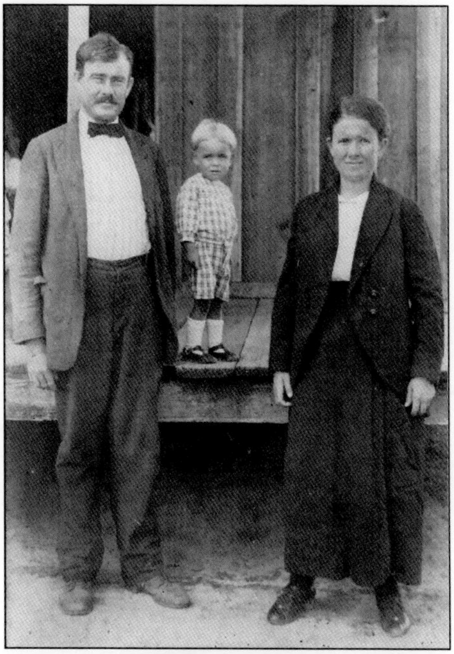

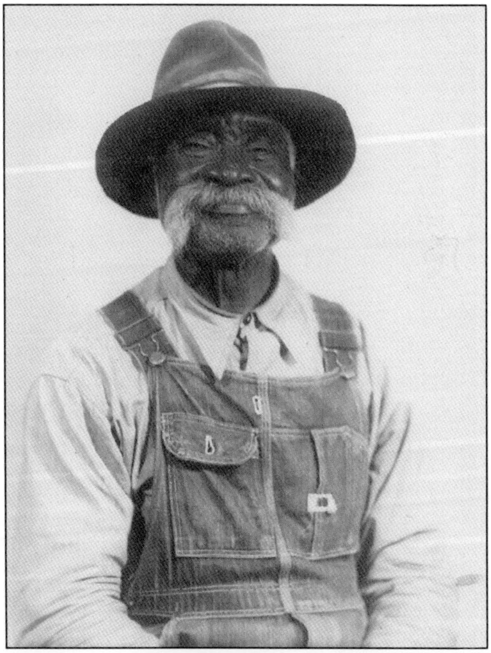

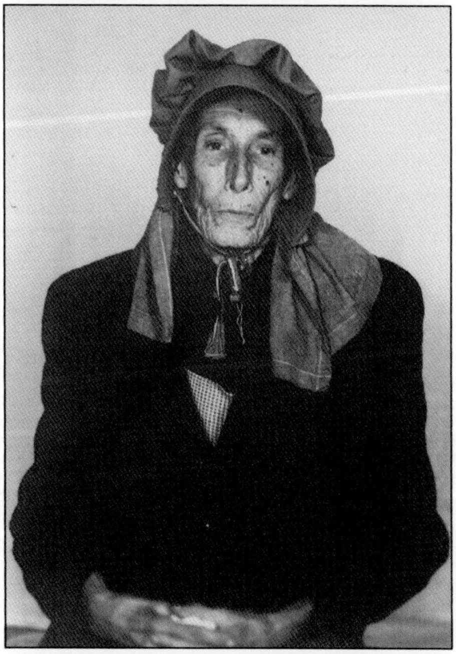

Overalls. Overalls (left) were some of the most commonplace and comfortable attire for early-1940s farmers and others. Loose denim pants held up by a bib and straps allowed farmers to move about their labor freely. Sam Grier poses for a formal portrait in his overall attire.

Bonnets. Women working in the fields, gathering fruits and vegetables, wore bonnets (right) to create a barrier from the hot Southern sun. Usually, bonnets were homemade of gingham and calico fabrics on treadle sewing machines using patterns handed down from generation to generation. Mrs. Kegler, also called "Granny Baker," had a formal portrait made in her prized bonnet.

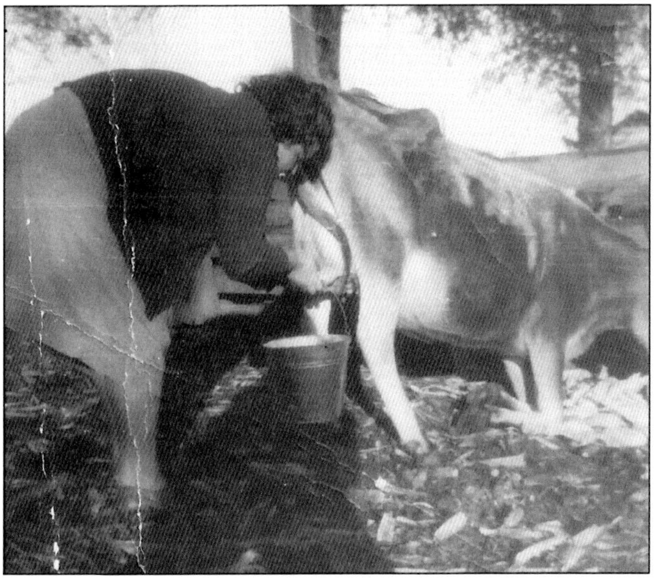

Jenkins Cow. In the early days of the 20th century, city folks got their bottled milk from the local dairy. However, families who lived in the country had at least one milk cow, sometimes two or three. The cows were fed well and were put in pastures that had the sweetest grass. It was a bad day (and bad milk) when the cow reached over the fence and snatched some bitter weed. Blooming clover, though a pretty picture in the field, created clover-tasting milk from the cow. (Courtesy of Maddox Memorial Library Archives.)

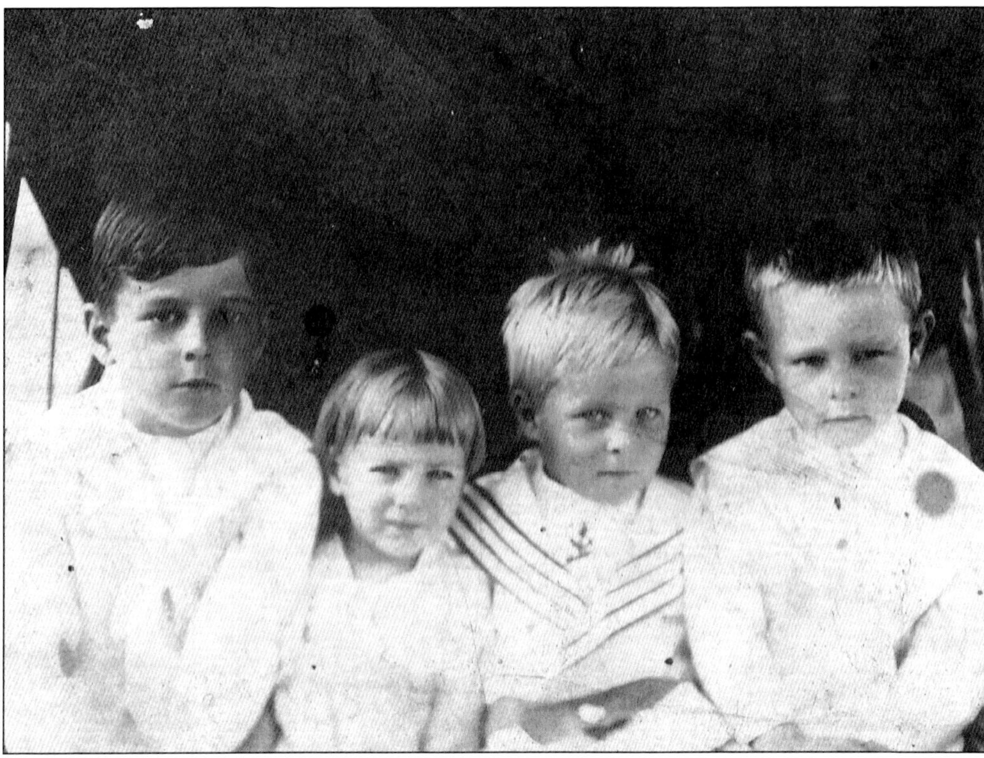

Urquhart Kids. Urquhart, a community in the northwest section of the county, was named for Dr. J.Q. Urquhart, a local physician in the 1880s. Winnie Davis Dunaway Jarrett reared 10 children, eight boys and two girls, in this rural setting after her husband, Perry Franklin "Pots" Jarrett, died in 1935. Five of the boys enlisted in World War II, leaving two to farm and support the war effort; the eighth son was too young to go. All five sons returned safely from the war. Pictured here in a buggy in their younger days are some of the Jarrett children (from left to right), Clay, Bronnie, Ralph, and Boyd.

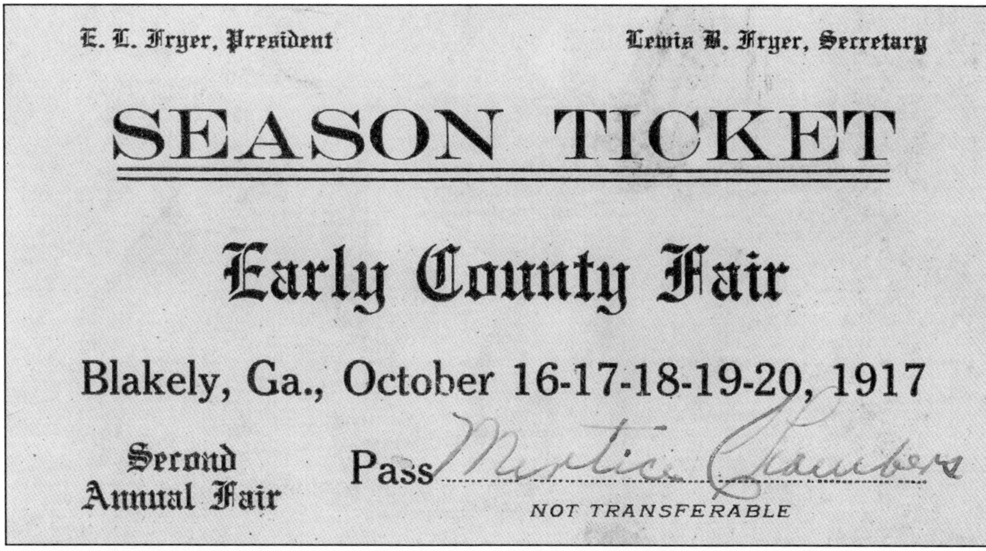
E. L. Fryer, President Lewis B. Fryer, Secretary

SEASON TICKET

Early County Fair

Blakely, Ga., October 16-17-18-19-20, 1917

Second Annual Fair

Pass

NOT TRANSFERABLE

SEASON TICKET. In the early 1900s, the Early County Fair was in full swing. Located on the corner of River Road and Redbud Street, the fair (with E.L. Fryer as president and Lewis B. Fryer as secretary) was a yearly weeklong event of, among other things, trotting horse competitions and baseball games sponsored by Flowers Lumber Company. With the railroad beside the track on the south side, transporting equipment and horses was an easy matter. It is said that "Shoeless" Joe Jackson at one time played on the baseball diamond, probably when he was a coach/player for Waycross. The Waycross team won the Georgia Little World Series. (Courtesy of Vicki Fryer Kornegay.)

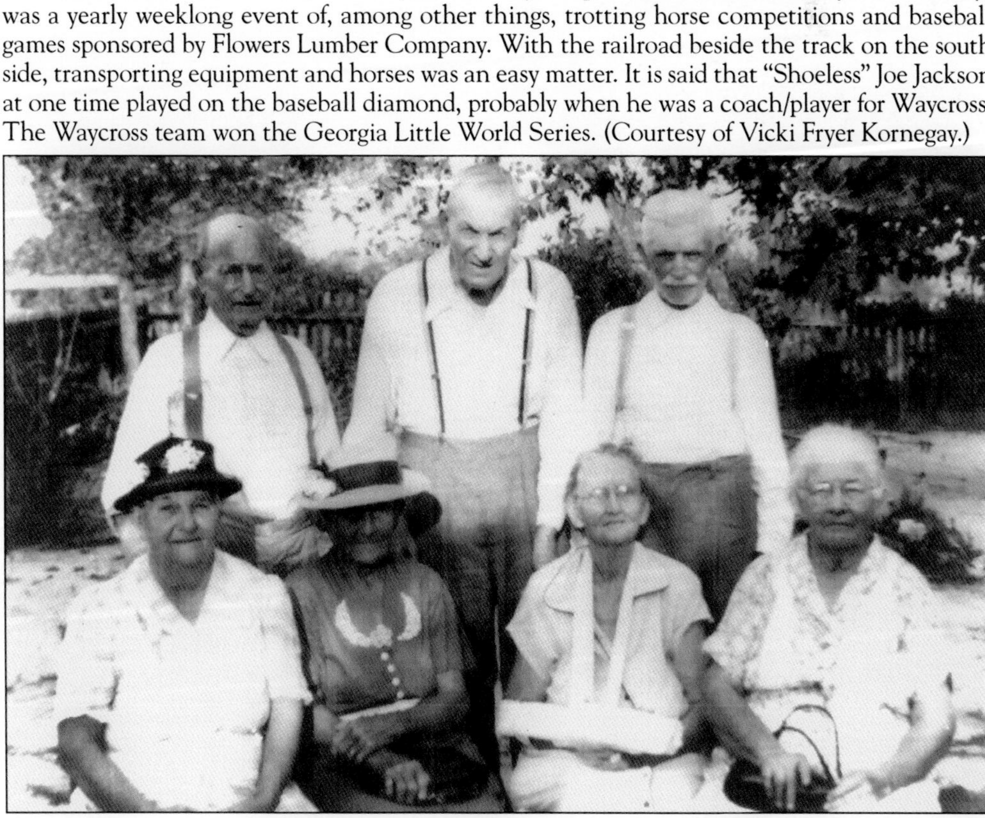

SOWHATCHEE FRIENDS. A gathering of old friends, relatives, and neighbors in the Sowhatchee community in the late 1940s brings together lovely images of lives well lived. Those pictured are, from left to right, (first row) Ella Wiley, Ola Chambers, Ida Lane Middleton, and Betty Ricks; (second row) Babe Chambers, James Madison Lane, and Joe Johnson. (Courtesy of Bernard Garwood.)

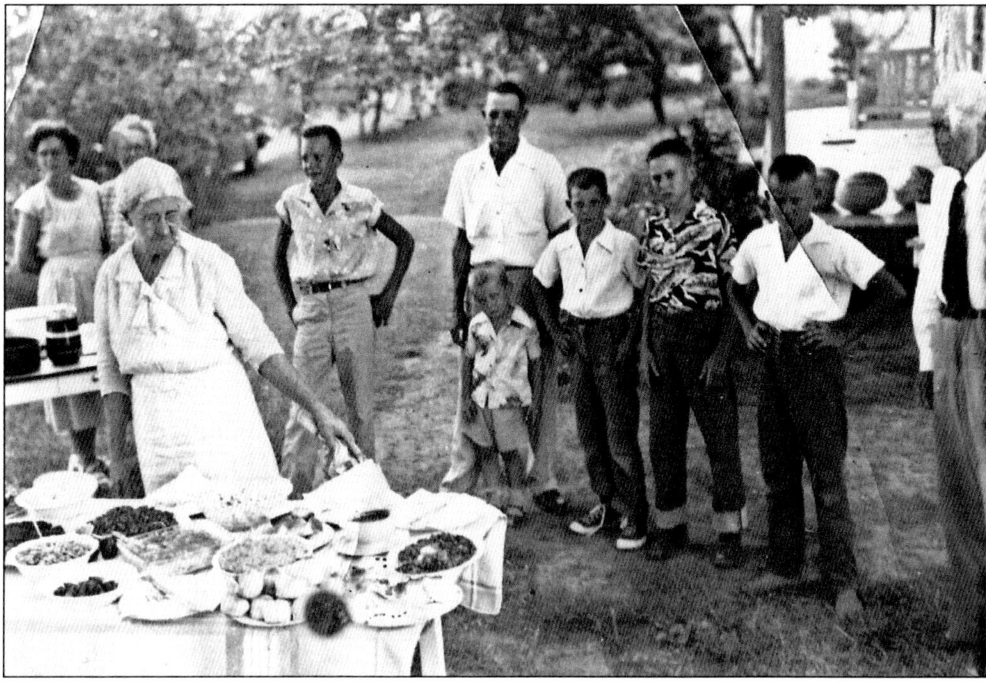

SUNDAY AFTERNOON AT GRANDMOTHER'S. On Sunday afternoons, families in town, as well as in the country, shucked the uncomfortable church clothes and hurried to grandmother's house. After a bountiful lunch, served on tables outside during good weather, the children went off to play their games, while adults settled down to catch up on family and community news. Grandmother Mary Brand Owen completes preparation for dinner for her extended T.H. Owen family and friends. (Courtesy of the Owen family.)

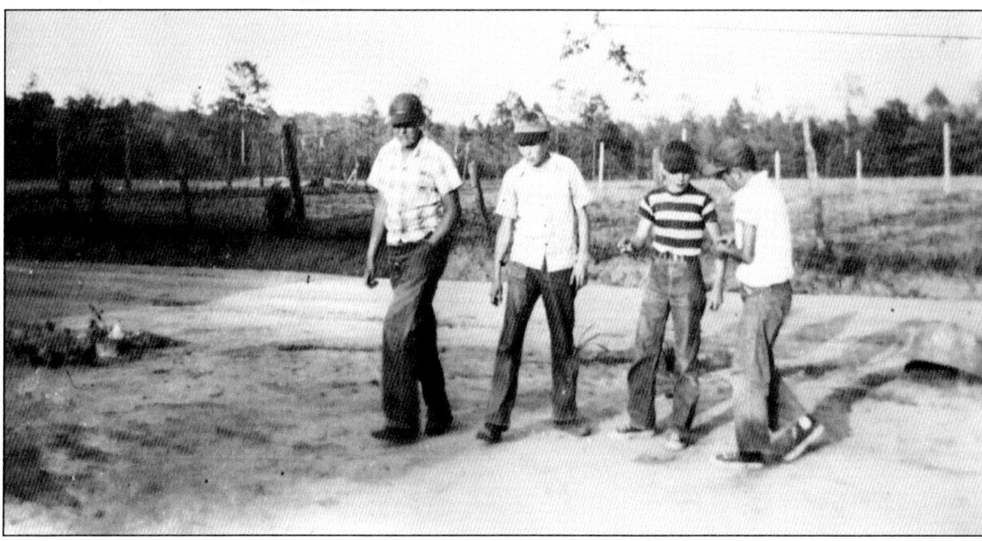

SHOOTING MARBLES. Beside a country road in Cuba, teenage boys engage in a game of marbles. Although the rules of the game vary by location, generally the main task is to eject the opponent's marbles out of a hand-drawn circle in the dirt, while keeping the first person's marbles within the circle. Simple games, like marbles, "jump-boarding," and tag, entertained children for hours. (Courtesy of Georgia Archives Vanishing Georgia Collection, EAR 99-82.)

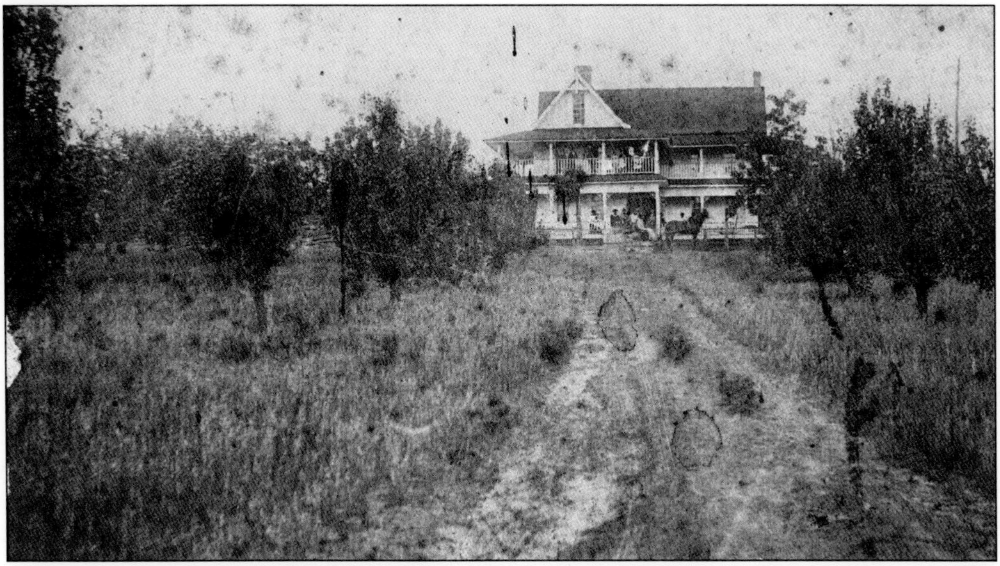

FAMILY MANSION. Nine miles north of Blakely on Highway 39, James H. Ross and his sons built a mansion between 1880 and 1890. The lumber was hand-planed at the Ross's sawmill. The Rosses raised horses from 1850 to 1926 and started the first school for African Americans in the community, the Ross School. On the farm, they grew peaches, figs, pears, mulberries, and apple trees. They also had a gristmill and blacksmith shop. James Ross was Jack Slaton's maternal grandfather. The Kolomoki Plantation now occupies the Ross acreage. James Ross was buried on Jack Slaton's farm. (Courtesy of Georgia Archives Vanishing Georgia Collection, EAR 85-82.)

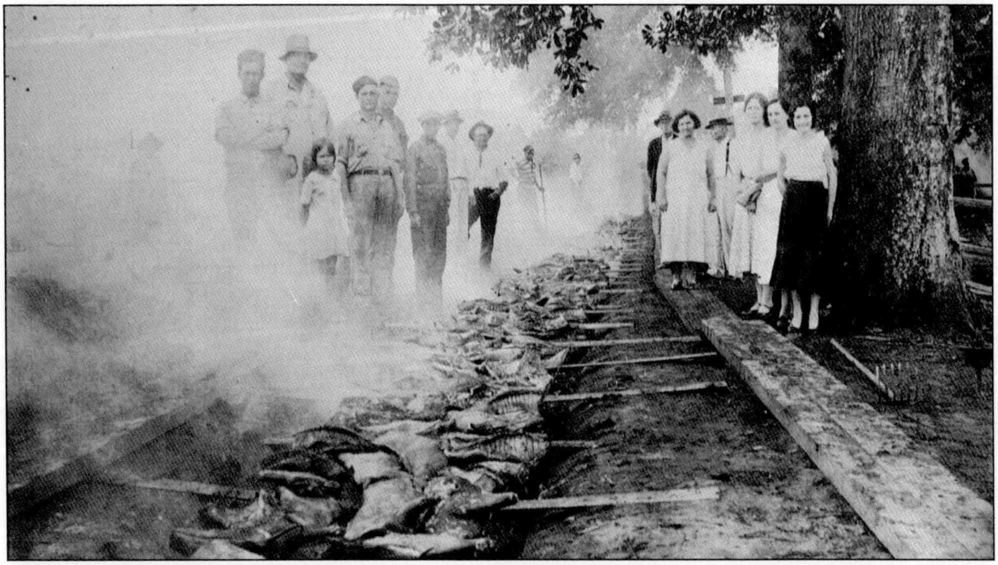

FOURTH OF JULY BARBECUE. On Independence Day 1932, barbecue was served on the square in Blakely. Warden Deck Williams (wearing the broad-brimmed hat) and other citizens, assisted by the convict in the striped suit, cooked the barbecue at the Early County Convict Camp, near Blakely. Shown in the photograph are, from left to right, Boyette Hayes, Warden Deck Williams, Aline Williams Starr, Ernest Chambers, Tom Whitley, J.D. George, N.J. Grist, Emmett Freeman, prisoner Lewis Jones, Charlie Hudson, Mrs. White, J.D. Sherman, Mrs. Dave Pearl, Eunice Weaver, and Edith Pearl King. (Courtesy of Georgia Archives Vanishing Georgia Collection, EAR 19-82.)

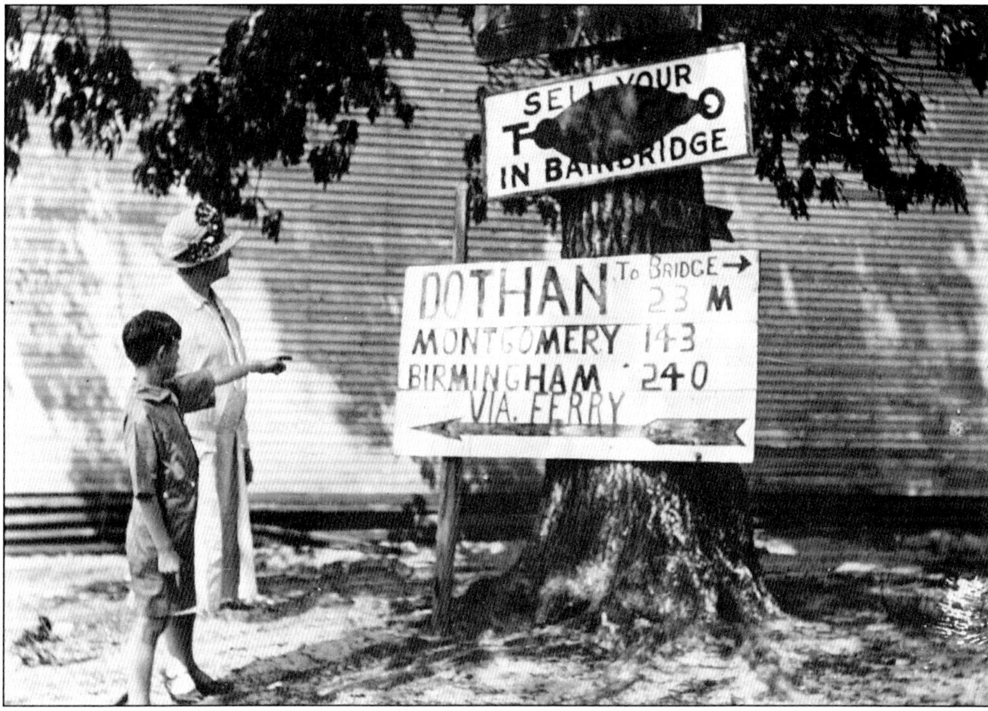

You Are Here. Direction signs attached to a big oak tree at W.C. Sheffield's Store inform travelers how far it is to the bridge crossing the river, 23 miles; to Montgomery, Alabama, 143 miles; to Birmingham, Alabama, 240 miles; and in which direction they should proceed to go to the ferry. While his mother looks on, Eddye Sheffield points out directions. Below, long after the washing of clothing was done on the banks of the creek and a quarter-century after big cast iron wash pots, beater sticks, and lye soap were used in cleaning clothes, washhouses sprang up in public places. Sheffield's Store provided a lean-to with tubs, water, and a fireplace to heat water. Women hired by the families would wash clothes while grocery shopping was done next door. (Both, courtesy of Georgia Archives Vanishing Georgia Collection, EAR 67-82.)

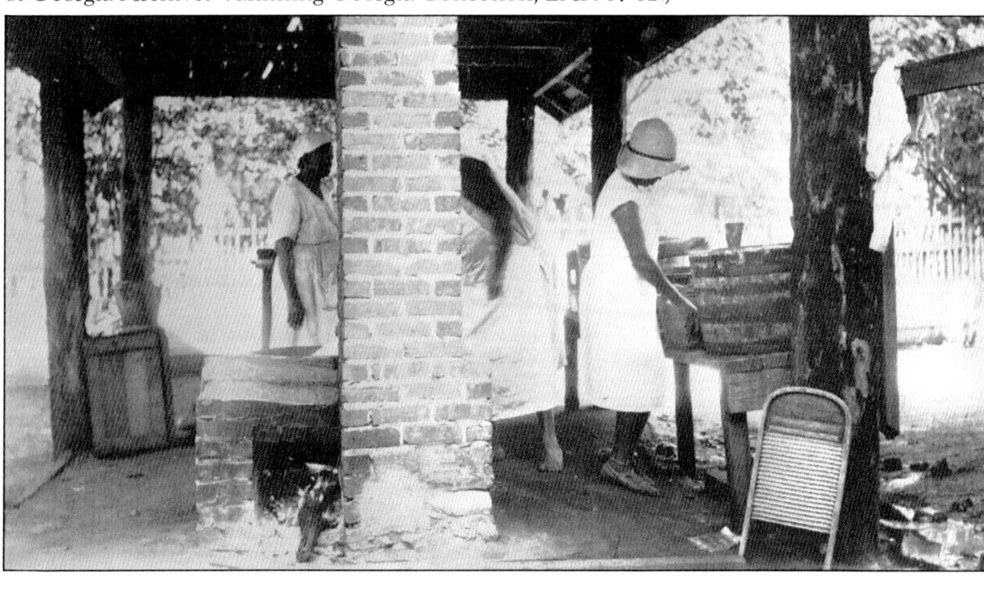

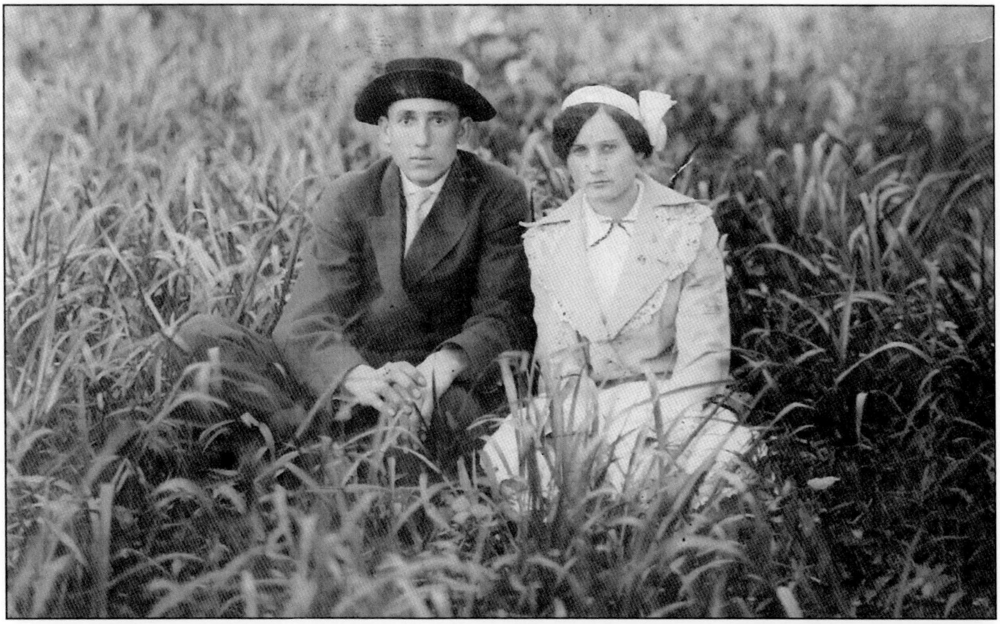

Soldier, Farmer, Athlete. Shelley Simmons, who grew up north of Blakely on Highway 39, was a soldier in World War I. His father, B.K. Simmons, was a country doctor working from an office near his home and owned some land and dabbled in farming. Shelley, returning from the war, became a small farmer and ran a mercantile store next to his father's office. His passion was baseball, and he played on a very successful local team. He is shown here with his wife.

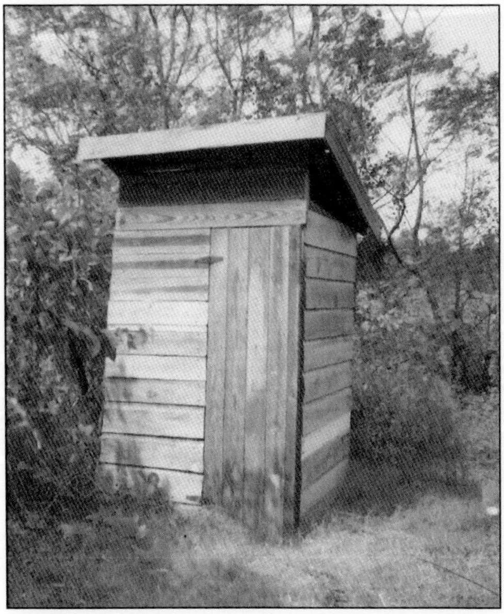

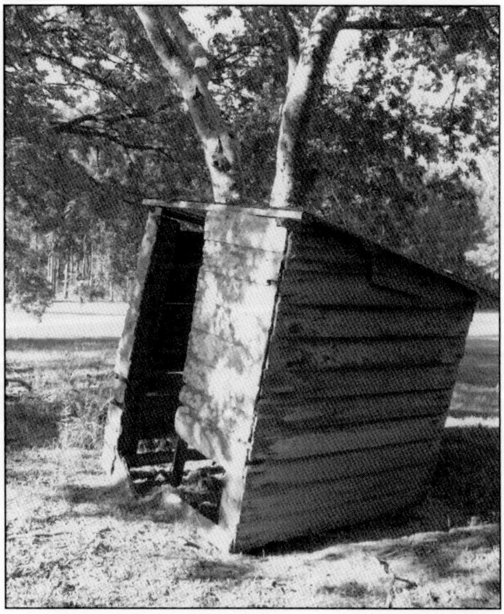

A Two-Seater. In addition to no electricity or running water in households, there was no such thing as an indoor toilet. Occupants either used the chamber pot (at night or in bad weather) or went outside to a secluded little outhouse. Some outdoor toilets had one seat, ("one-seaters"), and others had two ("two-seaters"). Of course toilet tissue had not been invented yet, so old Sears Roebuck catalogs were recycled! It was a cause for celebration when a family got electricity and water hookups . . . for many reasons.

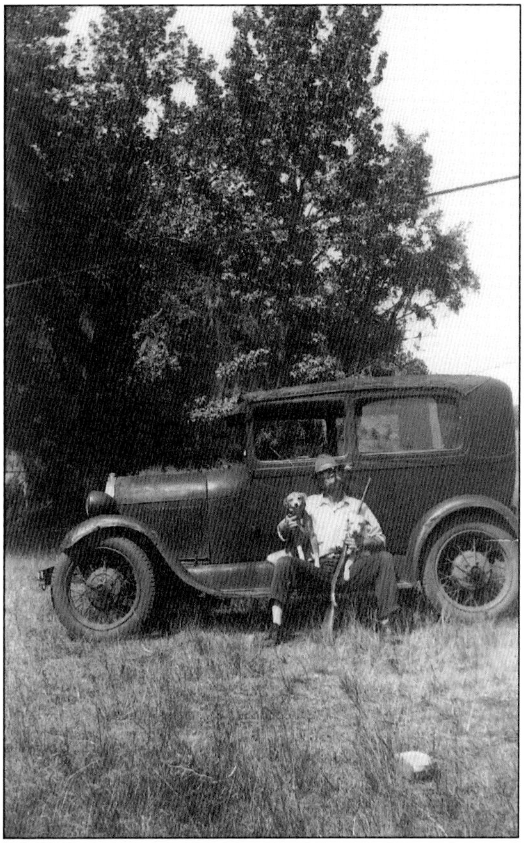

A Man and His Dog. Arthur L. Rabon lived on and worked a small farm near Sandy Bottom in the southern part of Early County. As families did in the 1930s, three families of Rabons, and even some neighbors, shared a car. It was used for grocery shopping, errands, doctor visits, church, and all the other day-to-day activities of the time. Mr. Rabon's two dogs, just back from a country run, seem ready to get home to rest in the shade. (Courtesy of Sarah Rabon Murkerson.)

A Wagon to Church. Along country roads in the south part of the county, an African American family loads up on the one-horse farm wagon to go to church. (Courtesy of Mr. and Mrs. John Pritchett.)

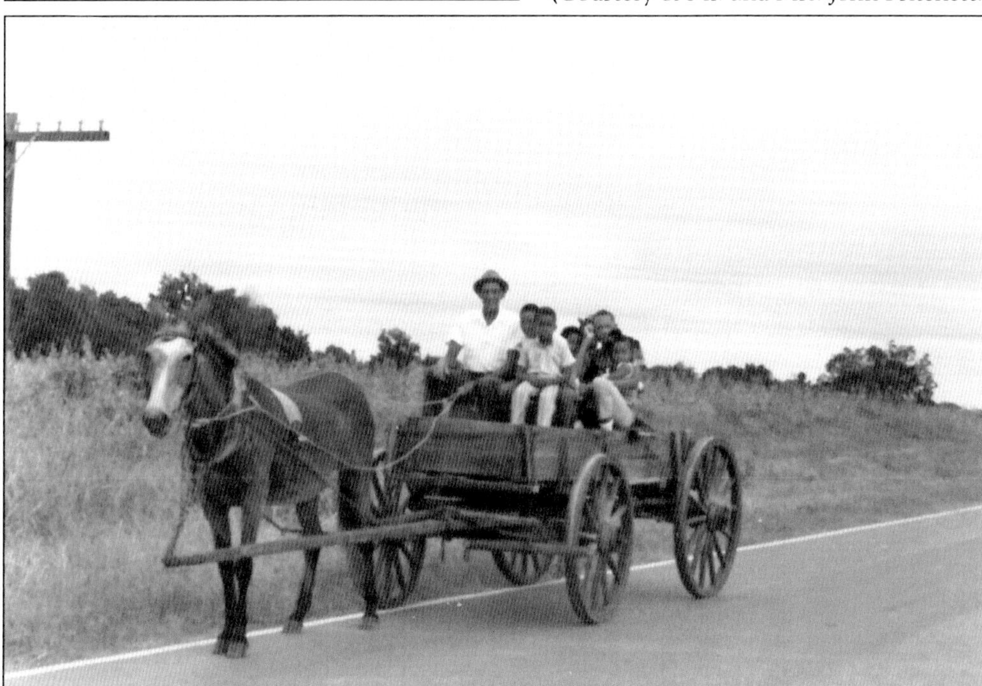

Five

Mind, Body, and Spirit

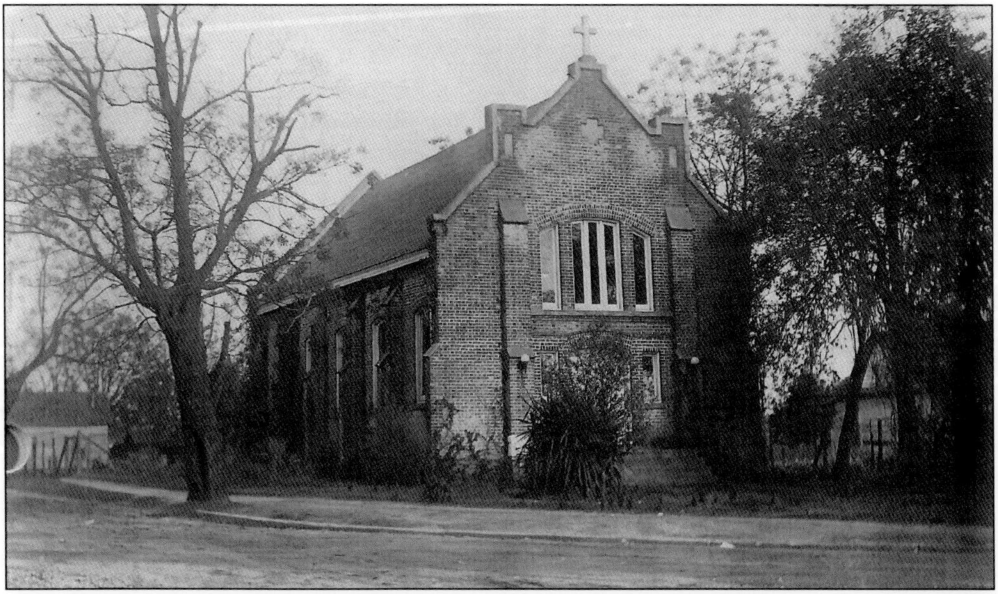

Holy Trinity. Rev. James B. Lawrence from Americus, Georgia, held communion in the Early County Courthouse in 1908. Lawrence then bought a lot on College Street, a block off the square to the west. Richard Holmes Powell, the father of Judge Arthur G. Powell of Atlanta, had lived on that site. Funds were raised, and the Holy Trinity Episcopal Church was completed in 1916. The church flourished, and at one time, lay leaders served the church. Among these were Dr. J.G. Standifer, E.E. Little, Philip Sheffield, and Wilton Howell. (Courtesy of Kathy Fraley.)

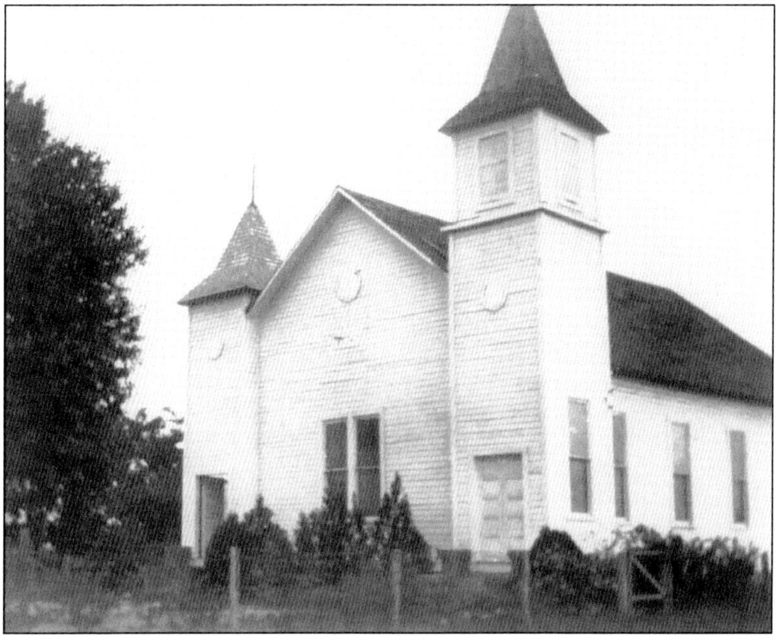

Jakin Baptist. In 1913, the members of the Baptist faith in Jakin met in the upper room of Harvey's Store and formed the Jakin Baptist Church. With help from Flowers Lumber Company, a frame building was completed in 1915.

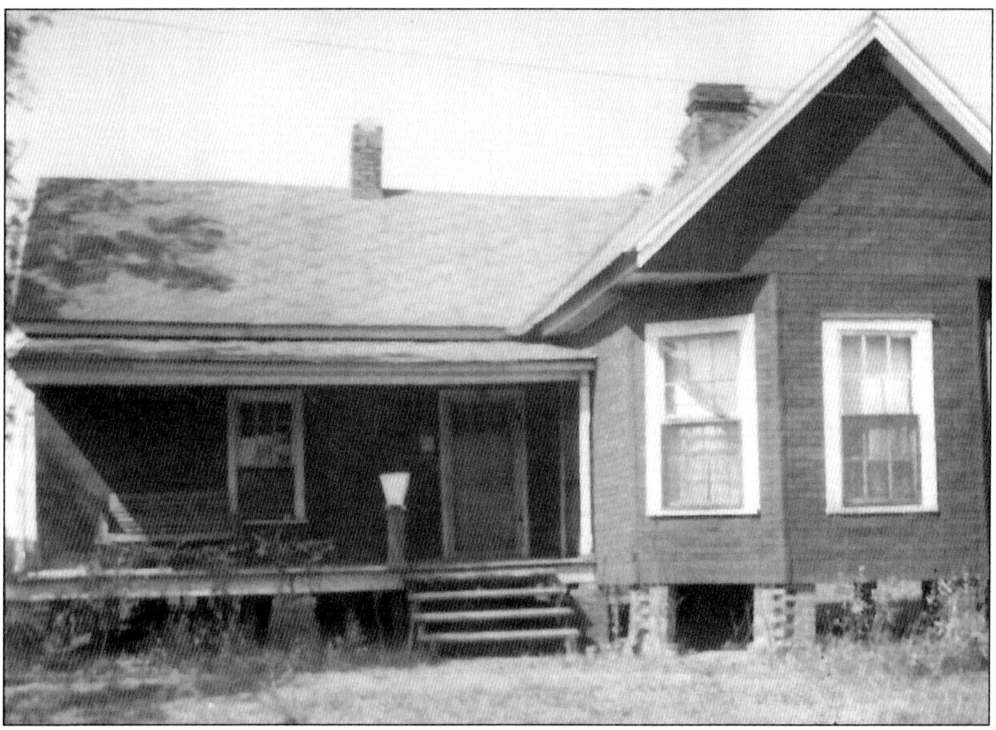

Wesley AME Parsonage. The *Blakely Observer* (organized in 1893), a rival newspaper of *Early County News* (founded in 1859), mentioned in its publication on December 28, 1893, that the AME church observed a Christmas celebration. Two years later, in 1895, according to the cornerstone, a church was erected on Church Street. In addition to *Blakely Observer and Early County News*, Blakely supported the *People's Voice*, a biweekly publication established 1894, which changed its name to *Blakely Reporter* in 1899. (Courtesy of Lucy Hilton-Maddox Memorial Library Archives.)

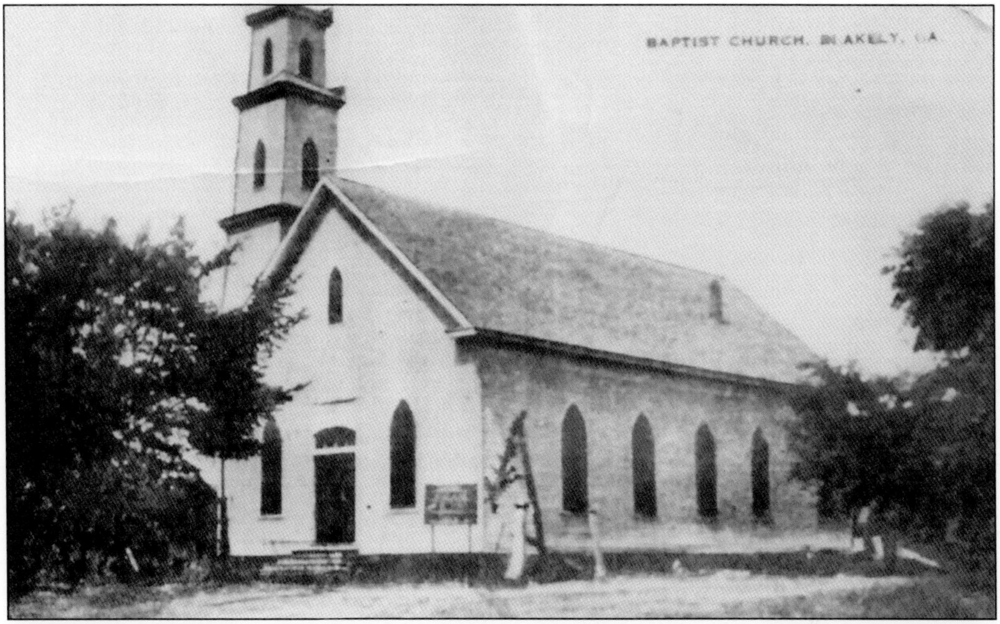

First Baptist Church. The church was constituted on Thursday, July 24, 1837. The name chosen for the church was Macedonia. The first church built was a 30-by-40-foot log house. Some 20 years after the first log church was built, a larger frame building was erected on the same site. The church cemetery grew up around the church. Then, in 1885, a new church (pictured) was built at the corner of River Street and Church Street, and it was used for about 27 years.

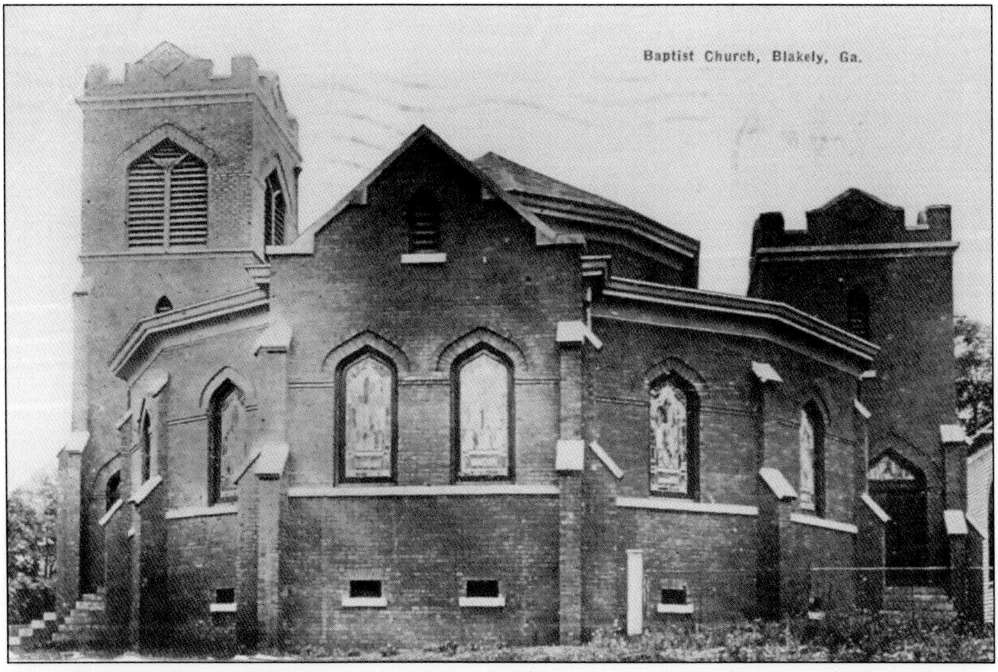

First Baptist Church Growing. In 1912, a brick structure, shown here, was built, and it has been in continuous operation since that time.

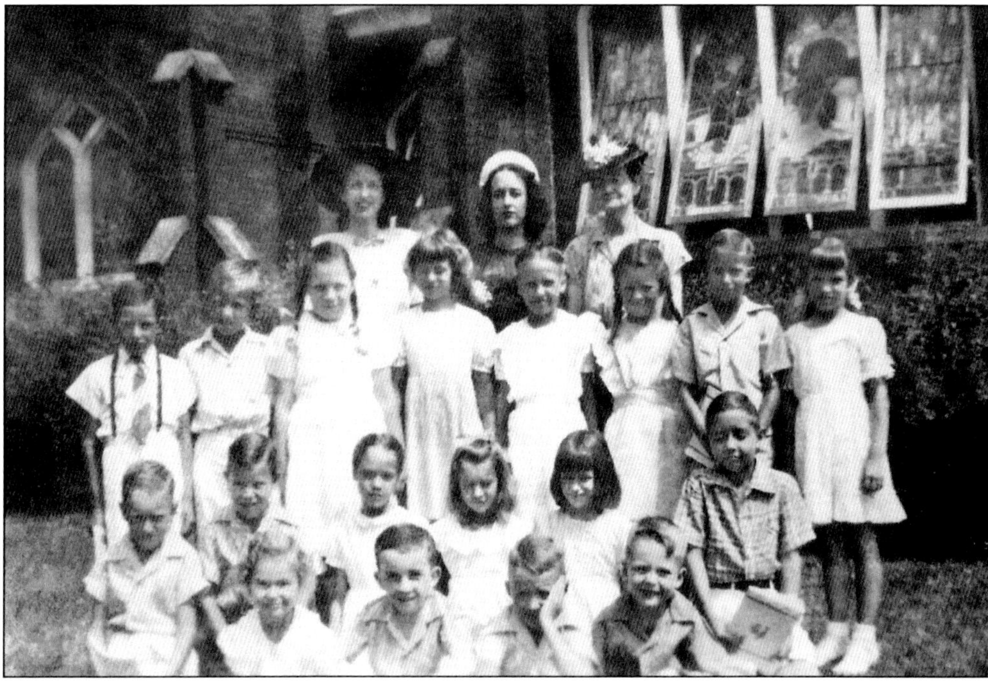

Summertime at First Baptist Church. With the windows of First Baptist Church open to catch a breeze, the youth of the church gather on the lawn in 1947. Those pictured are, from left to right, (first row) Janet Stovall, Bobby McLendon, Woodrow Houston, and Jimmy Brewer; (second row) John Pritchett, James Patrick Rice, Ina Frances Waller, Glyndell Thompson, Emylee Houston, and John Puckett; (third row) Roscoe Nash, Jimmy George, Joan Puckett, Susan Houston, Eunice White, Patricia Hudspeth, Jimmy Wasdin, and Priscilla Jones; (fourth row) Mildred Tarver, Virginia George Cain, Cora Avera White, and Clyde Griffin.

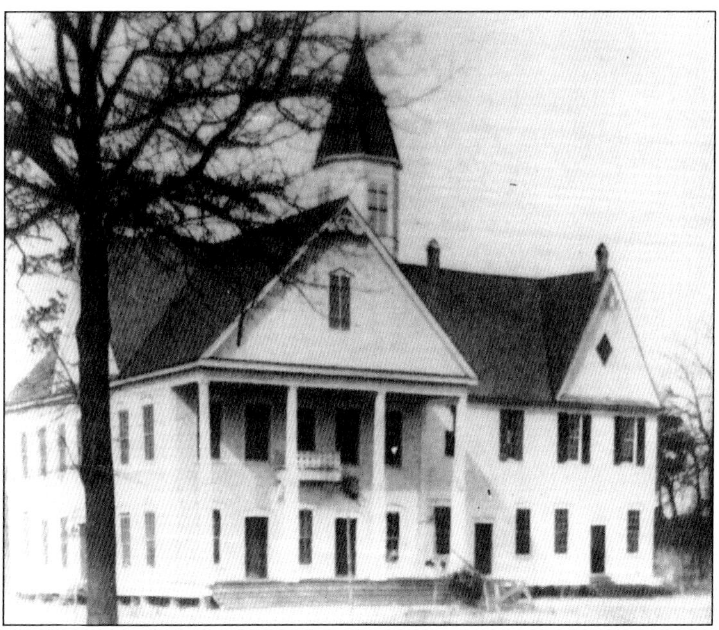

Bluffton Methodist. In 1886, the Methodist church in Bluffton was erected. The church was blown down but was rebuilt in 1919. The building in the background is the original Bluffton High School. Blakely native Delores Eubanks remembers in the 1940s a spring-fed creek down the steep hill behind the buildings. A dance platform and a swim hole provided entertainment for the rural town on the "Bluff."

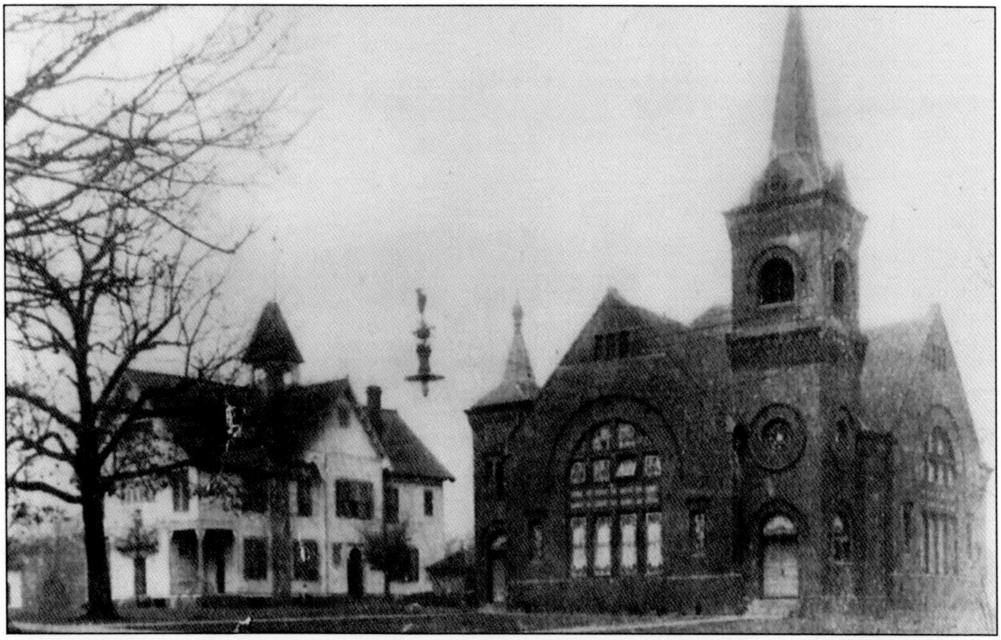

FIRST METHODIST CHURCH. In 1852 or 1853, Methodists in Early County united with the Presbyterians to build a church on the southwest corner of the public square. It was torn down in 1871, and members met at the old courthouse until a new frame church could be built on College Street in 1872–1873. As this wooden structure deteriorated, it was torn down, and a new brick church was completed and dedicated in April 1902. The Blakely Academy is seen in the background.

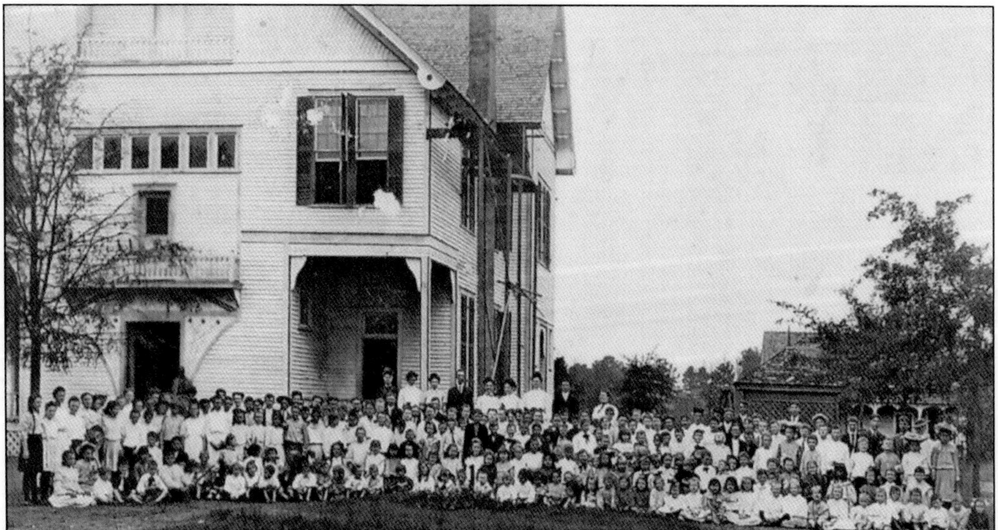

THE BLAKELY ACADEMY. The first Blakely Academy was started in 1827 with an act of the state legislature. It occupied several locations before moving to College Street: Arlington Road, River Street (Howard's Landing Road), and then South Main Street. It was renamed Blakely Institute by order of the Georgia State School Commission. In November 1892, it was located on College Street, next to the future site of Blakely Methodist Church. During the Spanish-American War, it was renamed Blakely Military Institute.

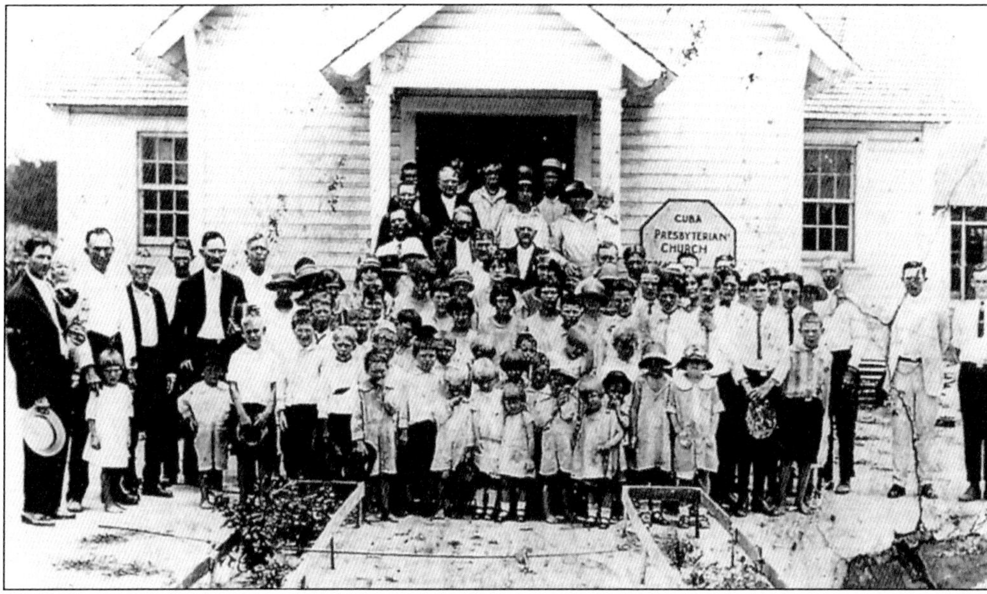

CUBA PRESBYTERIAN. On State Highway 27, south of Blakely, a new Cuba Presbyterian Church was dedicated on November 18, 1920. Annie May Cunningham from Texas, who stayed 18 months in Cuba, founded the church. Cunningham helped to create a permanent organization and also to build the only active Presbyterian church in Early County all at the same time. Dedication services, led by W.A. Watt, included hymns, prayers, and a sermon by Reverend Dr. Henderson of Albany. Dinner on the grounds followed.

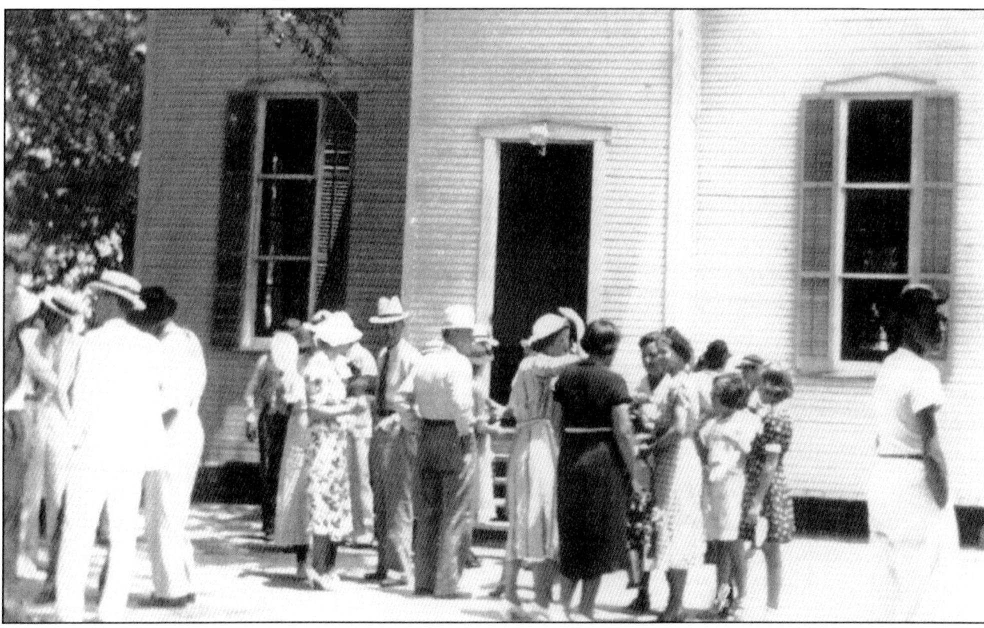

FELLOWSHIP. Members and visitors of the Old Midway Church catch up on the week's news after the Sunday morning sermon in the late 1930s or early 1940s. The children would remove their Sunday shoes and run off to an open space to play their games. Mostly the girls would wish for home and more comfortable clothes, and the boys yearned to dig into the fried chicken and biscuits waiting at home.

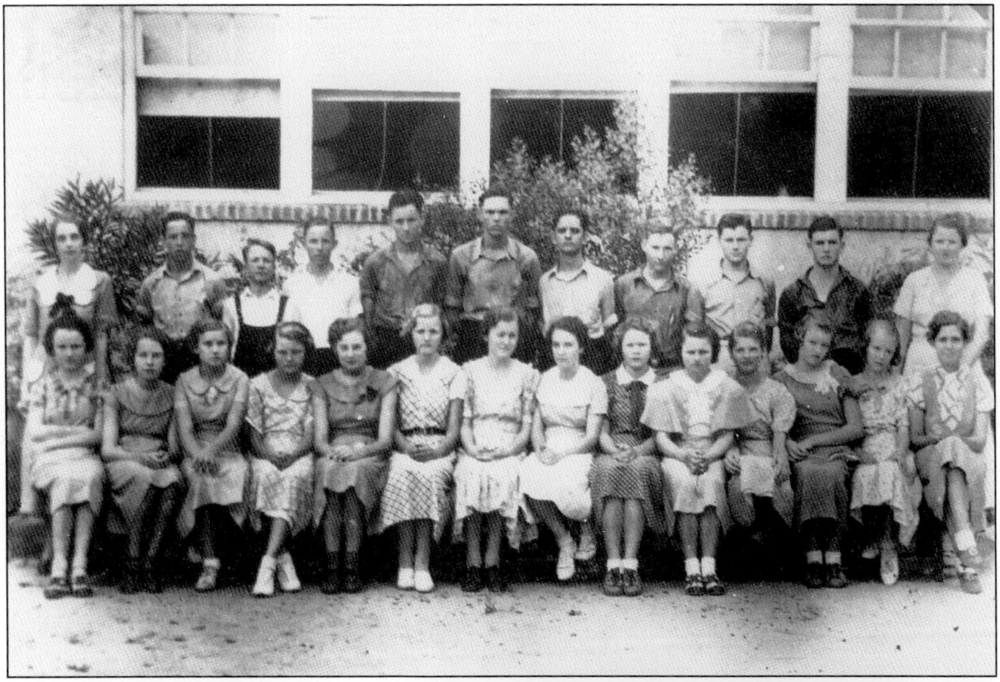

Hilton School. In the early 1930s, Hilton School was located 10 miles west of Blakely, just off Highway 62. Included in the photograph are Hazel McGrady, Jessie Smith, Flossie Martin, ? McDonald, Mildred Martin, Ouida Tabb, Othell Martin, Cecil DuBose, Ray Ham, Bill Knighton, Eddie Tom Tabb, Jack Paul, Rex Mills, Odell Knighton, John Scarborough, and John Lee Still. All other students and teachers are unidentified.

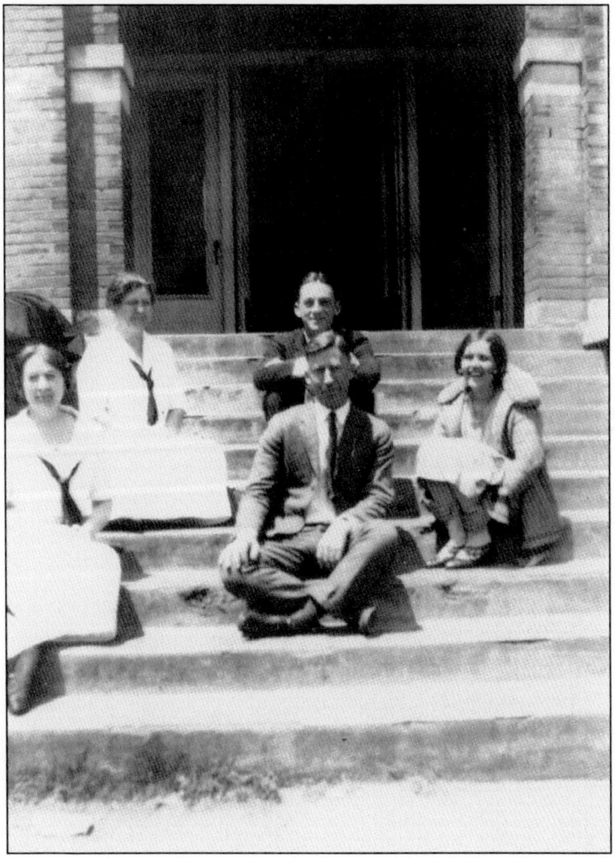

1925 Blakely High School Faculty. Revered by their students, the faculty members of the 18 seniors who graduated in 1925 were, from left to right, Una L. Jones, Ella Jones ("Miss Ella"), Mrs. J.D. Abernathy (Mrs. "AB"), E.E. McCarty, and McKenzie Mangham. The Early County High School auditorium was name for Mangham.

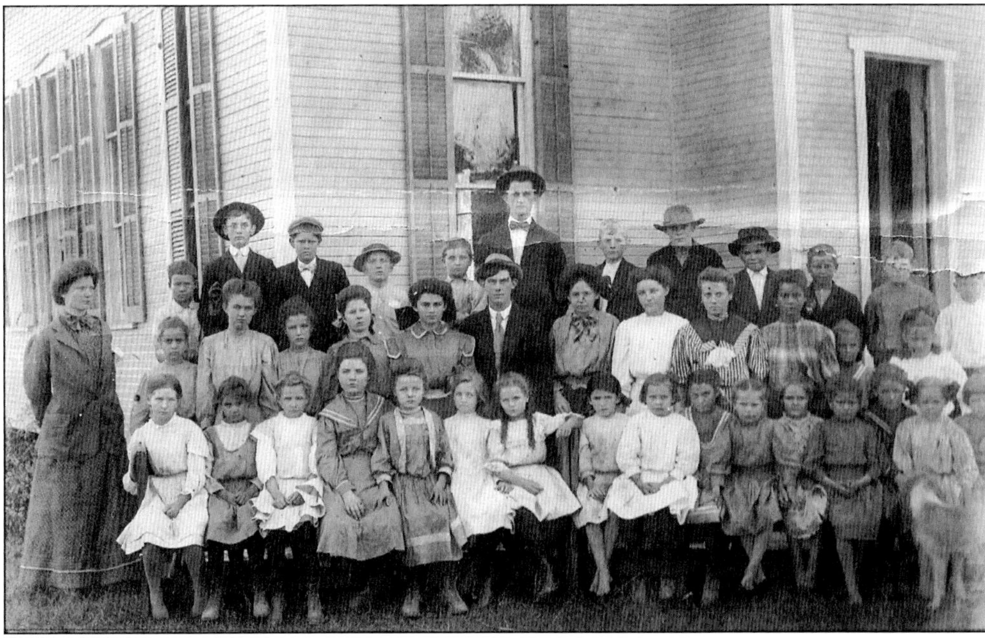

Midway School. The first school in the Jakin area began in the Open Pond Church Building. But soon, it moved to a small building at Danley Pond. Eventually, in the 1880s, a school building was erected at the centrally located crossroads of Bainbridge and Blakely Roads, which gave rise to the name "Midway." Pictured is a 1908–1909 group.

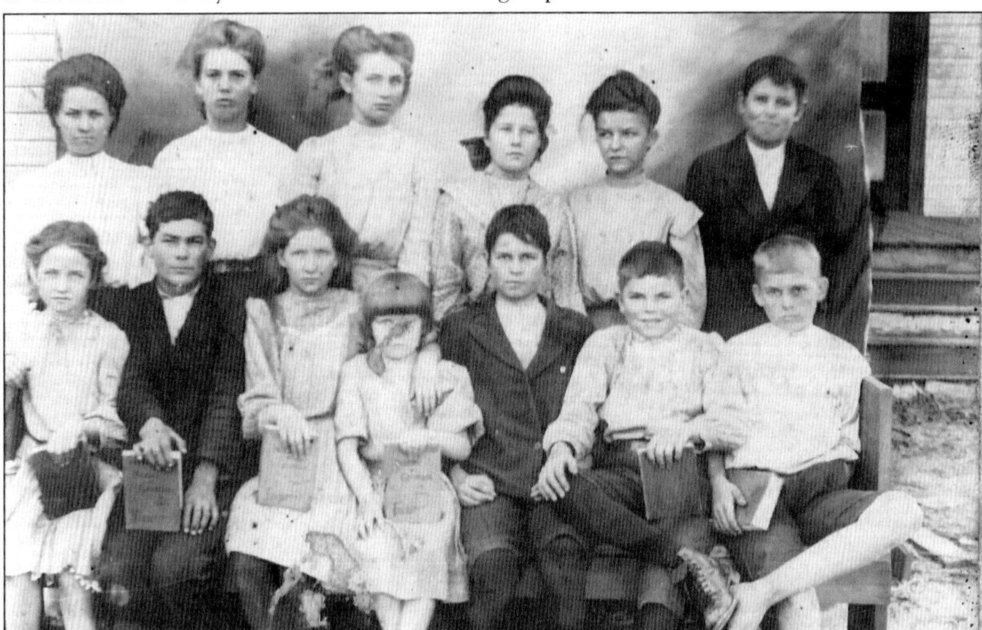

History Class. Sitting on a hand-built bench outside the school, a Midway School history class in 1911–1912 displays its history books. Those pictured are, from left to right, (first row) Mae McDaniel, Howard Easom, Ruth McDaniel, Gladys Harvey, Brock Avirett, Othni Minter, and Arver Mosely; (second row) Vera McClendon, Lonnie Warren, Leila Hodges, Tommie Minter, Maude Minter, and Earnest Avirett.

Cedar Springs Academy. In 1886, the first steps were taken for establishing a school at Cedar Springs. Prof. J.L. Kelly opened the school and continued there until he retired in 1901. Prof. C.W. Twitty served as the next principal. This drawing appeared in the *Blakely Reporter* on November 3, 1903.

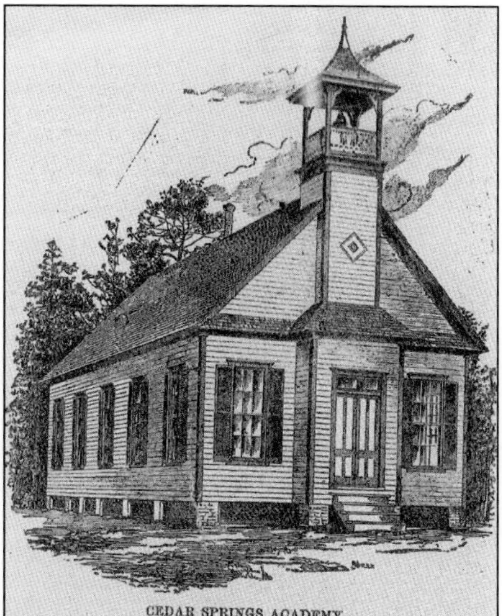

CEDAR SPRINGS ACADEMY.

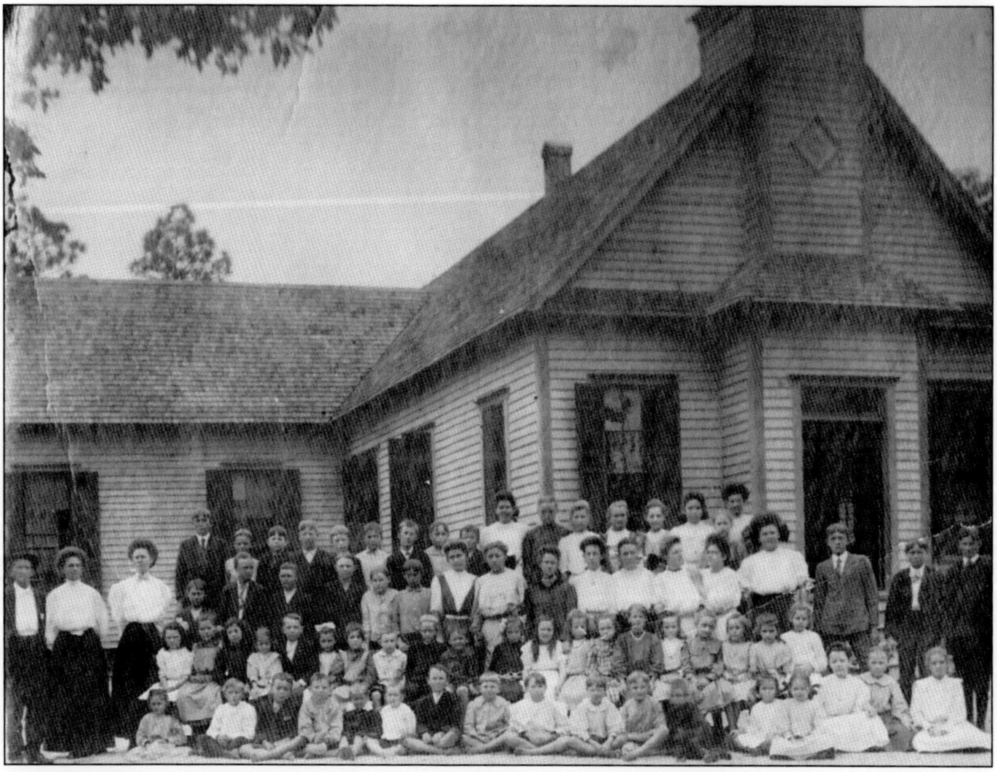

Academy Becomes Famous. Cedar Springs Academy was always a "pay" school. Young people who wanted to attend school came from as far away as 100 miles and attended as boarders. Two boardinghouses opened up to accommodate the out-of-town students. It was said that students who attended this academy were successful at West Point, Annapolis, Wesleyan, Milledgeville, and the Medical College of Georgia. The Georgia State Board of Education issued a plaque to the school chronicling the fact that the academy was the first school in Georgia to transport children to school. This photograph was taken around 1909–1910.

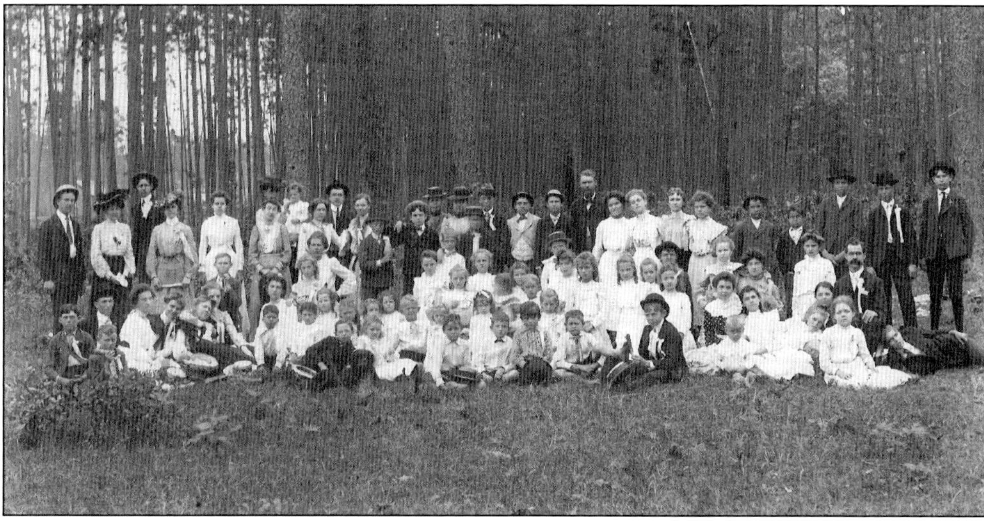

JAKIN PRIVATE SCHOOL. In 1904, Jakin citizens gathered to celebrate the end of the school year. Enjoying a picnic were members of the Mosely, Minter, Harvey, Hodges, Merritt, Aviritt, Fort, Hudson, McDaniel, Warren, Kirkland, Ward, Evans, Bryant, Eason, Perry, Newberry, Hill, and Reese families, among others. Flowers Lumber Company built the free school for children of employees.

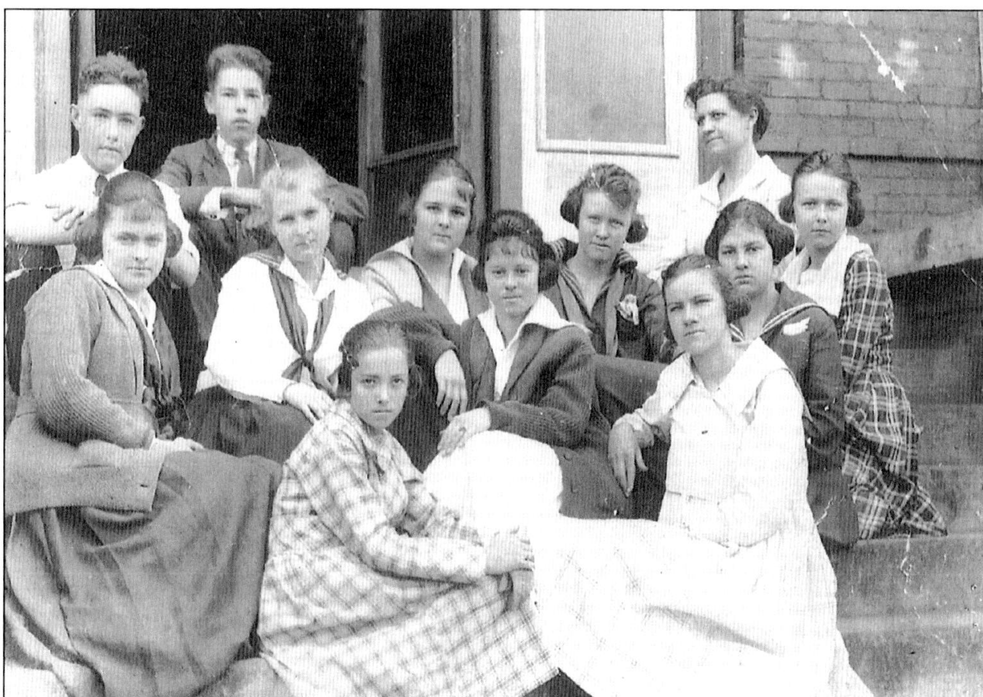

LATIN CLASS. Ella Jones's Latin class is seated on the steps of the north entrance of Blakely High School around 1920. In the group are Hoyle Fleming, Margaret Deal (Boyett), Beulah Williams (Bryant), and Ella Jones.

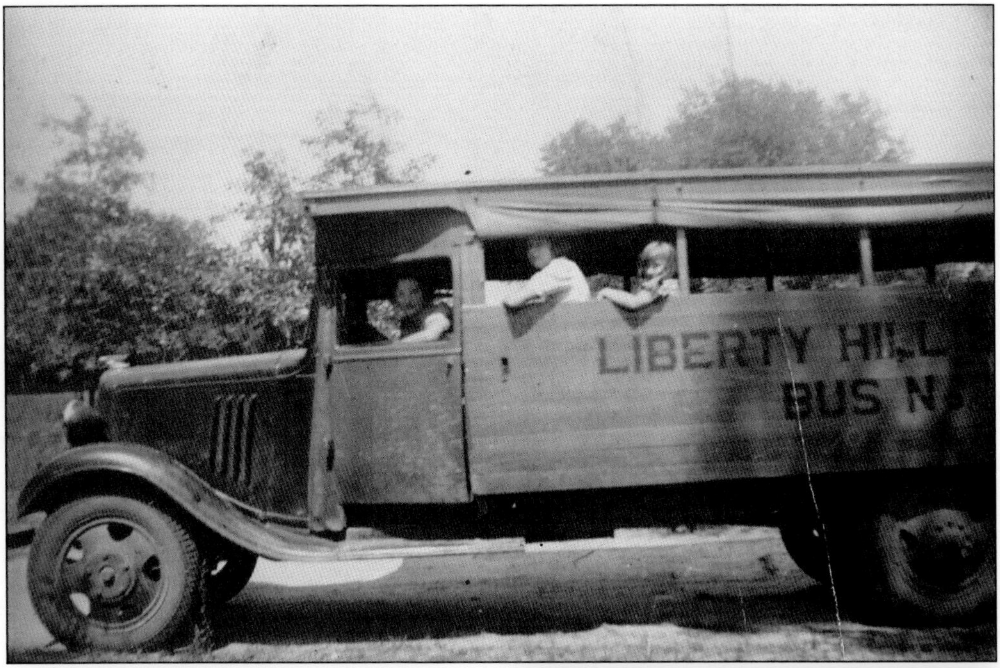

LIBERTY HILL BUS. In 1919, when Liberty Hill School was established, children walked to school, most for only two or three miles. Classes were taught by Gertie Bishop from Richland, Georgia. Teachers taught all levels of students, first grade to seventh grade. Driven by various people over the years beginning in 1920, the one-horse school wagon had a canvas top and seats built down the sides. The photograph shows Annie Bridges as the driver of this 1938 school bus. She was reportedly the first woman school bus driver in the state. (Courtesy of Georgia Archives Vanishing Georgia Collection, EAR 0005.)

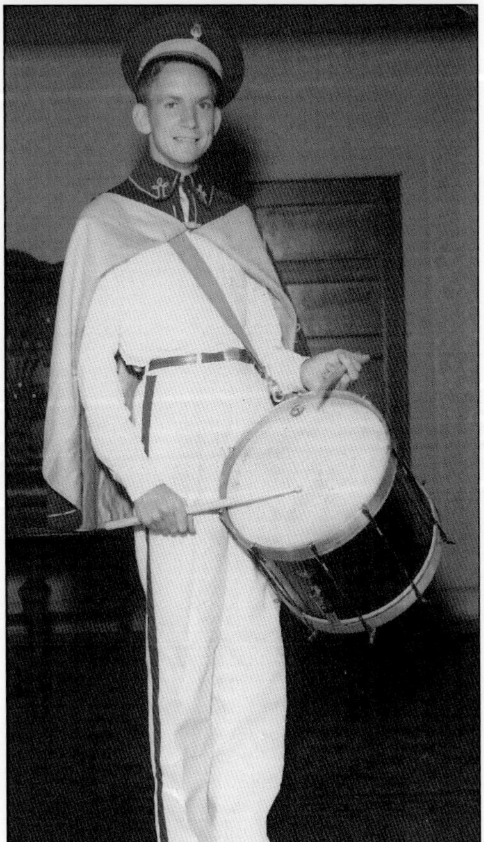

HUGH. Marching in the Blakely High School Band, Hugh Eubanks won the drum competition at Music Festival. The band marched in the *Biscuit Eaters* parade in Albany, celebrating the movie by the same name. After graduating from high school, he joined his brother Herman in his commercial photography business. Over the years, he and his wife, Delores, served the community as they worked out of their home studio on College Street, covering weddings and community activities as well as taking portraits of family groups. (Courtesy of Delores Eubanks.)

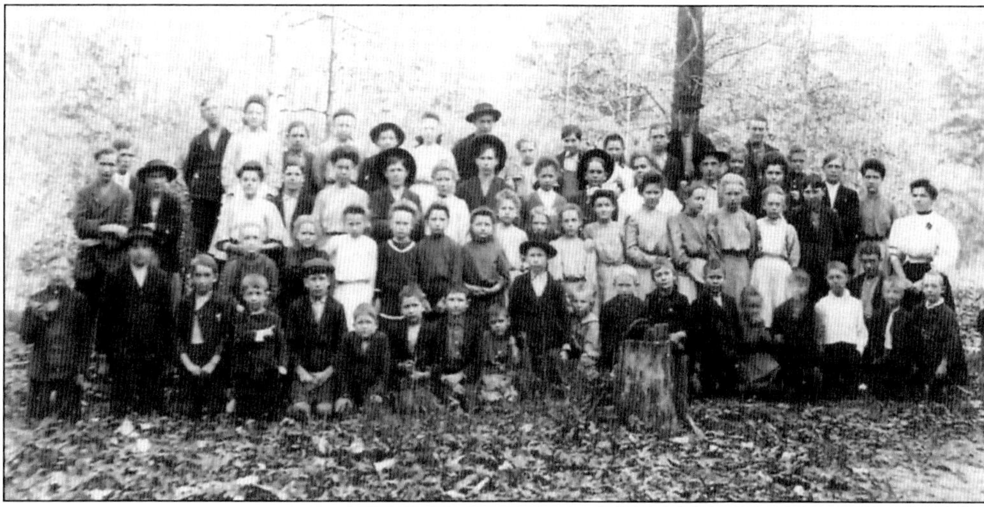

New Hope School Group. On the back of this yellowed, vintage photograph of a New Hope School group in 1910 is a touching message to Ethel Pounds by "a friend sincere and true." It states the following: "When you are sitting sad and lonely reflecting over the past, just remember love, my dear and the boy that loved you best. If you love me like I love you, no knife can cut our love in two, written by a friend sincere and true, hoping to be remembered by you." The postcard was signed, "H.D.," but the last name is unfortunately not legible.

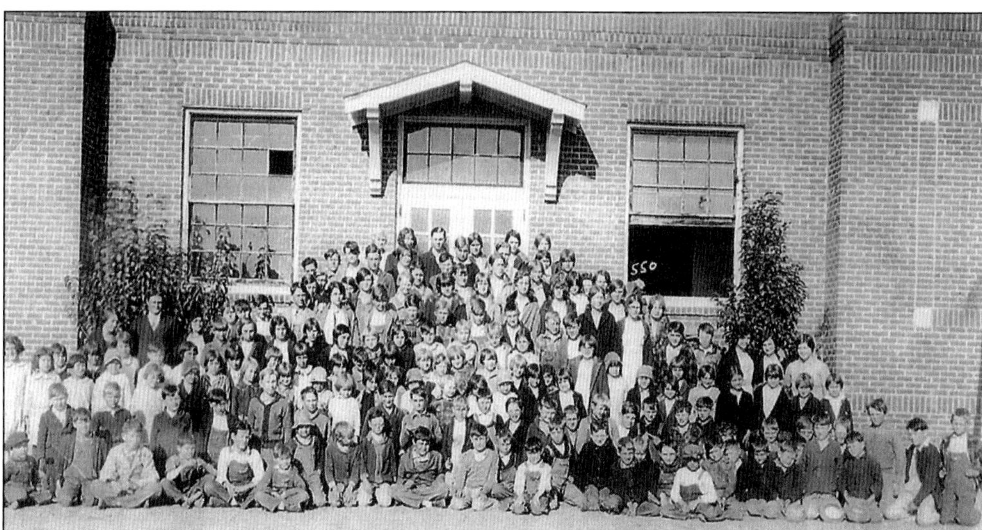

New Hope School. Early teachers at New Hope School, between Blakely and Damascus, were T.G. "Bud" Harvey Jr. and Vesta Minter. In 1930, the school had Bill Brown as principal, and the teachers were Liddie B. Smith, Lella Lewis, and Grace Balkcom.

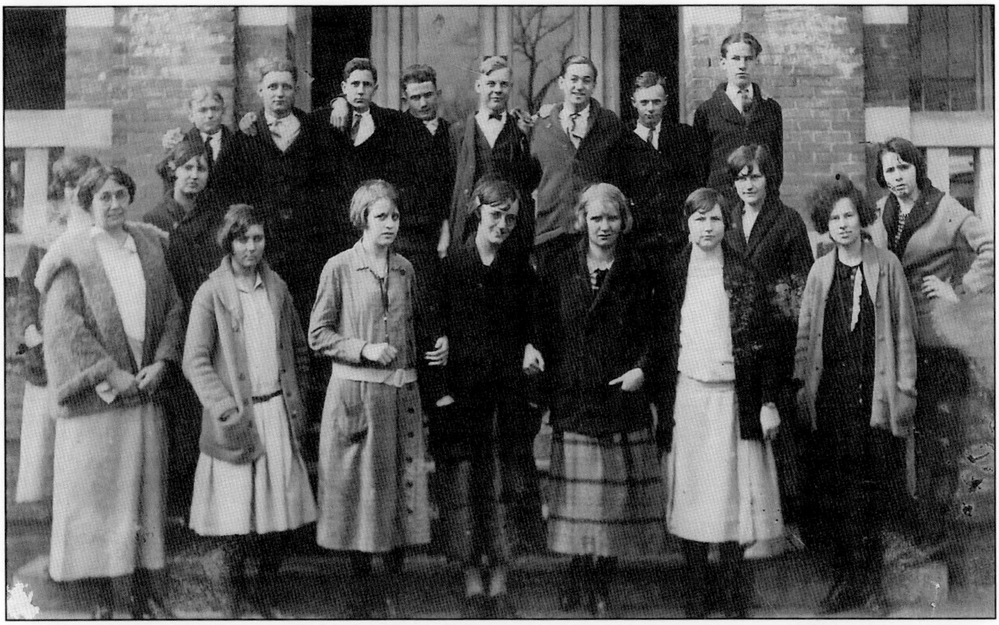

CLASS OF 1925. Blakely High School graduated 10 girls and eight boys in 1925 in the midst of the Roaring Twenties, an era of unprecedented affluence. But, in 1920, the American farmer had suffered from the collapse of agricultural prices, and unfortunately, the 1920s down on the farm were anything but roaring.

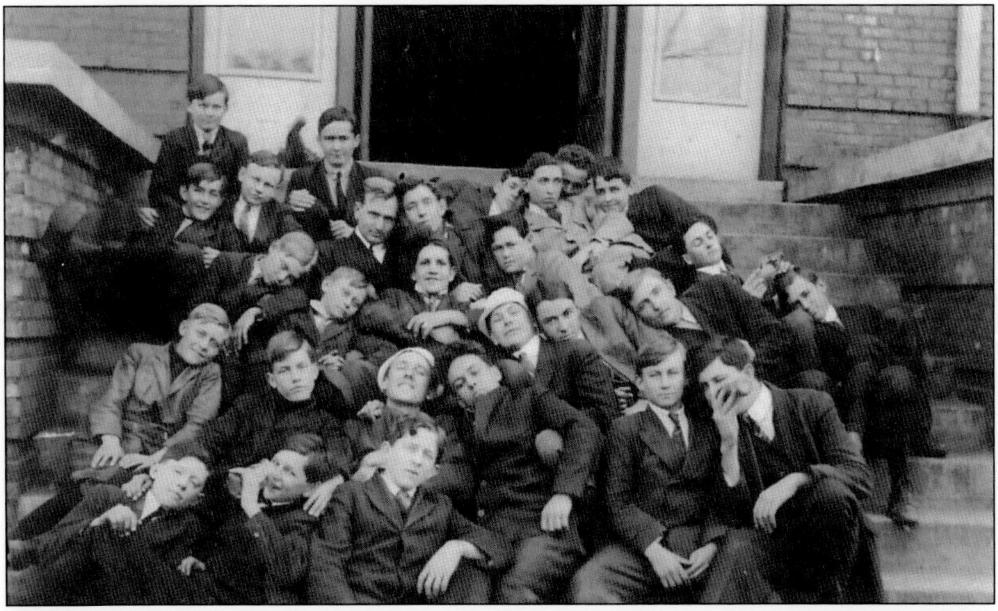

THE MIDNIGHT CLUB. The class of 1925 had as their motto, "Let the old world wiggle, we've got her by the tail." The sprawling "Midnight Club" (purpose unknown) seems from the photograph to be a rowdy bunch that was dedicated to having fun, which fits right in with the attitude of the 1920s.

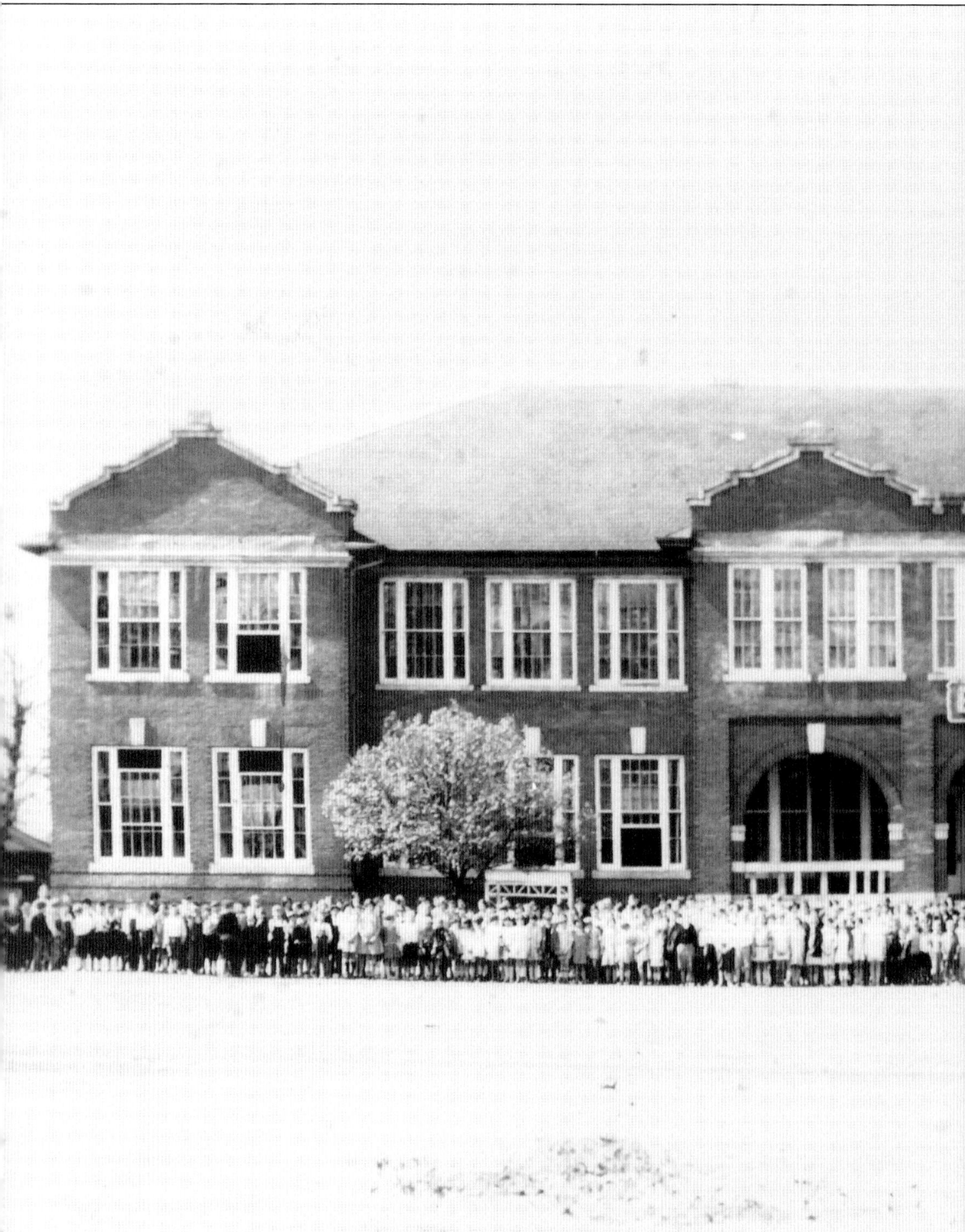

Blakely High School. In 1913, Blakely had a new brick schoolhouse that replaced the old Blakely Institute on College Street. The large, two-story building, with white trim around the doors and the tall six-over-six paned windows, was the pride of Blakely. Complete with steam heat, indoor

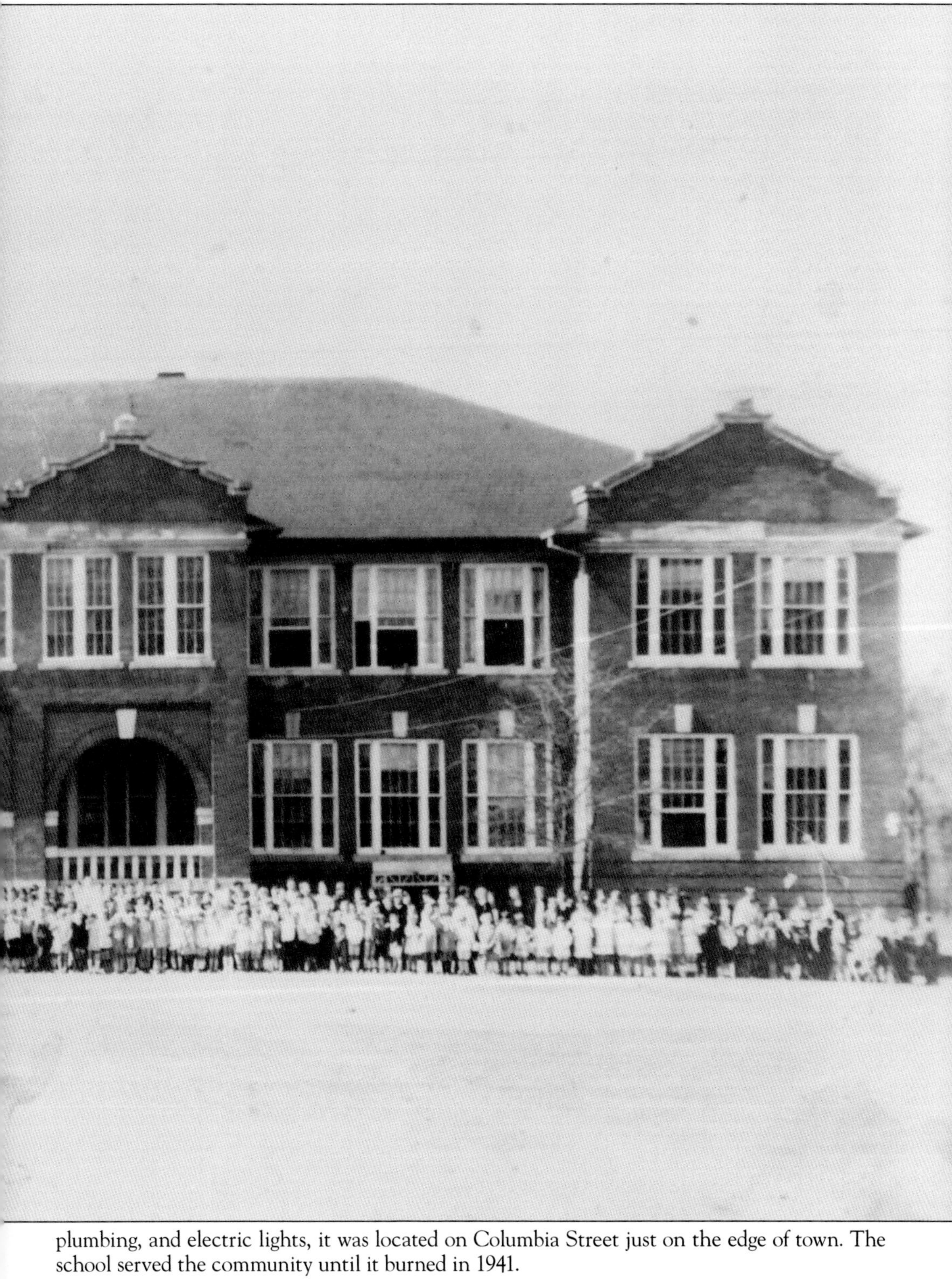

plumbing, and electric lights, it was located on Columbia Street just on the edge of town. The school served the community until it burned in 1941.

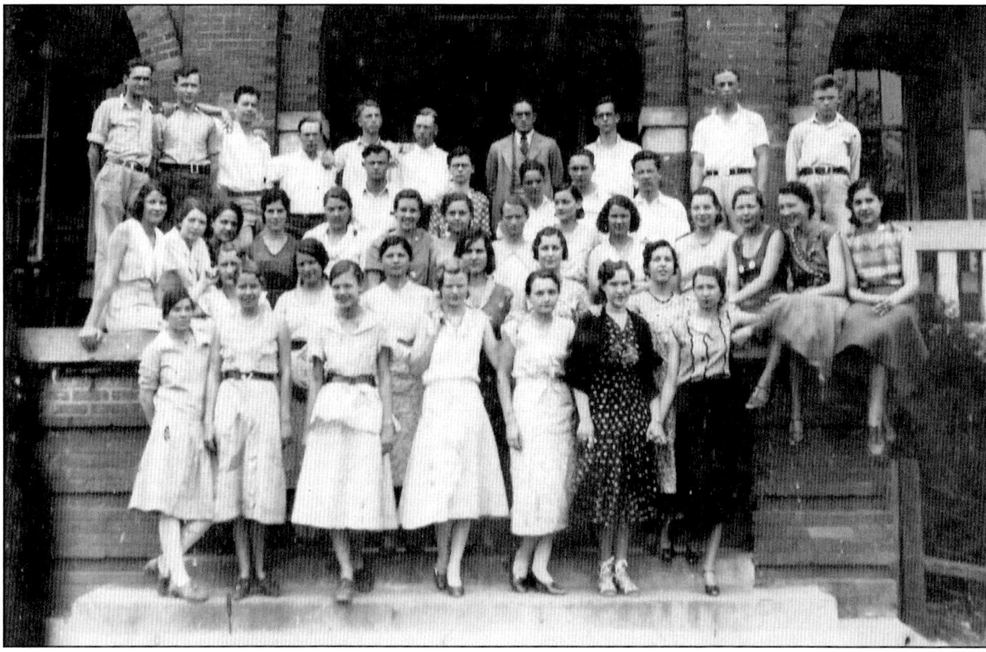

CLASS OF 1932. It was September 1921 when the class of 1932 enrolled in first grade with Mrs. Emmett Freeman as the teacher. They were to be together for 11 years, even though some students were added and some were lost. By 1932, there were 28 girls and 14 boys. The baccalaureate sermon was delivered at the First Methodist Church, and graduation exercises took place at the school auditorium on Friday night, May 27, 1932. Schools at the time had only 11 grades.

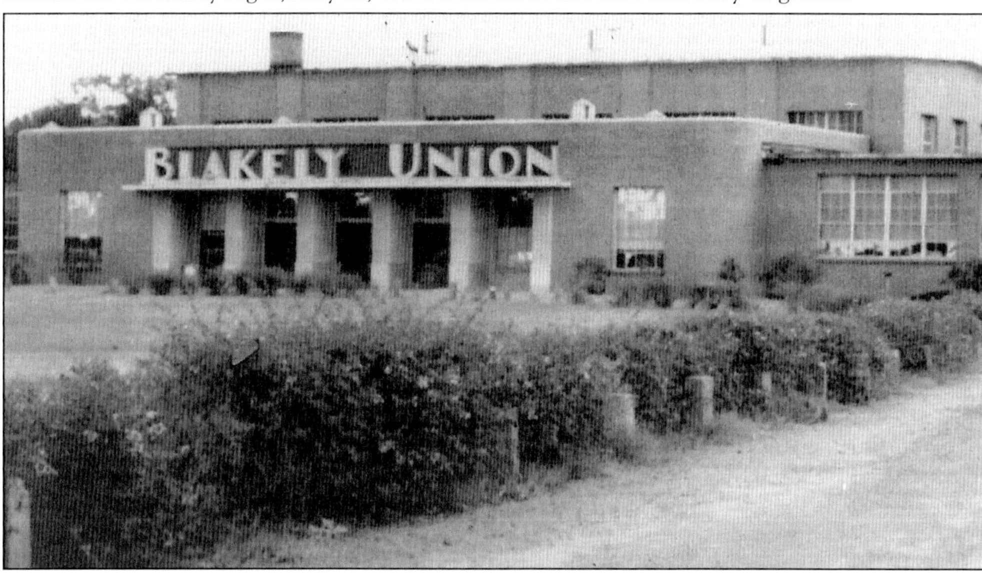

BLAKELY UNION. The first graduating class at Blakely Union High School was in 1946, which was before the building was even completed. After the Blakely High School building burned in 1941, the "shell," the white frame building that was the gymnasium, was used for grammar school classes. The older students attended classes all around town in public buildings and private homes. Blakely Union continued to provide education for Blakely students until the last class graduated there in 1966 and a new high school was built across the street.

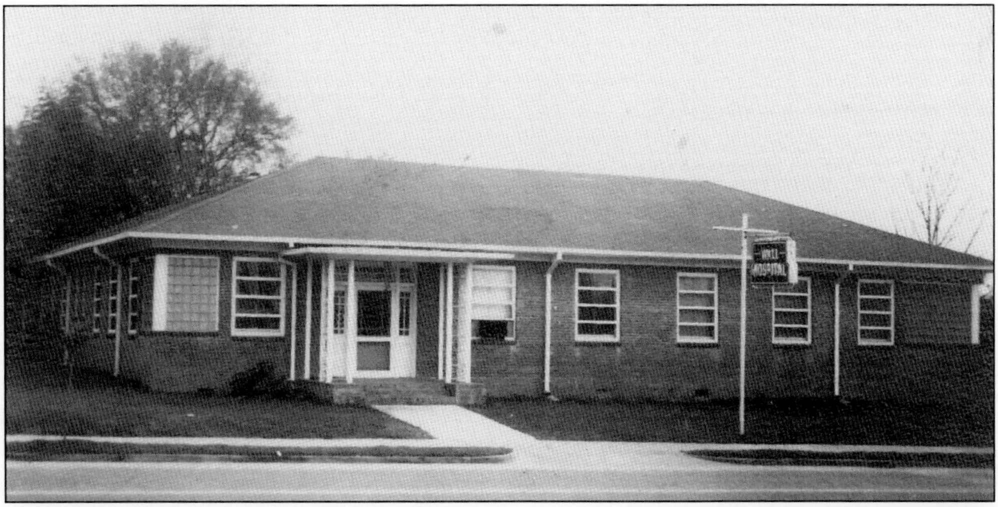

Wall Hospital. Dr. William Henry Wall built his 15-bed hospital on Columbia Street in Blakely. It opened for patients on September 27, 1947. Dr. Wall had served in the Georgia State Senate for a term in 1945–1946 and returned to serve again in 1951–1952. Reportedly, later the hospital became a convalescent home run by Lillian Carter, the mother of former president of the United States Jimmy Carter.

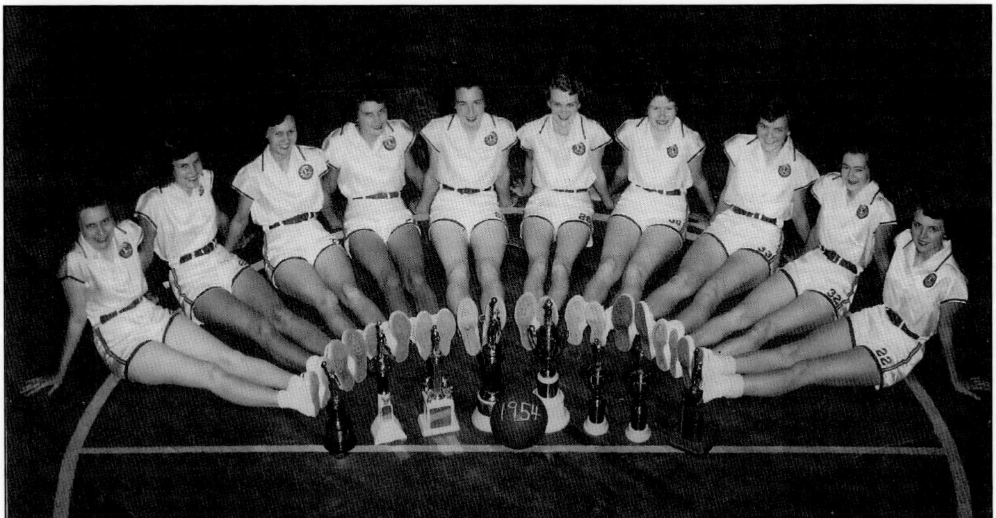

Lions Club Team. Dressed in sharp uniforms, the Blakely Lions Club basketball team played "just for the fun of it." Competing against such teams as Cuthbert, Bainbridge, and Albany, they brought home lots of trophies. These women of the community were, from left to right, Dot Willis, unidentified, Virginia Tedder, ? Sheffield, Bernice Horne, unidentified, Lottie Alston, unidentified, Margaret Bush, and unidentified.

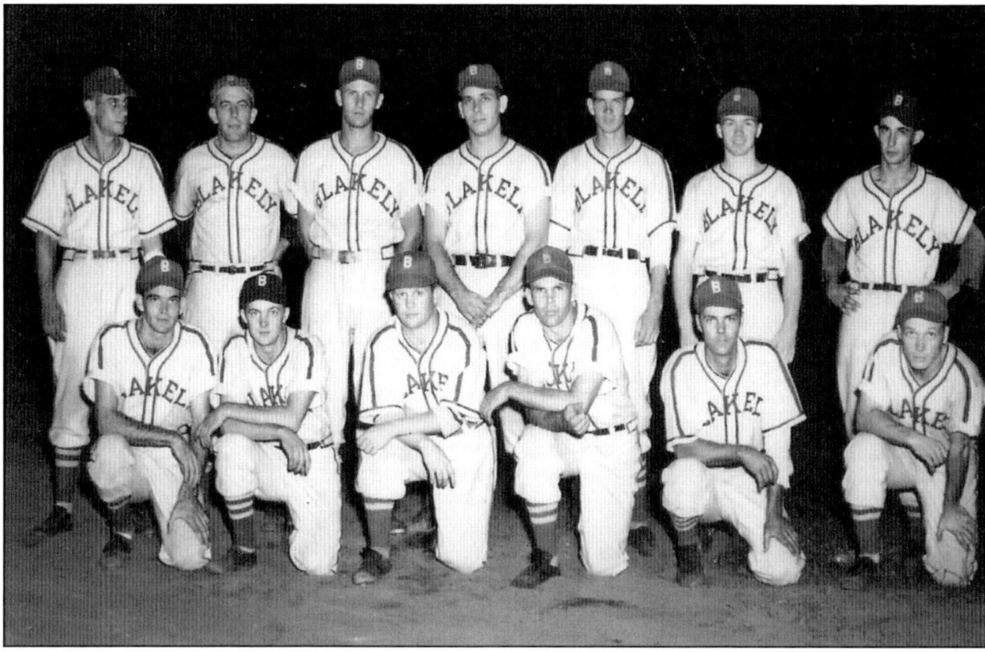

FLINT RIVER LEAGUE. Probably the best baseball player to come out of Blakely, Georgia, was Jack (Harry R.) Clifton. Graduating from the University of Georgia in 1940, he never pitched a losing game. Though he played in a league that included Yogi Berra, a sore arm ended his professional career. He came to Blakely and played for Blakely Tigers, which became the champions of the Flint River League in 1949. A brush-back pitch to opponent Otis Johnson in 1951 left Johnson in a coma, and he later died. In an interview many years later, Jack said of Johnson, "It was always a burden and it still is. I think about it quite often." Above, players are, from left to right, (first row) Dan Rhew, Ralph Horton, Duck Smith, Jack Clifton, Charleston Jones, and Billy Horton; (second row) Jack Gilstrap, Aubry Baker, Bo Clifton, Tick Knowles, Al Rivenbark, Joe Clark, and Billie Currie. (Both, courtesy of Mrs. Jack Clifton.)

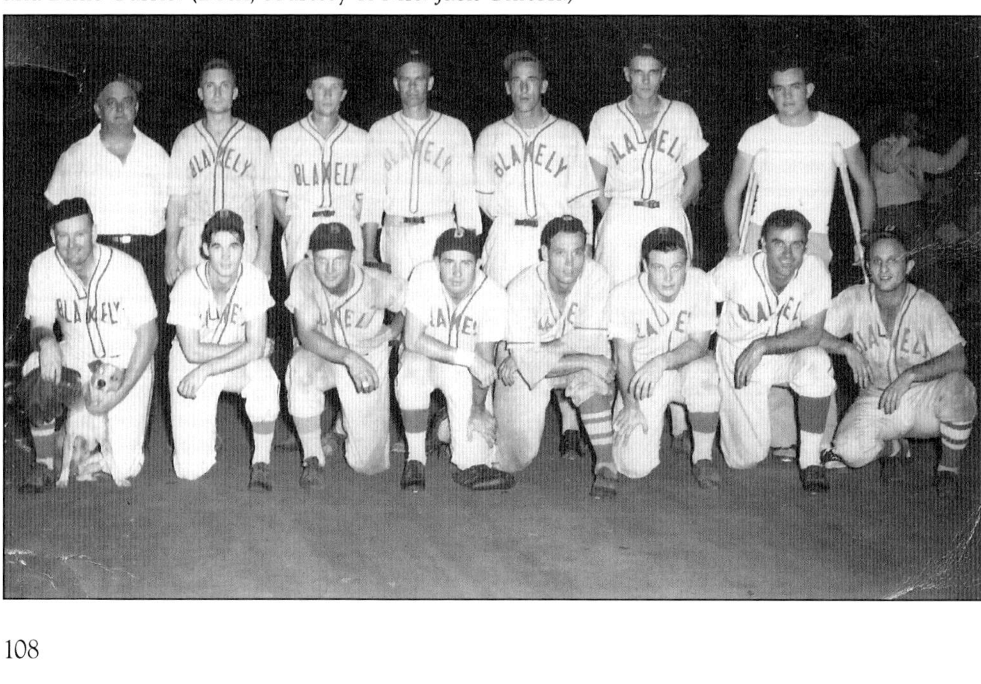

For the Love of the Game. The Blakely Democrats softball team included, from left to right, (first row) Grady Holman, Billy Hinton, Billy Currie, Jack White, Howell Reid "Eight-Rock" Stovall, Wilton Radney, and Ralph Brown; (second row) "Lefty" Nowles, John Holman, Earl Chandler (pitcher/manager), Sam Clinkscales, Tommy Owen, and Mac Balkcom.

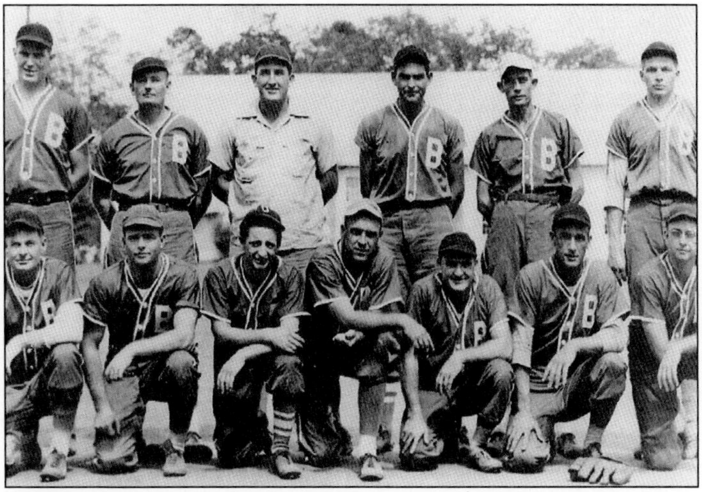

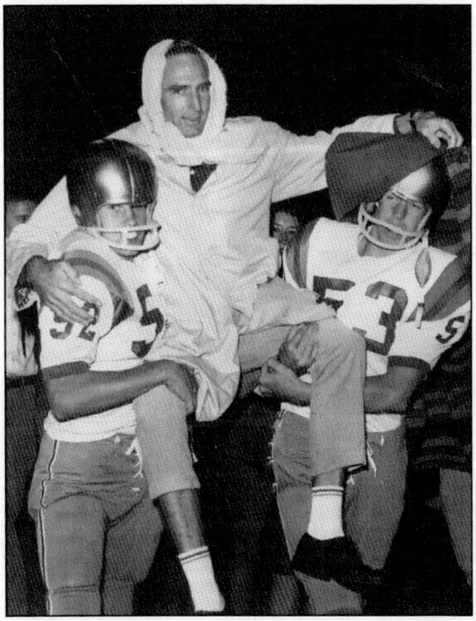

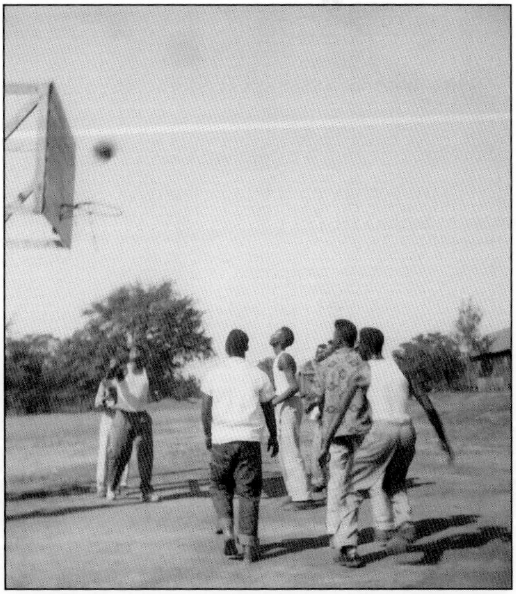

State Champs. Tradition was the word used to describe Early County High School football (left). Memorable teams played there, many winning sub-region and region titles. But just one team walked away with it all. With a 12-0-1 record, the Bobcats of 1964 won the first state football championship. Head coach Ray Knight is carried off the field by Mike White (left) and Carroll Waller after the championship game in Lovett.

Washington High Basketball. It was not unusual for school basketball teams to practice and play varsity games on dirt courts (right). When county schools began to consolidate and centralize in the late 1950s, a few gymnasiums began to be built in central locations. Washington High School players practice the sport on the grounds at the school. (Courtesy of Maddox Memorial Library Archives.)

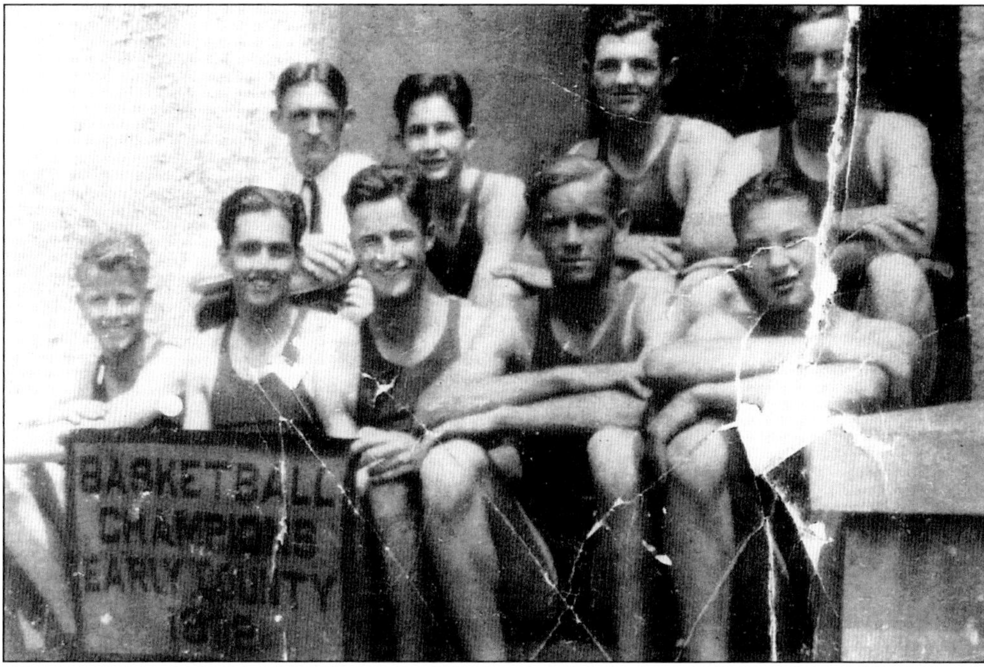

Local Champions. Coach L.T. Foshee led his local boys in Hilton to the 1932 county basketball championship. Team members include, from left to right, (first row) Hugh L. Martin, Gordon Slappy, Cecil Hall, Martin Still, and Junior Smith (second row) Coach Foshee, Wilmer Smith, Harold Foshee, and Idus Chambers.

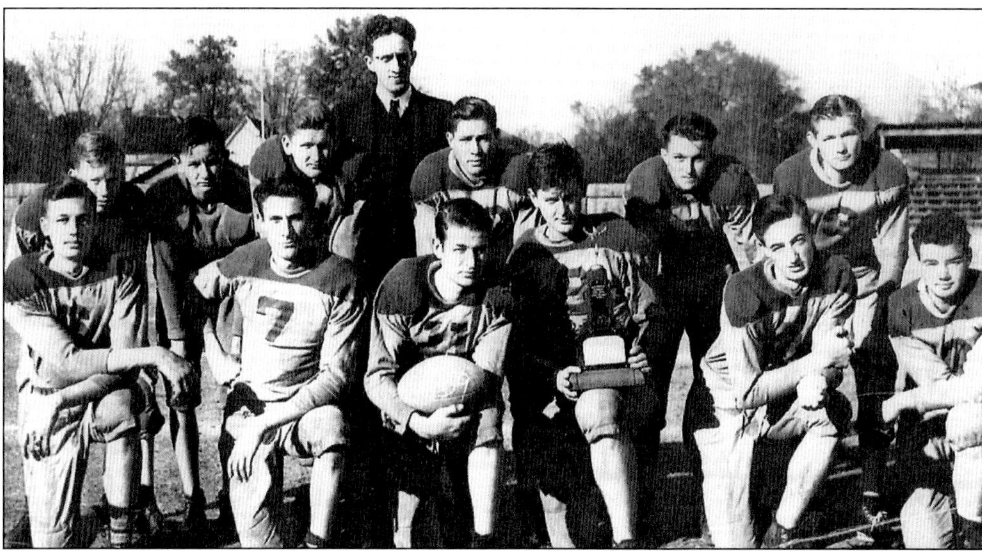

Hammack's Team. Dr. Jack Standifer saw football games at Staunton Military Academy in 1905 and thought his hometown, Blakely, should have a team. Raising $300 from the town, he outfitted the team and named it the Bobcats. The 1939 Bobcat team, coached by Butch Hammack, was a high-scoring team and won all its games but lost in the playoffs. Players are, from left to right, (first row) Howard Sherman, Harry Sirmons, Moody Chandler, William Mosely, Arthur Sherman, and Billy Spence; (second row) unidentified, John Mosely, Zack Smith, unidentified, Edgar Pearson, and Harold Willis. Coach Hammack is standing.

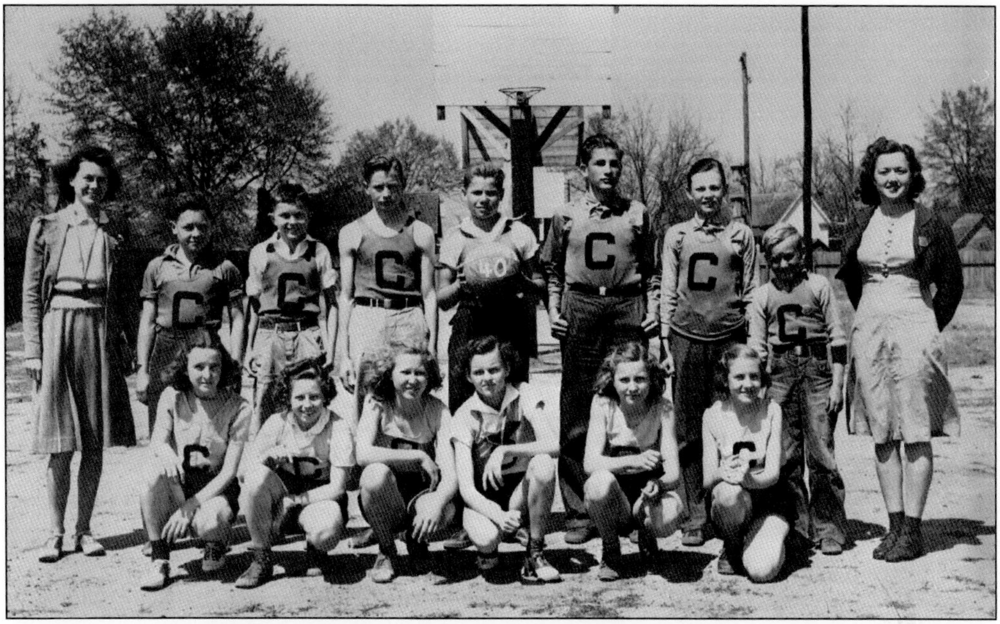

Colomoki Coeds. Having practice and even games on a dirt court was a commonplace sighting 1939, when these seventh-grade boys and girls were playing. The Colomoki School, a big, brick building, was north of Blakely and just off Highway 27. The school was closed in the early 1950s when county schools were consolidated. (Courtesy of Georgia Archives Vanishing Georgia Collection, EAR 95-82.)

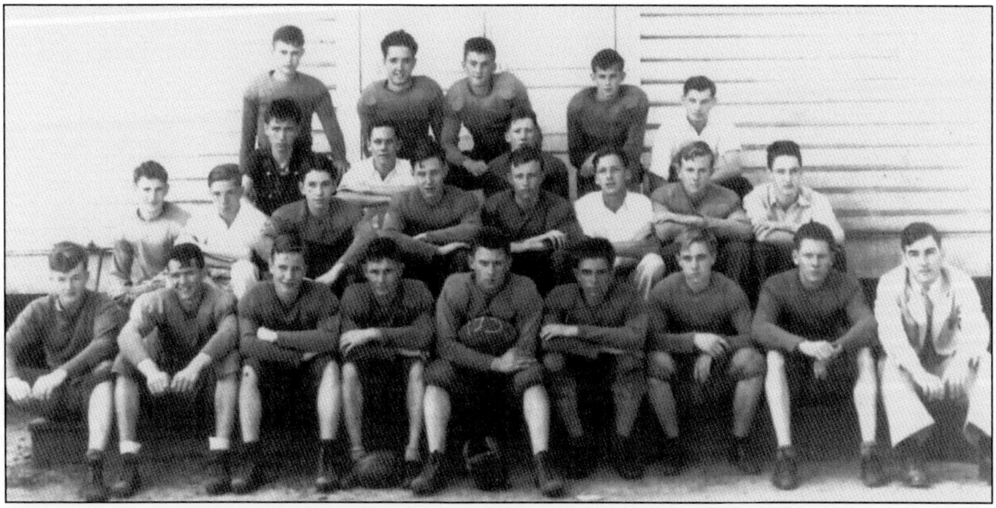

Bobcat Team, 1932. Sitting on the steps of the "shell," the old white gymnasium that served Blakely High School, coach David Hazelhurst and his team line up for a photograph. The team only played six games that year and won one over Ashford. The team members are, from left to right, (first row) Stanley Sherman, Norman Alexander, Bruce Williams, Johnny Lee Still, Jack Hayes, William Clearman, Richard Grist, Lamar "Red" Pritchett, and Coach Hazelhurst; (second row) James Hobbs, Jeptha Lee, Leonard "Lent" Houston, Collier "Bubba" Gay, Hubert Clark, Raymond Duke, R.L. Thornton, and Collier Davidson; (third row) James Warrick, William Mashburn, unidentified, and Phillip Spence; (fourth row) Ralph Hobbs, Archy Walker, Bernard "B" Herring, and Alex Howell.

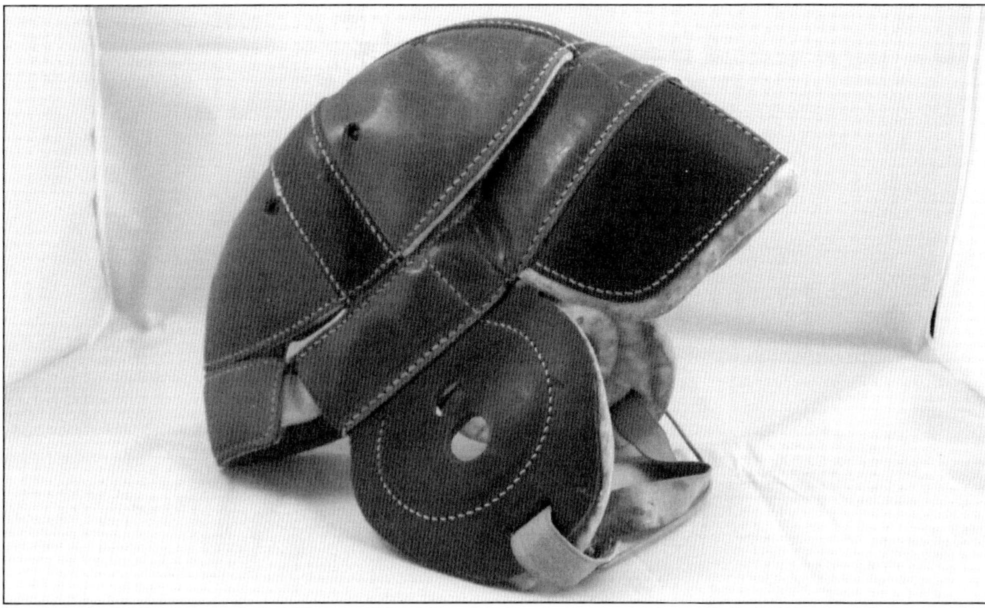

Leather Helmet. In the fall of 1921, when the first football uniforms were purchased for the new team, only one helmet was bought. The person who carried the ball wore the helmet. The team lost its first game to Dothan but found later that one of the big team's stars, Johnny Mack Brown, became an All-American player for the University of Alabama and played in the Rose Bowl. Brown went on to become a famous Hollywood cowboy. Dr. Jack Standifer introduced Blakely High School to football and called the team the Bobcats. (Football helmet courtesy of the Boyett family.)

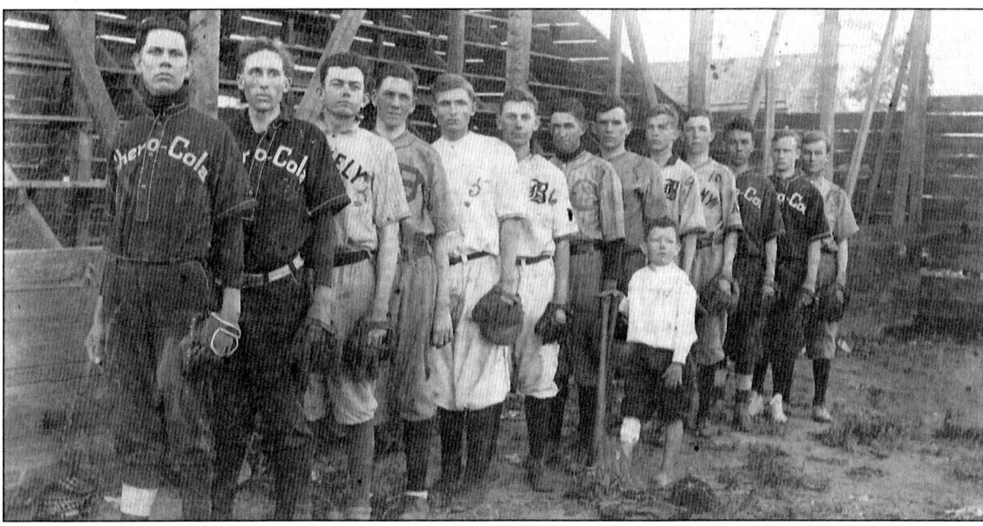

Blakely Baseball Team. Chero-Cola Bottling Company, located on North Main Street just off the square in Blakely, sponsored the players and provided the shirts for the Blakely baseball team. The company formed in 1904 and was a short-lived predecessor of Royal Crown (RC) Cola, produced by the same company. Team members are, from left to right, Daniel Davis, Shelly Simmons (pitcher), Watson Ricks, Bethea Beard, Chester Chandler, Edwin Brooks, Many Beard, ? Whitchard, Cortez Bush, Earl Fleming, Lane Coachman, Guy Walthrop, and assistant coach Eifla Beasley. The ball boy in front is "Red" Whittington.

Six

Around the Town

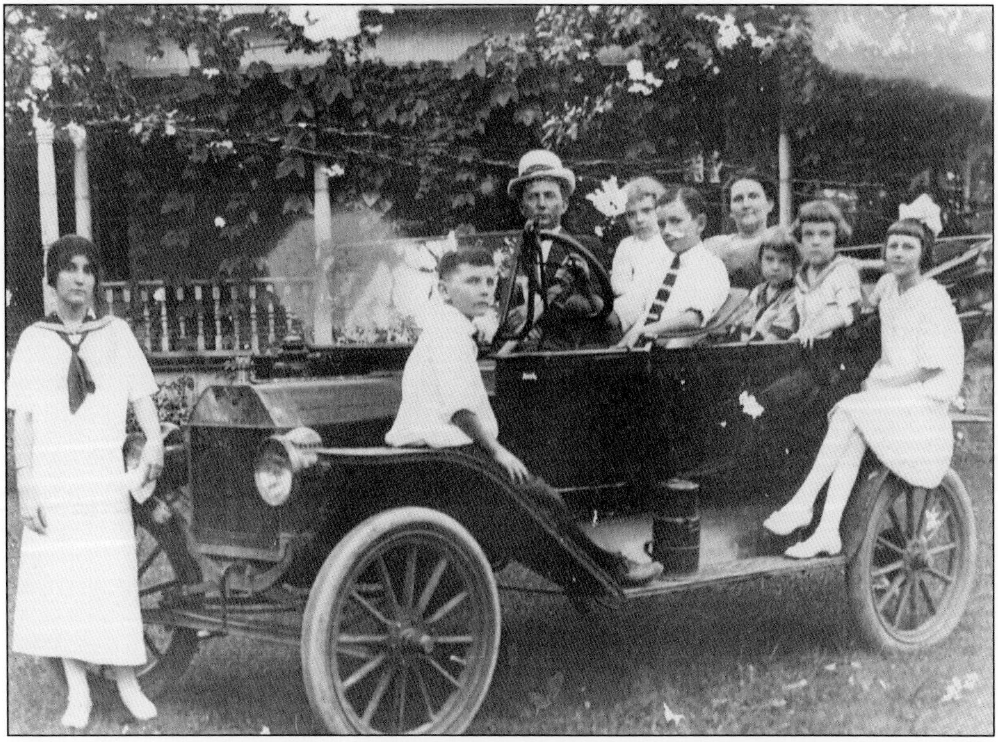

Model T. Proud of its car, the C.S. Middleton family loads up for a family portrait in 1915. "Mother Ida's" house is in the background. Those standing by and sitting on the automobile are, from left to right, Lucile, 17; Harvey, 11; and Sibyl, 13. In the front seat are, from left to right, C.S. Middleton "Papa Charlie," about 44; Hazel, 8; and Max, 15, driving. In back seat are, from left to right, Ida Lane Middleton "Mother Ida," about 39; Melvin, 6; and Harold, 8.

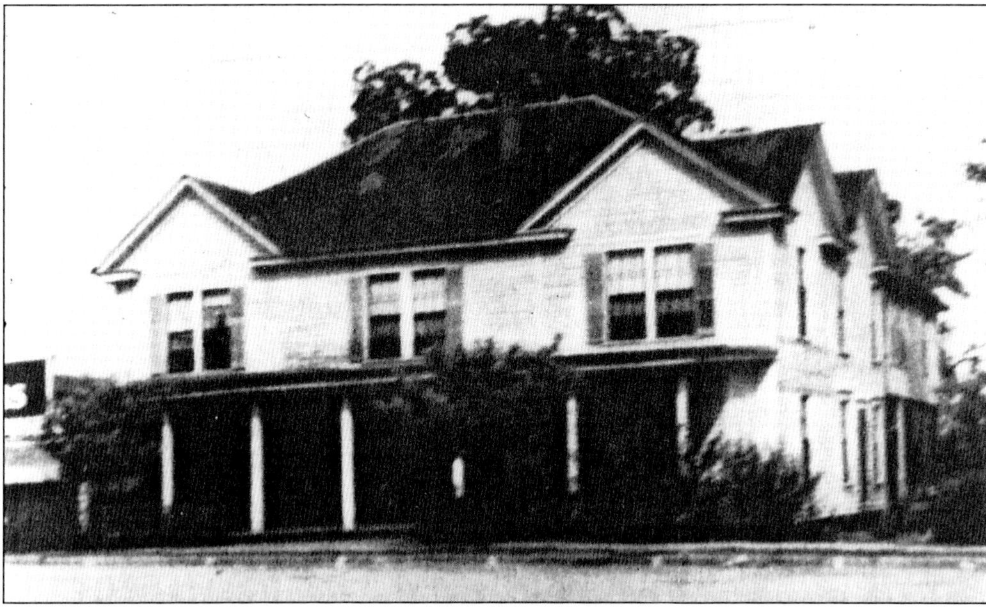

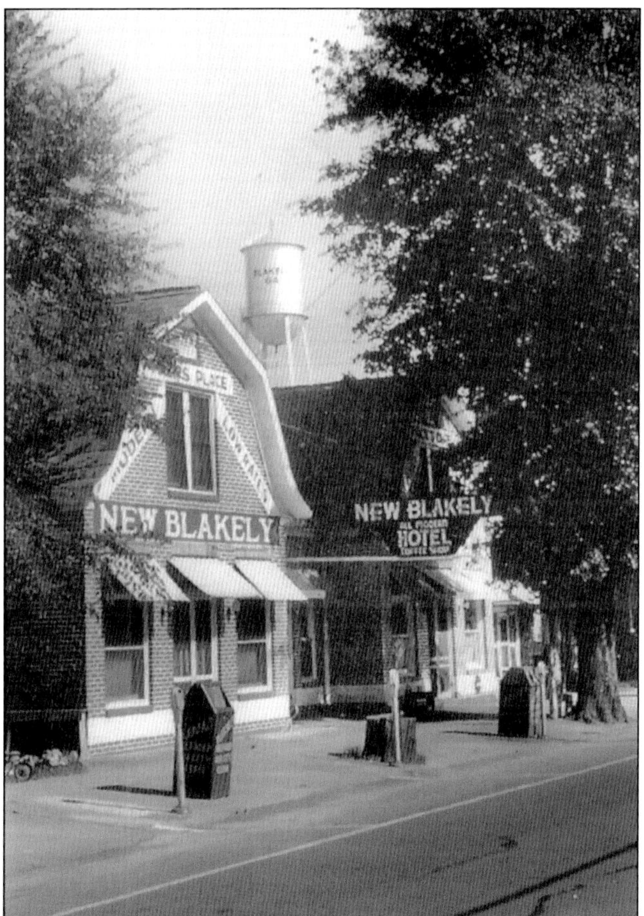

EARLY HOTEL. Turning east off Court Square, a traveler encountered Early Hotel on the north side of Magnolia Street, not even a block off the square. The hotel was a prelude to encountering Dr. Holland's Hospital, which eventually became the site of the offices for the Early County home economist and the county extension agent. Later, Blakely Fire Department was moved from Court Square to the hotel site.

NEW BLAKELY HOTEL. Mack Strickland's hotel on North Main Street rented rooms by the night or by the week. The hotel also accepted boarders at times. Meals were served in the downstairs dining room and were open to the public. It also served the community by providing a place for large parties, receptions, and business meetings. Delores Eubanks remembers, "My high school graduation class [early 30s] had our senior party at the hotel."

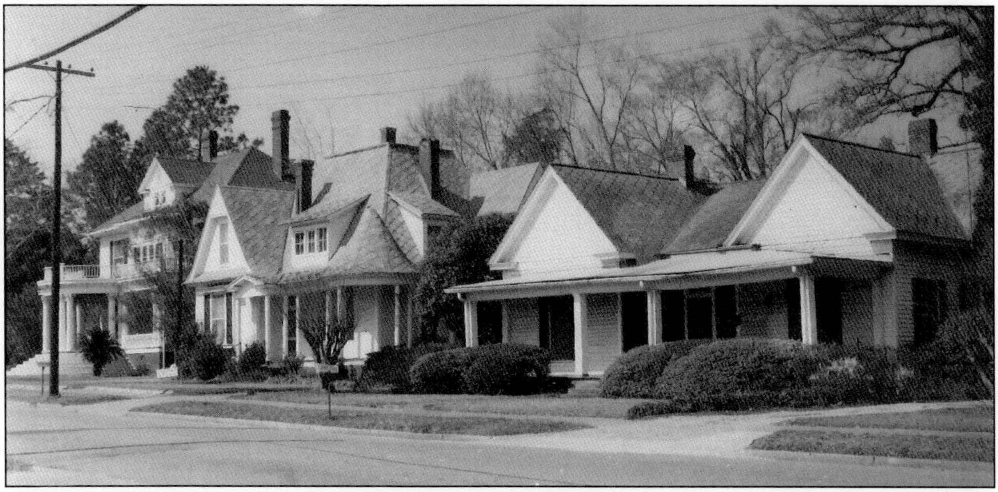

Three Ladies. Among other beautiful homes on College Street were, from left to right, the Hand, Deal, and Murdock homes. Erected just after the turn of the century, all of the homes changed hands several times over the years. The only home still standing is the Deal house. The Hand home burned, and the Murdock house was torn down.

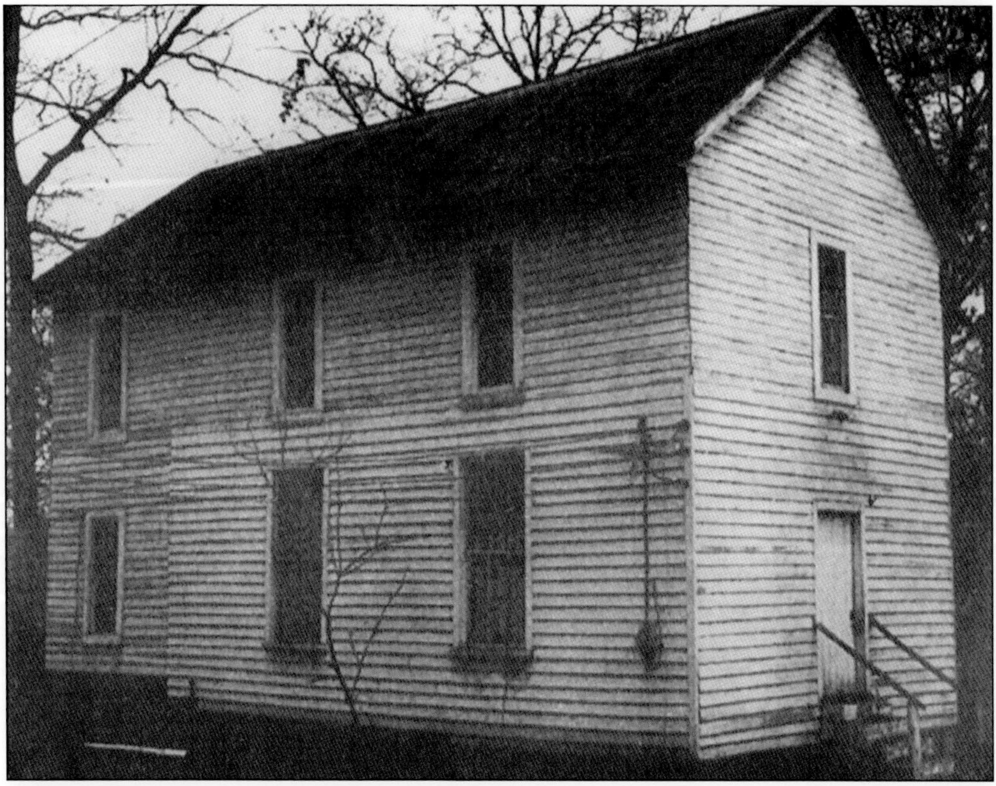

Cedar Springs Courthouse. This community house was a busy place in the early 1900s. It was the scene of small gatherings, such as wedding showers, club meetings, and quilting bees. Behind the building, fishermen cooked their catch of the day for the community. On other days, the smoke of the barbecue fires would waft through the town, enticing Cedar Springs citizens to bring their covered dishes and join their neighbors for food and fun.

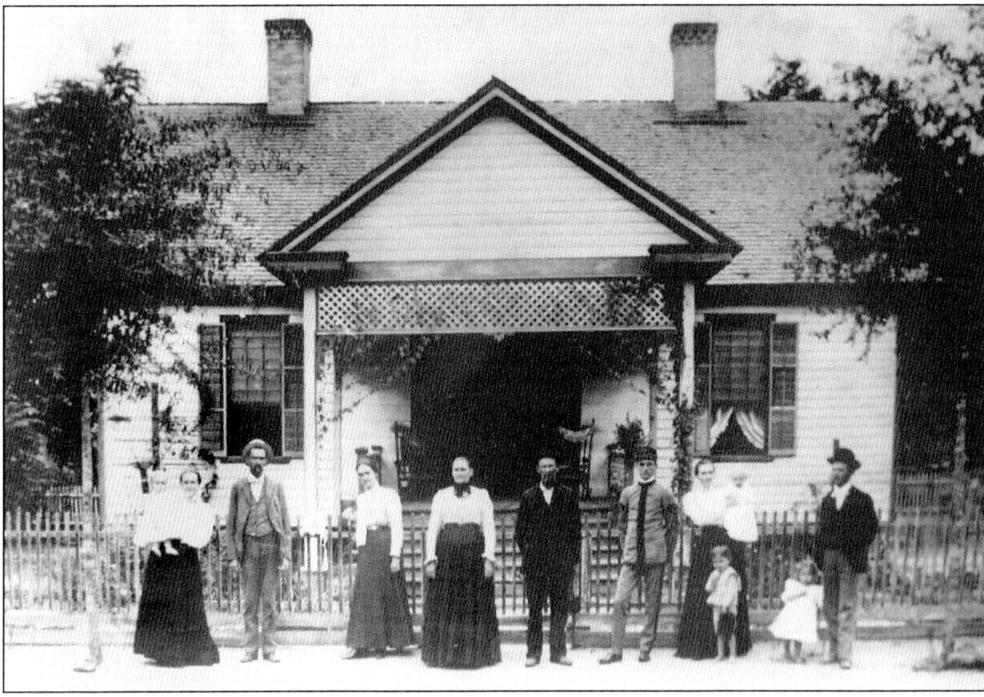

The Lane Home. Built in 1900 in Sowhatchee, the J.P. Lane home still stands in good condition. Joseph P. Lane was the son of Joseph W. Lane and the grandson of Joseph Lane, a pioneer to Early County. Grandfather "Joe" was a prosperous plantation owner and served three terms in the Georgia House of Representatives in the late 1800s. He was also instrumental in the building of the "Grand Ole Lady" and the Coheelee Creek Covered Bridge. (Courtesy of Mr. and Mrs. Gene Regan.)

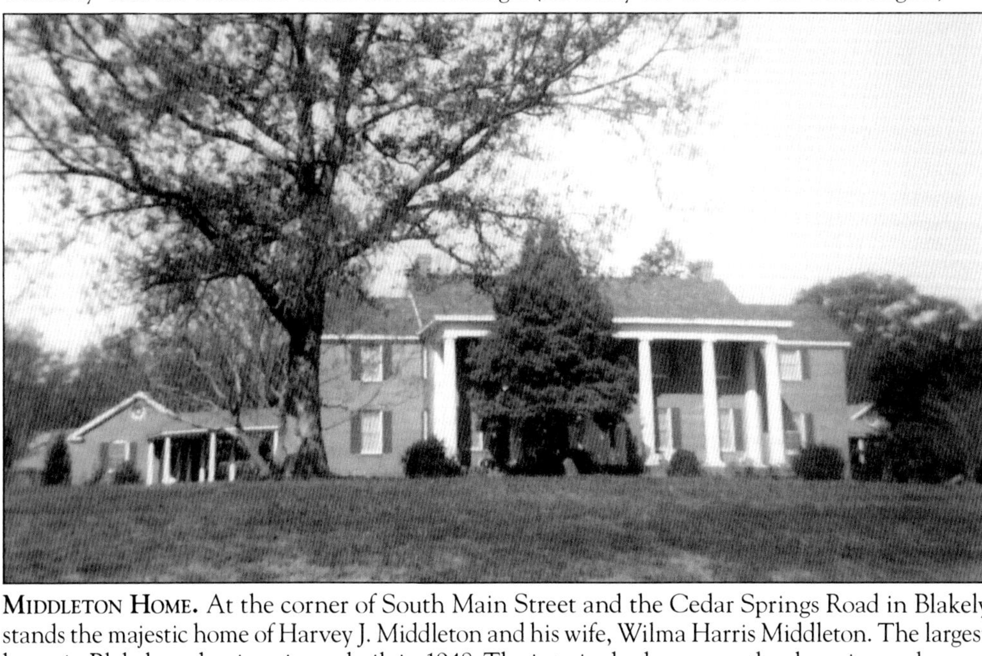

Middleton Home. At the corner of South Main Street and the Cedar Springs Road in Blakely stands the majestic home of Harvey J. Middleton and his wife, Wilma Harris Middleton. The largest home in Blakely at the time, it was built in 1948. The interior had, among other luxuries, mahogany paneling and woodwork and hand-painted wallpaper. (Courtesy of Mr. and Mrs. Gene Regan.)

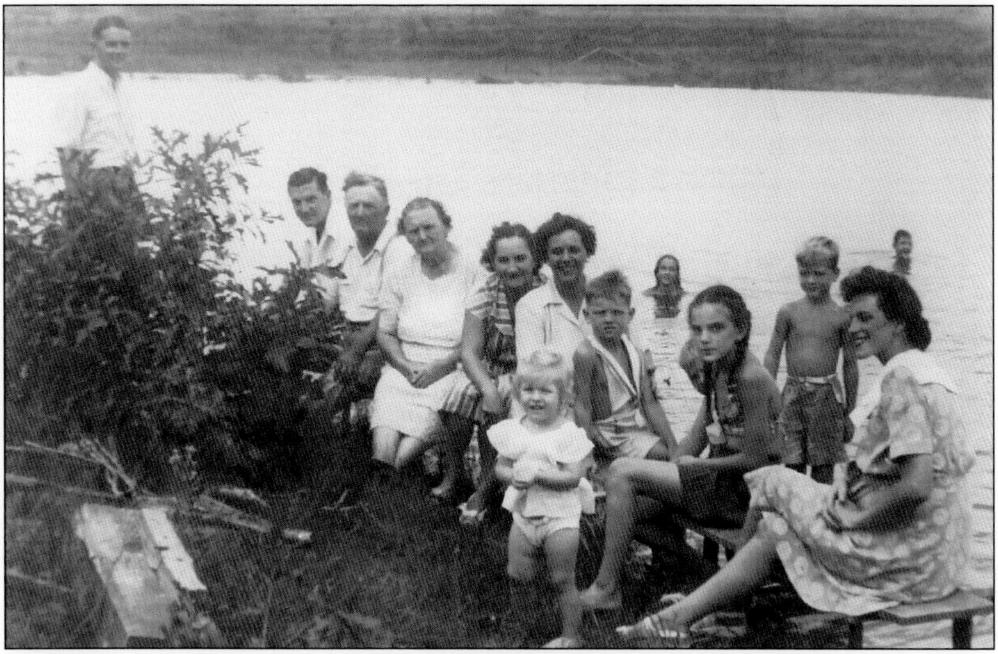

Country Club Drive. In the 1950s, Dr. C.S. Middleton built a fishpond for his wife, Ida. Overlooking the small pond was a small house. Family members gathered for this 1945 photograph of the pond. Later the property, including the pond and home, was purchased by the Town and Country Club. (Courtesy of Mr. and Mrs. Gene Regan.)

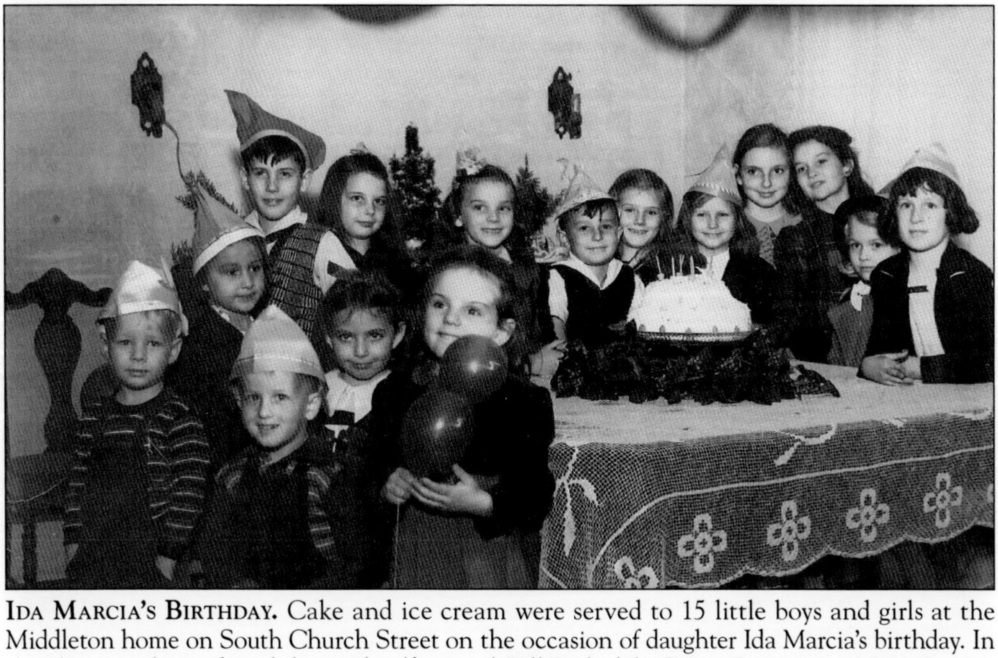

Ida Marcia's Birthday. Cake and ice cream were served to 15 little boys and girls at the Middleton home on South Church Street on the occasion of daughter Ida Marcia's birthday. In the photograph are, from left to right, (first row) Bill Barksdale, Royce Davenport, Minia Lanier, and Marilyn Middleton (holding balloons); (second row) Sibyl Middleton, Cecil Dunkin, Mead Maddox, Ida Marcia Middleton, Edwin Boyette, Marjorie Carswell, unidentified, Marshaline Giles, Evelyn Temples, Ann Collins, and Jane Fuqua. (Courtesy of Mr. and Mrs. Gene Regan.)

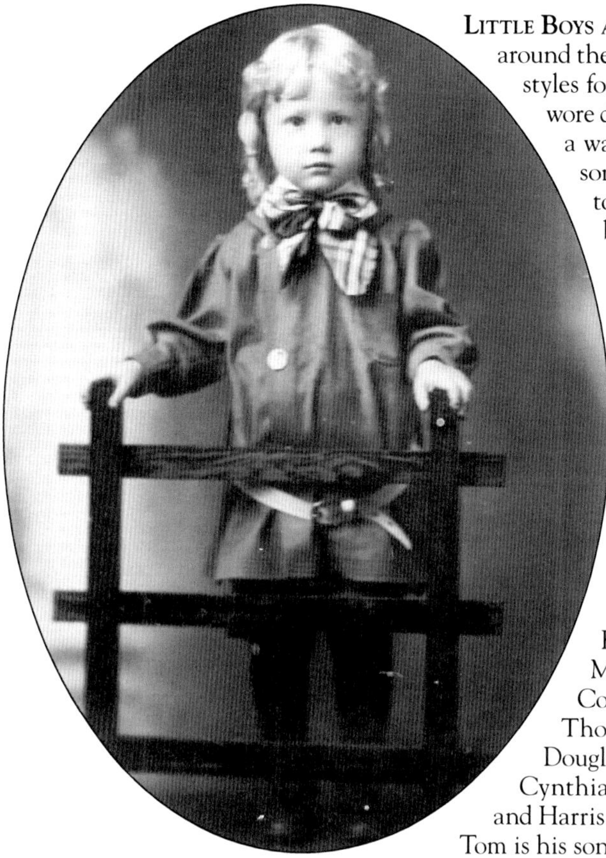

LITTLE BOYS AND DRESSES. Clothing styles for boys around the turn of the century blended with the styles for girls. Boys had long curls and often wore dresses that were shapeless and without a waist. They wore smart sailor suits and sometimes lace collars, which gave way to ruffled collars a few years later. As a boy, the clothes of A.D. Harris, who was later a leading citizen in Blakely, reflected the style of the period.

THE HARVEY HOME PLACE. With lots of Victorian trim, the home of Tom Harvey of Jakin was the site where he and his wife, Valeda Virginia Minter Harvey, raised 10 beautiful children. Married on March 14, 1883, in Early County, their children were Mary Adair, Thomas Grady, John Quitman, Berrien Douglas, Winnie Valeda, Wallace Watson, Cynthia Dot, Jessie Gladys, Milton Minter, and Harris Graham. Pictured on the porch with Tom is his son Milton in 1907.

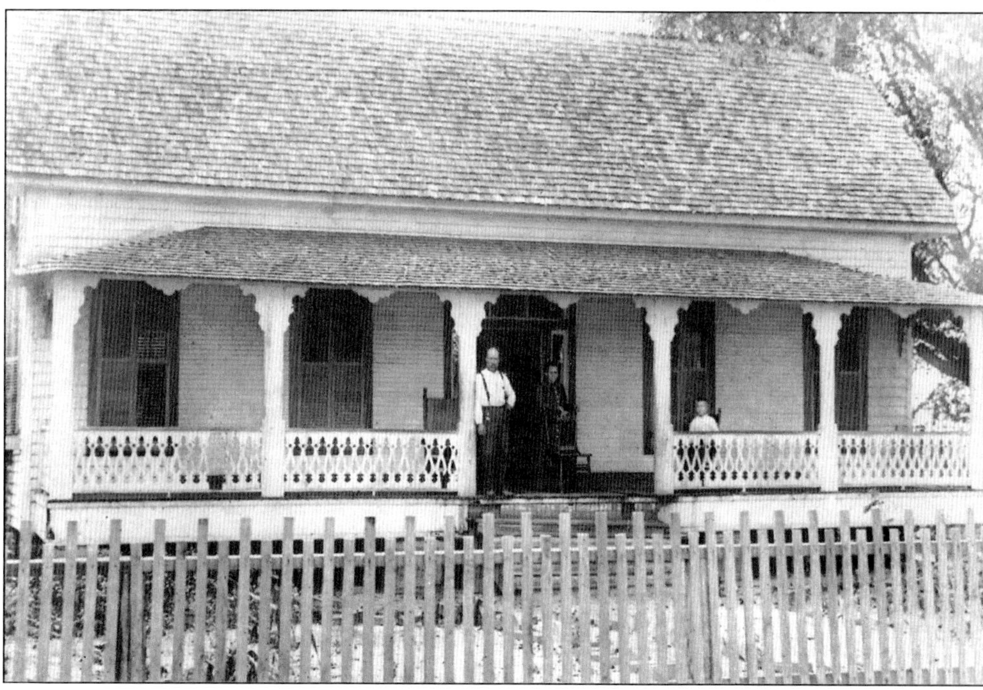

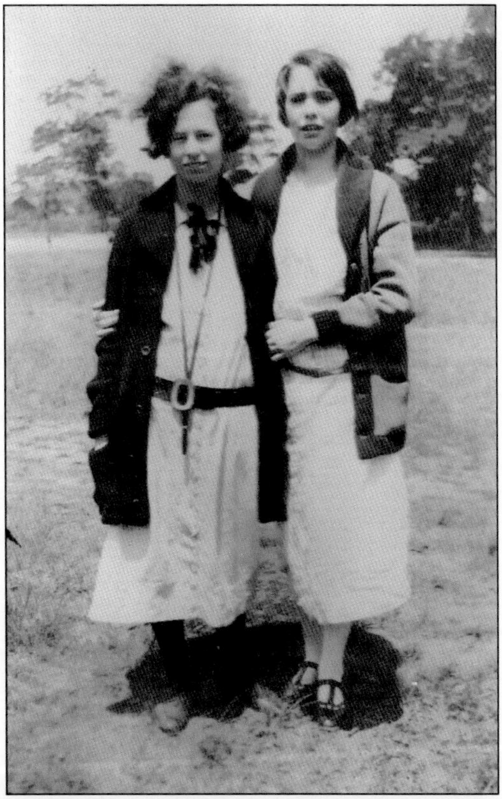

Roaring Twenties. Dorothy Jones (left), the valedictorian, and Neta Barham, the salutatorian of the class of 1925, exhibit the height of fashion for the time. Short hairstyles were popular; shapeless and loose clothing were the rage; and everyone wore mid-calf length skirts and dropped-waist dresses. Boyish, flat-chested fashions were ever-increasing in popularity and were the epitome of the spirit of the reckless rebel.

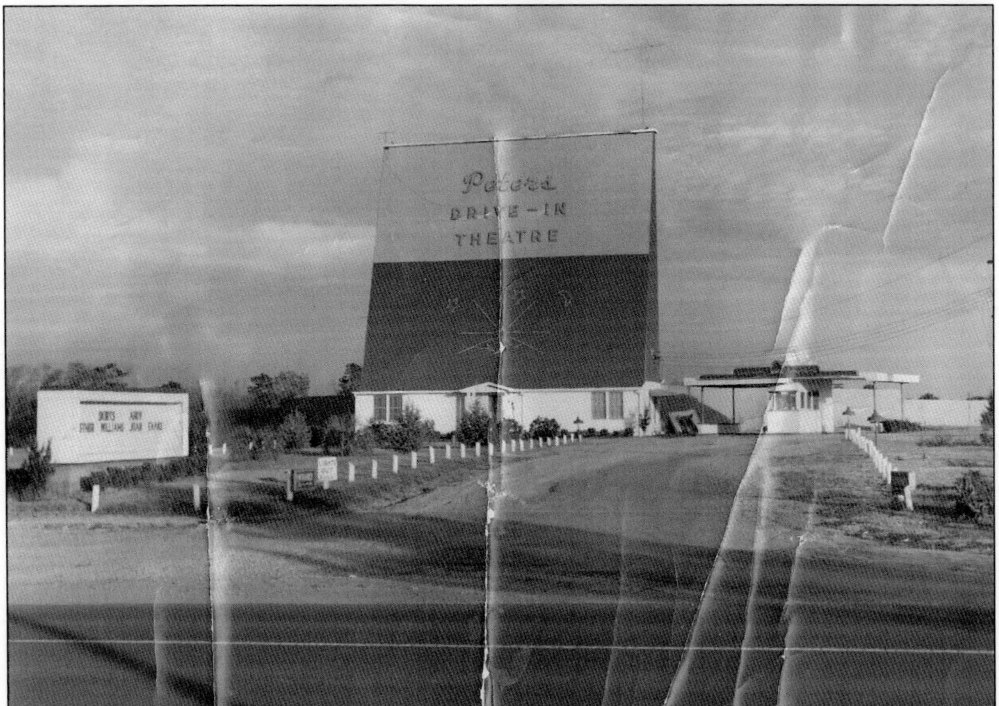

Peters Drive-in. Ten-cent Sno-Cones and pop corn, hamburgers, hotdogs, and good wholesome westerns, love stories, and musicals awaited anyone who could come up with 39¢ (or hide in someone else's trunk) to enter Peters Drive-In. On Wednesday nights, it was only $1 per car! On Sunday nights, cars lined up on Highway 27 waiting to get in to see the new movie. Close to the drive-in was Café 27, run by Trudie Balkcom. (Courtesy of Mr. and Mrs. Billy Peters.)

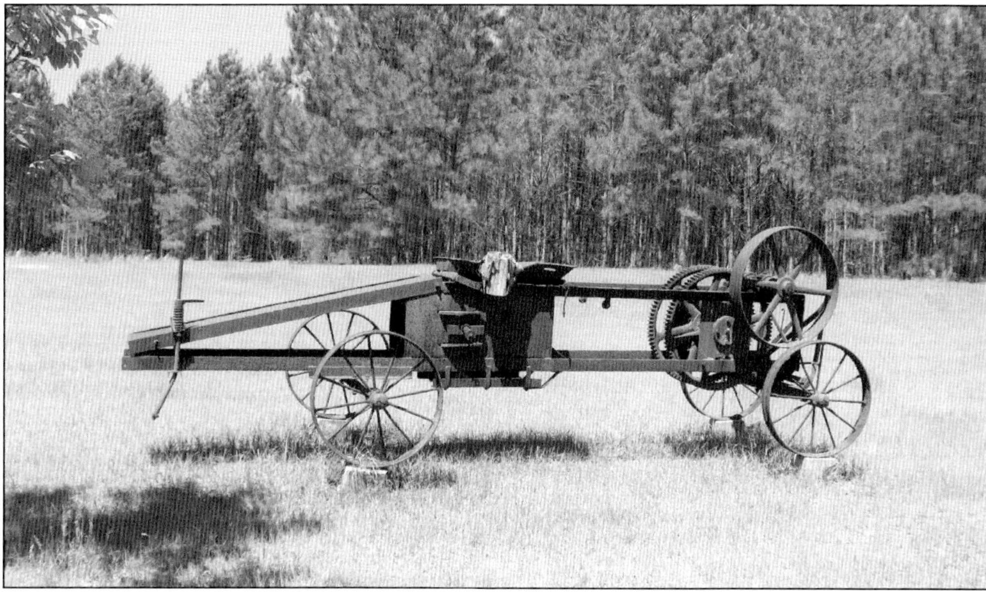

Abandoned Sculpture. Deteriorating barns, farm equipment, outbuildings, and ancient unpainted wood homes dot the countryside in Early County and lend themselves to drawings and paintings by the plethora of artists around the area. The weathered tin roofs of the buildings stand as a testimony to country living and activities of the county in the first half of the century. The rusty old hay press could very well be a piece of sculpture as it catches the light and casts shadows that are elegant and sensuous.

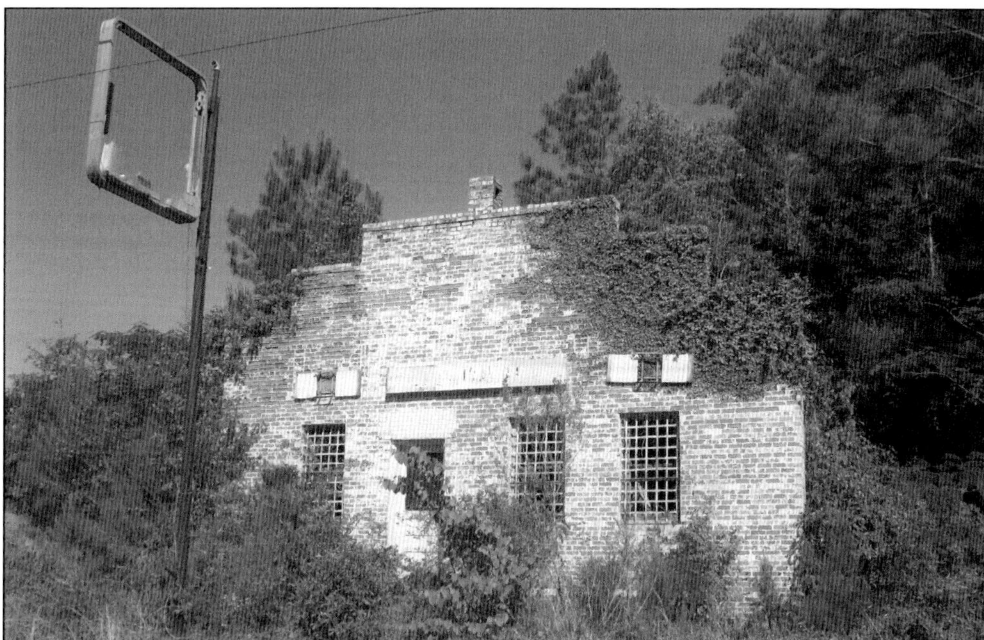

Trading Post. The brick facade of a store just north of Cedar Springs shows that the place had many different names, evidence of a number of different purposes. Seniors around Blakely remember it as Claude Golden's store, a hardware store; others remember a trading post. All remember it as a store that was across the road from Cedar Springs School.

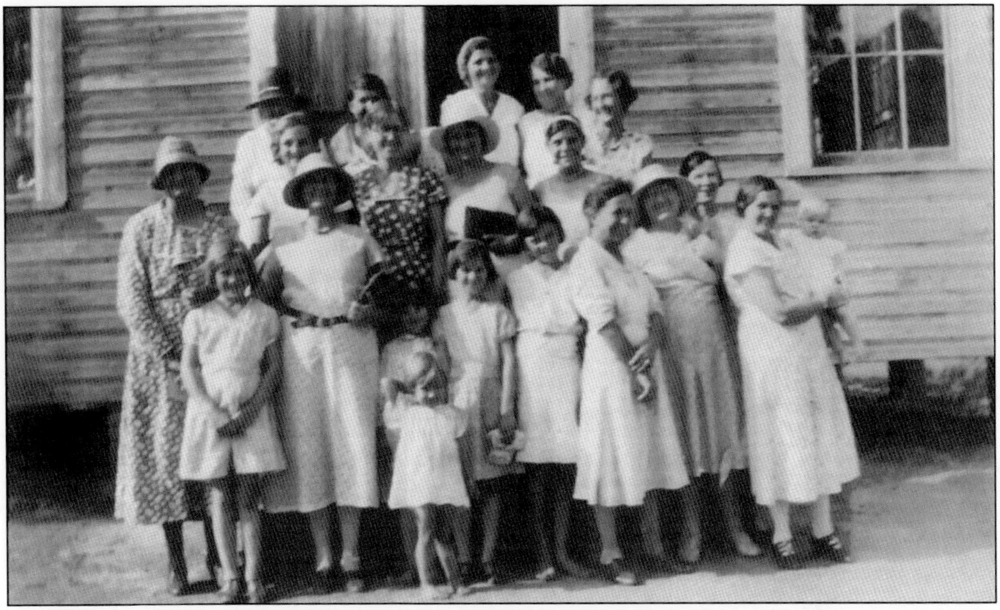

Langston Chapel. There was a time when many small churches of various denominations were scattered around the countryside in Early County. The Lady's Circle at Langston Chapel gathered for a photograph in front of the church. The Methodist church was located about two miles west of Blakely on Freeman Road. (Courtesy of Ephaly Bowman.)

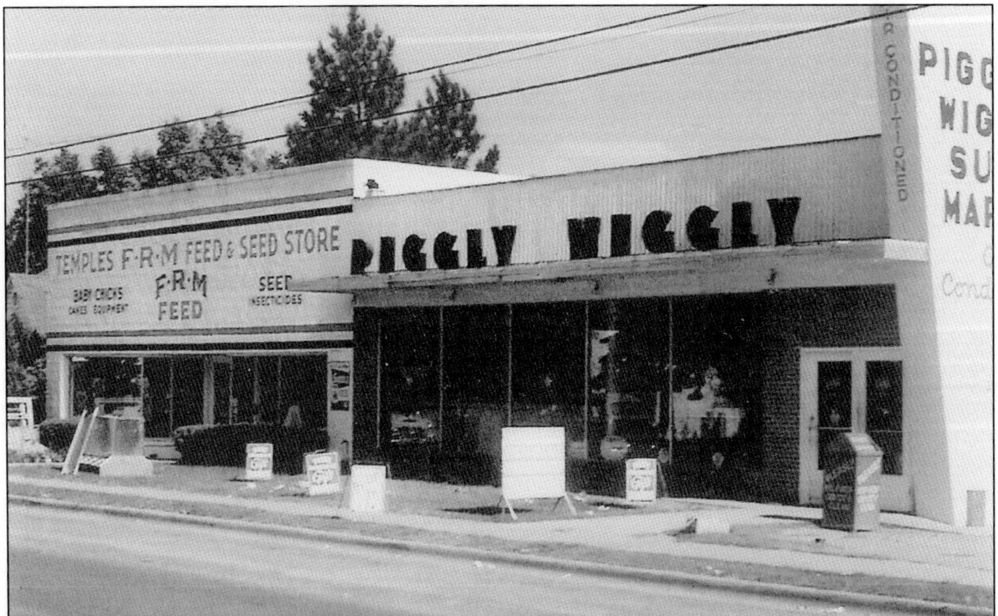

On Magnolia. A block off Court Square on the road east to Arlington stood Temples Hardware (feed and seed) and Piggly Wiggly. Operated by Ralph Scarborough and Frank Davis, "the Pig" served local housewives for 30 years. The store survived a blast from across the street when an explosion caused by a gas truck's leaking fumes that somehow ignited destroyed Davenport Motor Company. Ralph Scarborough later bought out the feed store and enlarged his grocery.

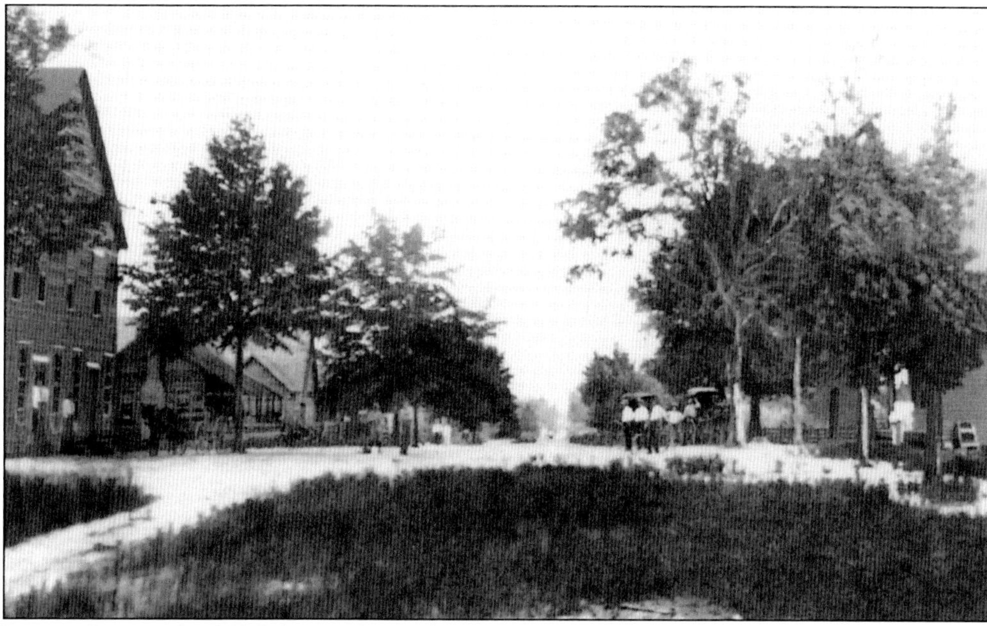

LUCILE. Just south of Blakely, Lucile Road meanders south away from Blakely. The remnants of a community called Lucile stand testament to the changing county. Folklore says that Lucile was first called Racketville but had its name changed to Lucile for a child that was born in the community. In the old, dark photograph, one can see the large building to the left, which is said to be the Woodmen of the World Building. (Courtesy of Amelia Easom.)

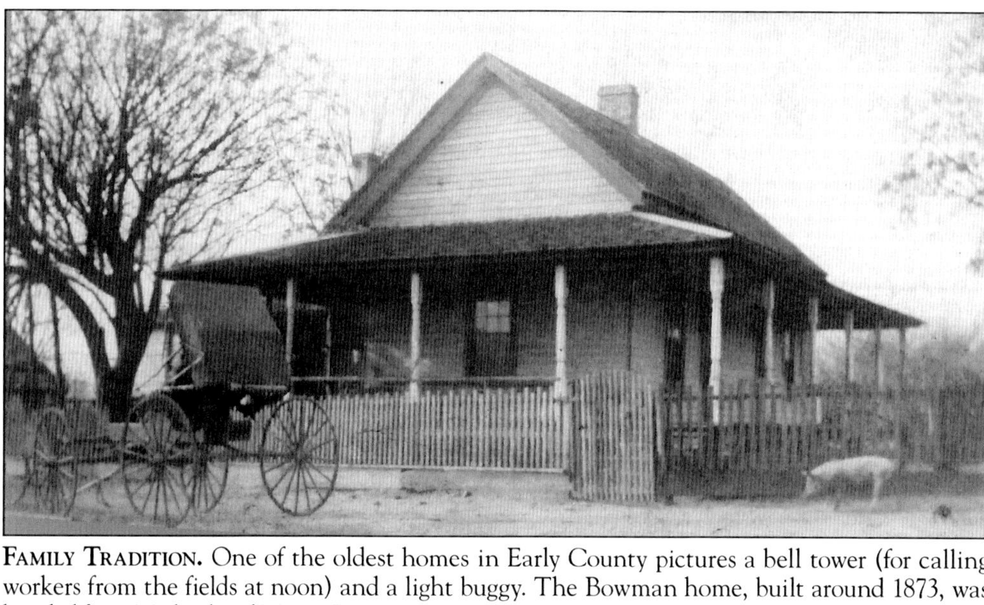

FAMILY TRADITION. One of the oldest homes in Early County pictures a bell tower (for calling workers from the fields at noon) and a light buggy. The Bowman home, built around 1873, was handed from Michael and Mattie Bowman to Joe Bowman and then to Ephaly Bowman, continuing the old tradition of keeping the home place in the family. The Bowmans were a family of farmers residing on Chancey Mill Road west of Blakely. (Courtesy of Ephaly Bowman.)

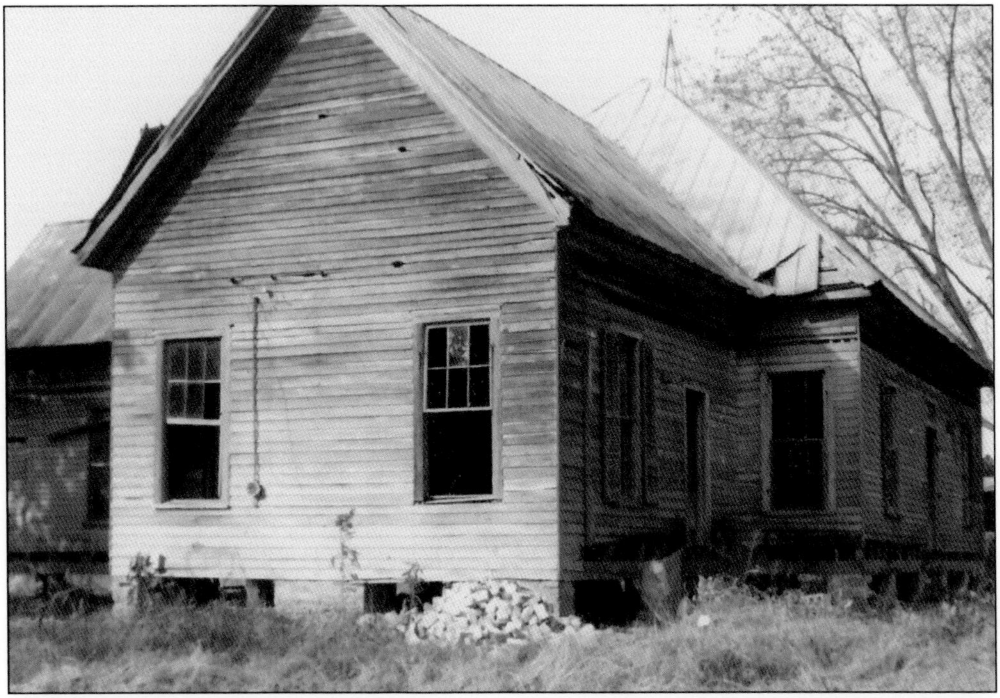

Saving the Home Place. A weathered wreck, the home stood empty for 20 years, seemingly abandoned and left to fall to the elements. Generations of Jarretts had lived in the home, which was originally built in 1894 by Henry J. Hayes for the marriage of his son Walter E. Hayes Sr. In 1932, the house became the home of Perry Franklin and Winnie Dunaway Jarrett and their family. The spacious house then became the home of William Boyd and Verena Sheffield Jarrett. In 1989, the last child born in the home, Rudy Jarrett, and wife, Ann Akers Jarrett, had the home moved. Restoration included moving the home, in two pieces, seven miles to Chancey Mill Road. Returning the house to its original splendor, they have saved their ancestral home. (Both, courtesy of Rudy and Ann Jarrett.)

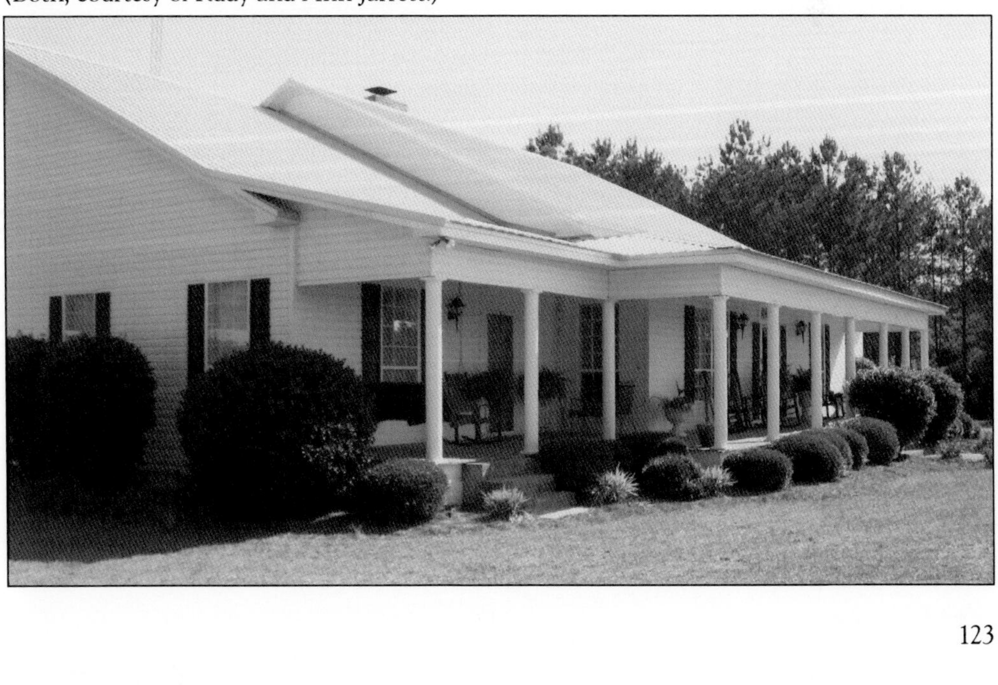

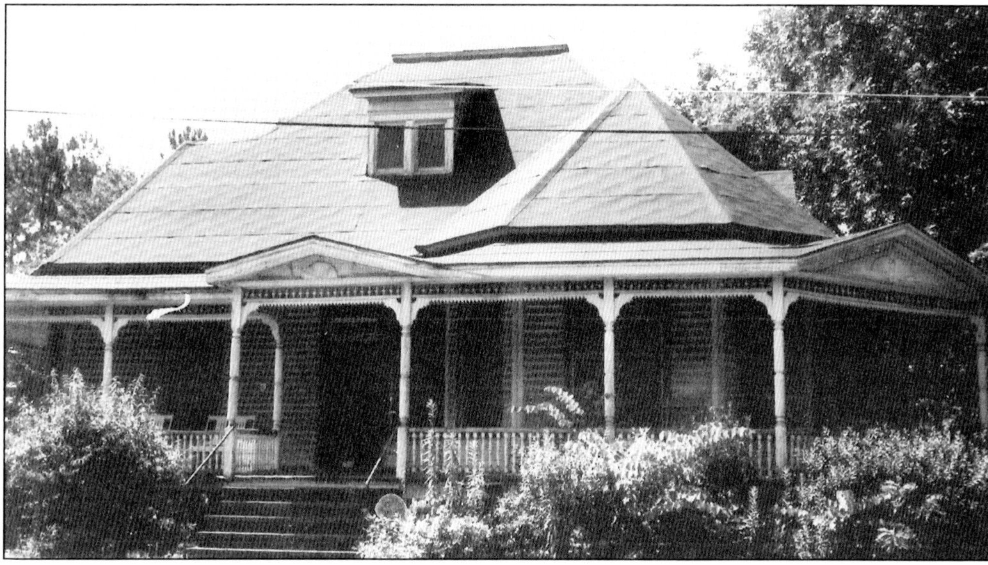

Flowers Home. The lumber business, with its related industries, added to the economic growth of Early County. The cutting of hardwood forests created big business in the early years of the century. The lumber company owners and managers had to have a place for the families to live. Three of their homes were reportedly built just west of what is now Flowers Drive. The home pictured here was just north of Columbia Street. Later, it was the home of Lois Robinson Allen. Two other Flowers homes were built on the old Dothan Road and on Freeman Road, just west of Flowers Drive.

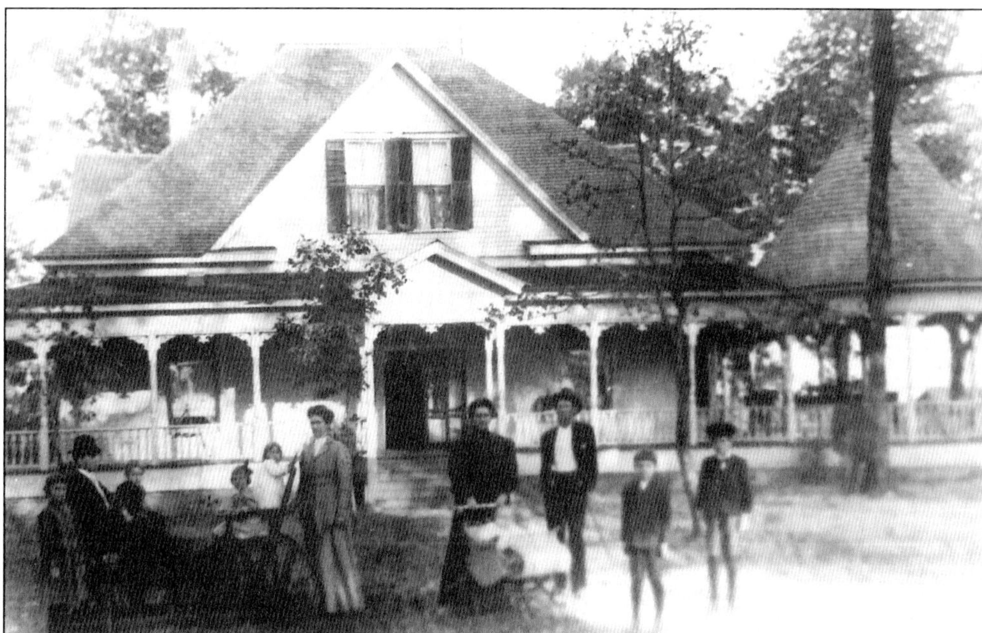

C.S. Middleton Home. This landmark on the corner of South Church Street and Cedar Springs Road for more than a century was eventually demolished. Neighbors and family members knew the home as "Mother Ida's" for Ida Lane Middleton. Another Middleton home was built on the same site. (Courtesy of Mr. and Mrs. Gene Regan.)

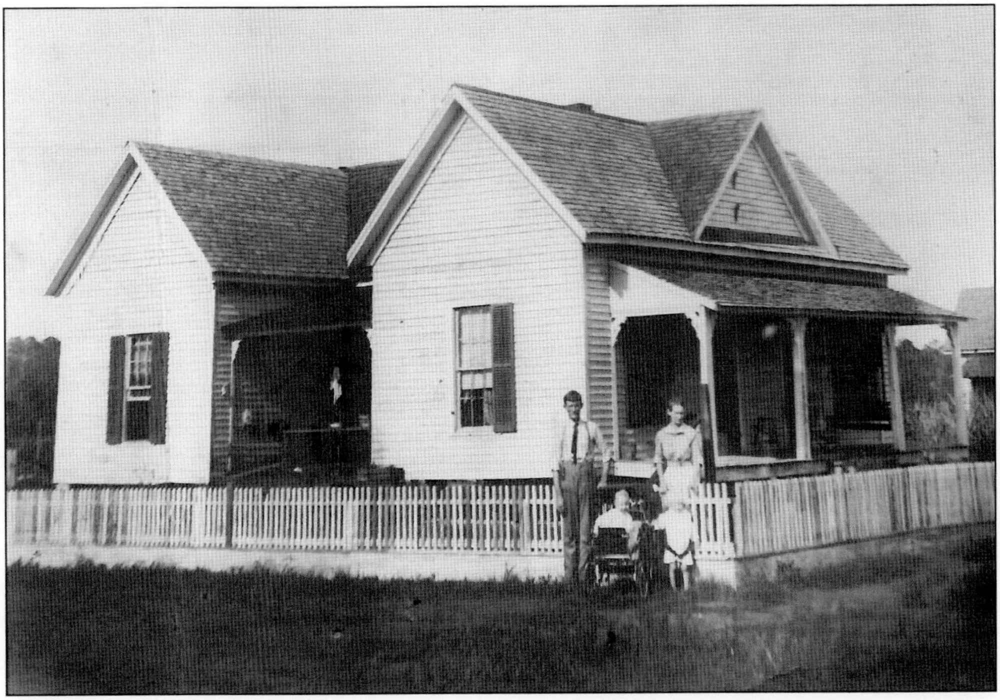

Williams Home. On Liberty Street just off the square, the home of Josiah Williams and Sarah Elizabeth Jernigan Williams was surrounded by a white picket fence. The Williams children Raymond (left) and Leonidas enjoy their two-seater toy car outside the fence around the year 1915. The Williams Restaurant, located across from the train depot on north Cuthbert Street, was owned and operated by the Williamses.

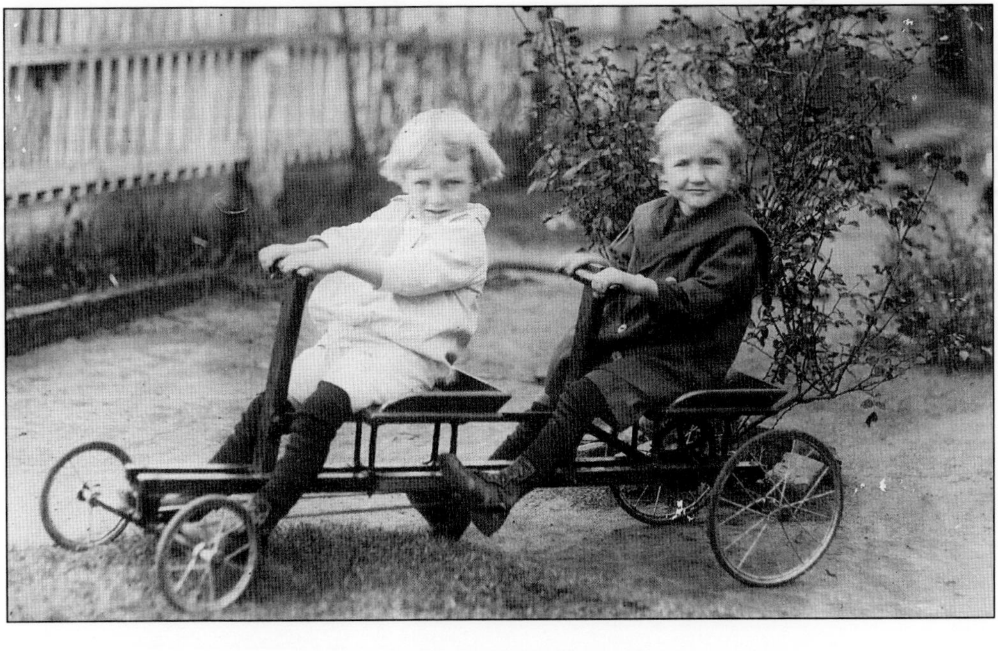

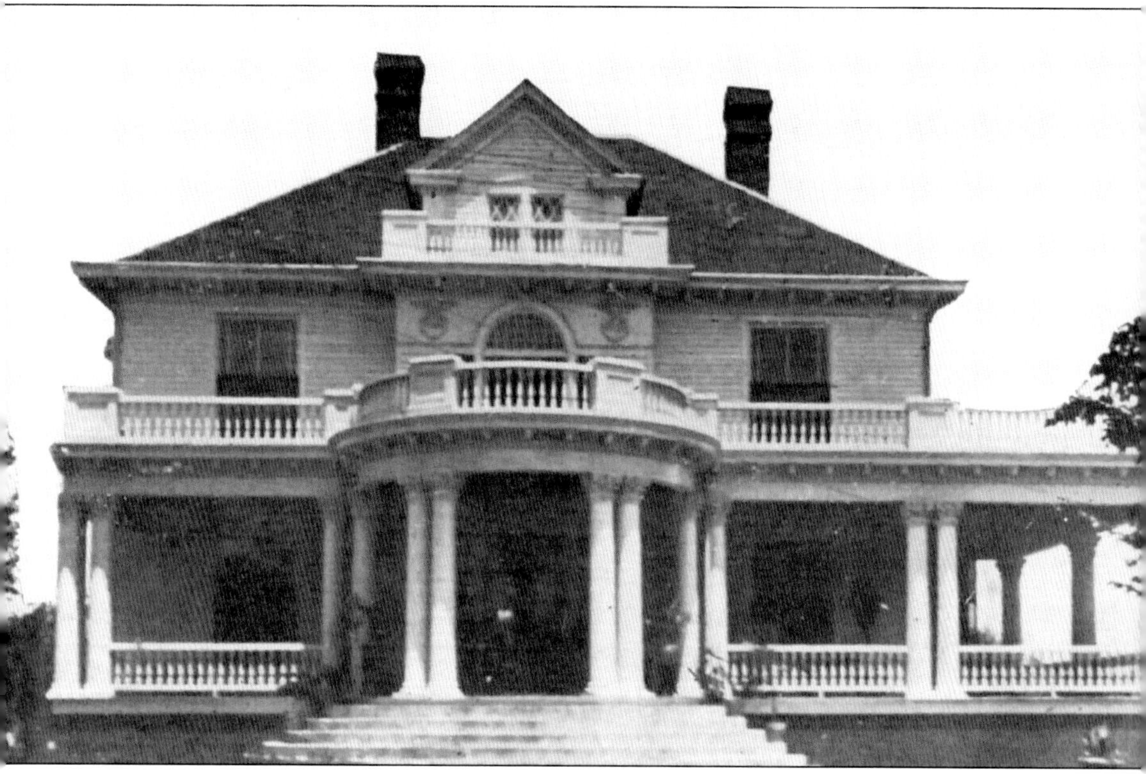

HAND-FRYER HOUSE. Built in 1910 by Dr. J.H. Hand, this two-story frame home was lived in by Dr. Hand and his family. Rossie Smith, niece of Dr. Hand, inherited the house, and she and her husband, Carl Fryer, occupied it for a number of years. The beautiful home, with its stained glass windows, curved front steps, and fluted columns with Corinthian capitals, was later occupied by the Gleaton family and the Pace family. The College Street home burned in September 2002.

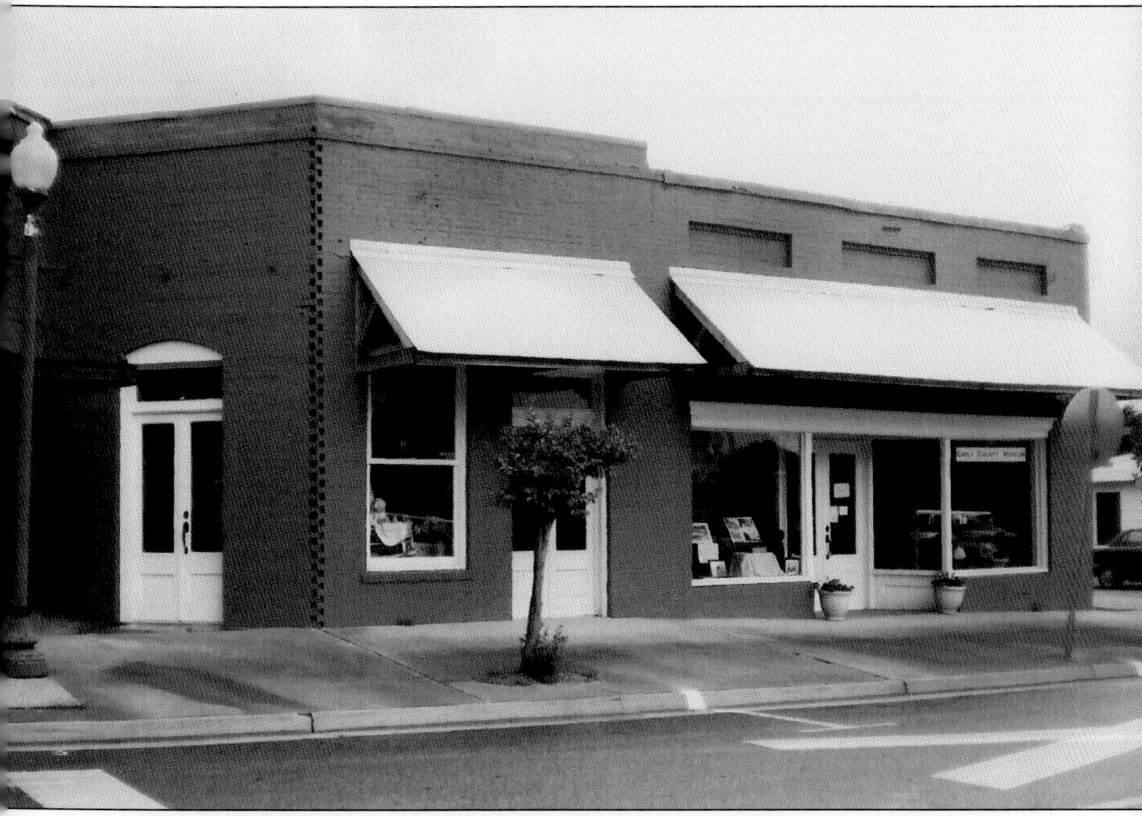

Early County Museum. Located in buildings built before 1915, the Early County Museum site was formerly occupied by William C. Cook Jr., Dr. Pepper Bottling Company, two different drugstores, a feed and seed store, and a mercantile and grocery store. C.E. Boyett Sr. Clothing Store, Mulkey Trim Shop, Claude Day storage, and Willis TV Shop also occupied the buildings over the years. Opened in November 2007 with two buildings, the museum has grown and expanded and now includes a "Tribute to the Farmer" Building and a meeting room for the community to use. The museum has benefitted by having Julianne Megahee Hudson as our staff member who keeps things running smoothly. This publication was made possible by the generosity of Georgia Pacific.

MISSION STATEMENT

The Early County Museum is committed to preserving and promoting our cultural heritage by sharing its historic collections with present and future generations.